Between Rules of War and Rule of Law

Dorte Hühnert-Hugendubel

Between Rules of War and Rule of Law

Legitimation as a Strategic Practice in Norm Transformation

Springer VS

Dorte Hühnert-Hugendubel
Institut für Gesellschaftswissenschaften,
Duisburg
Universität Duisburg-Essen
Essen, Germany

Diese Arbeit wurde von der Fakultät für Gesellschaftswissenschaften der Universität Duisburg-Essen als Dissertation zur Erlangung des Doktorgrades (Dr. rer. pol.) genehmigt.
Name der Gutachterinnen und Gutachter:
1. PD Dr. Daniel Lambach
2. Prof. Dr. Tobias Debiel
Tag der Disputation: 22.01.2025

ISBN 978-3-658-49120-8 ISBN 978-3-658-49121-5 (eBook)
https://doi.org/10.1007/978-3-658-49121-5

This Springer VS imprint is published by the registered company Springer Fachmedien Wiesbaden GmbH, part of Springer Nature.
The registered company address is: Abraham-Lincoln-Str. 46, 65189 Wiesbaden, Germany

To all women—daughters, mothers, and sisters—in academia

To my sweeties,
Stella and Rabea

Acknowledgements

They say it takes a village to raise a child. What's true for raising children is also true for writing a dissertation—it takes a village! While most of the time, working on a project like this is a solitary task, it never felt lonely. I was fortunate to be surrounded by a wonderful and supportive personal dissertation "village"—and I am deeply grateful to each and every one of you.

First, I would like to thank my two supervisors: Daniel Lambach, for allowing me the freedom to find my own path; and Tobias Debiel, for your honest and insightful comments on my work. At the *Institute of Political Science* at the *University of Duisburg-Essen*, where I found my academic home, I am especially grateful for the supportive environment. To Jutta Wergen and *Coachingzonen*—thank you for listening, advising, walking alongside me, and encouraging me to trust my own direction. To the PhD group at the Institute, thank you for the rich exchange about both research and life with a dissertation.

A very special thank you goes to the women who accompanied me on this journey—my powerful shero colleagues, companions, and friends. Sarah Kohler, thank you for the discussions, the friendship, the reassurance, and the collaborative work. To the *Motivationsmädels*, thank you for the routines that stayed even after our meetings ended, for your open ears, and for creating the feeling of working individually but never alone. Patricia Rinck, thank you for your trust, your thoughtful comments, and your honest assessments.

Finally, my greatest thanks go to the most important people in my life. I could not have completed this dissertation without the unwavering support and unconditional love of my family. To my parents, Gisela and Achim, thank you for your unshakable belief in me, your constant safety net, and your support in every aspect of life. To Jens and Anna, thank you for your encouragement, reassurance, and valuable outside perspective. To Stella and Rabea, thank you for grounding me and reminding me what truly matters in life. And to Max, my person—thank you for the good times and the hard times, for your love, and for loving me anyway.

About the Book

This study reconstructs the legitimation practices used by the Presidents Bush, Jr., and Obama in the transformation process of detention-related norms during the war on terror. Building on an extensive scientific debate on norm conflicts during the war on terror, the research problem concerns the breach between U.S. use of force and application of violence against terrorists and the argued commitment to protective norms on legitimate violence. The study examines the research question how the Presidents George W. Bush, Jr., and Barack Obama practiced legitimation to foster the transformation of violence-regulating norms in the war on terror? The case of indefinite detention is not only characteristic for the described problem of U.S. conflict of interest but also for a well-documented transformation in detention law. Thus, the empirical analysis reconstructs strategic legitimation activities of the Presidents Bush and Obama to come to a comprehensive conception of a legitimation practice in norm transformation processes. In this regard, the war on terror is understood as a security-political discourse during which the normative order of legitimate violence is transformed over time and in terms of quality from containing to enabling the use of force and application of violence. This study takes a deeper look into legitimation activities of state actors in terms of legalization and justification, which are aimed to bridge the gap between the use of force and application of violence on the one side and the restrictive prescriptions of norms on legitimate violence on the other side. Concerning the use of and contribution to theory, this study seeks to merge insights from IR norm research and legal scholarship with the conceptual focus on norm transformation. Following a pragmatist abductive interpretive approach, the single case study uses a combination of evidence-based analysis of actions and events over time and qualitative content analysis of presidential speeches. The empirical case study examines how President Bush and President Obama used legalization and justification activities towards the norm transformation in detention law concerning GTMO detainees. The resulting patterns in activities in and on the material world and in rhetoric added up to a comprehensive conceptualization of a strategic political practice of legitimation in norm transformation processes.

Contents

About the Author

Dorte Hühnert-Hugendubel is a political scientist specialized in International Relations, norm research, and U.S. foreign policy. She has worked as a research associate at the Chair of International Relations and Development Policy at the Institute of Political Science at the University of Duisburg-Essen and as a research assistant at the Peace Research Institute Frankfurt. Dorte Hühnert-Hugendubel holds a Master's degree in International Studies and Peace and Conflict Research and a Bachelor's degree in Politics and Economics. She has studied at the Goethe University Frankfurt, Westfälische Wilhelms-Universität Münster, and at the Science Po Rennes. In 2016, she was awarded the Christiane Rajewsky Prize for Young Researchers by the Arbeitsgemeinschaft Friedens- und Konfliktforschung (AFK). In addition to US foreign and security policy, her research interest lies in the development of orders of violence in the international system (hierarchies/heterarchies), norms research, practical theory and international law policy in states of emergency.

Abbreviations

AUMF	Authorization for Use of Military Force against Terrorism
CIA	Central Intelligence Agency
CSRT	Combatant Status Review Tribunal
DTA	Detainee Treatment Act
EO	Executive Order
GC	Geneva Conventions
GTMO	Guantanamo Bay Detention Center
ICRC	International Committee of the Red Cross
IR	International Relations
MCA	Military Commissions Act
NATO	North Atlantic Treaty Organization
NGO	Non-Governmental Organization
NYT	New York Times
PMSC	Private Military and Security Companies
POW	Prisoner of War
UAV	Unmanned Aerial Vehicle
UK	United Kingdom
UN	United Nations
US	United States
USA	United States of America
USSC	United States Supreme Court
WWII	Second World War

List of Figures

List of Tables

1 Introduction

"History has called our Nation into action. History has placed a great challenge before us: Will America, with our unique position and power, blink in the face of terror, or will we lead to a freer, more civilized world? There's only one answer: This great country will lead the world to safety, security, peace, and freedom." (George W. Bush, Address to the Nation, 2002: 939). The question, though, is—how? Torture, extraordinary renditions, targeted killings, and indefinite detention of terrorist suspects are not singular incidents in U.S. security policies in the war on terror but characterize the war on terror as a phase of fundamental conflict between security interest and norms on legitimate violence (Liese 2009; Walen/Venzke 2007; Venzke 2009). This conflict is discussed regarding fundamental contradictions by political and legal science. Judging U.S. acts of violence in the war on terror as illegal, critical legal scholarship more fundamentally debates the role shift of the United States from the founders of the post-World War II restrictive normative order of legitimate violence to the breaker of violence containing-norms (Crawford 2010; Hurd 2016; O'Connell 2010; Reus-Smit 2007). Focusing on the state of emergency after 9/11, political and legal scientists debate contradictions between constitutional and international legal principles and U.S. attempts to argue for exceptions to rules with terms like *enhanced interrogation* and *unlawful enemy combatants* and for exceptional spaces outside the scope of national and international law, like Guantanamo Bay Detention Camp (GTMO)[1] (Agamben 2004; Alexander 2013; Butler 2006; Fletcher 2004; Johns 2005; Steyn 2004). IR norm research is concerned wiht these contradictions regarding the performative actions of the United States engaging in

[1] In the context of this study, I use political terms and abbreviations, as used in presidential speeches. The use of these terms does not constitute an expression of opinion or an endorsement of political or military terms or policies connected with these terms.

D. Hühnert-Hugendubel, *Between Rules of War and Rule of Law*,
https://doi.org/10.1007/978-3-658-49121-5_1

norm dynamics of making, breaking, eroding, regressing, or even killing protective norms in the war on terror (Evers 2017; Heller/Kahl 2013; Jose 2016; Kutz 2014; Rosert/Schirmbeck 2007; Senn/Troy 2017). Not only violence-containing norms are in a legitimacy crisis in the war on terror, but also the power position of the United States, their reputation, and reliability are critically discussed based on U.S. legitimation attempts of the use of force and application of violence in the war on terror (Dunne 2007; Hurd 2007b; Reus-Smit 2007). Trying to consolidate the conflict between the strategic want to use violence against terrorists and the prescription of violence-containing norms to refrain from massive force, U.S. political actors engage in strategic legitimation activities to gain support for the use of force and the application of violence in the war on terror.

Based on this problem and adding to these debates in political and legal science, I propose an actor-centered and action-focused approach to political legitimation as a strategic effort to engage in norm transformation. These U.S. legitimation activities I consider strategically placed to promote the transformation of violence-containing to violence-enabling norms to realize national security interests and govern other states' use of violence. Following a practice-oriented approach, the research question of this study asks, how the Presidents George W. Bush, Jr., and Barack Obama practiced legitimation to foster the transformation of violence-regulating norms in the war on terror? Applying a practice-oriented approach based on Adler and Pouliot (2012), I examine U.S. legalization and justification activities as competent performances and adding up to a practice of legitimation in the case of indefinite detention in Guantanamo Bay Detention Camp. Researching this question, I am foremost interested in U.S. government attempts to consolidate security political interests with normative prescriptions through legitimation activities and the effects on the violence-regulating norms. The case of indefinite detention is not only characteristic for the described problem of U.S. conflict of interest, but also for a well-documented transformation in detention law. Thus, the empirical analysis reconstructs strategic legitimation activities of the Presidents Bush and Obama to come to a comprehensive conception of a legitimation practice in norm transformation processes.

In the following, I present the research question and place the research interest in a wider scientific debate on legitimacy, legitimate violence, and state legitimation attempts in the war on terror. Building on these theoretical assumptions, I explain the research design and present the contribution of the empirical study to a conceptual appraoch to a practice of legitimation in norm transformation.

1.1 Research Question and Research Interest

As the critical legal and political debates on indefinite detention show, the U.S. detention policy in Guantanamo conflicts with robust protective international norms, namely, the *Geneva Conventions*, the *Torture Convention*, and *The Universal Declaration of Human Rights*. Regarding domestic law, the detention-related issues discussed the most are constitutional rights and legal principles such as *habeas corpus* and *due process*. These critical debates are mainly concerned with the legality, the effects of detention policies on the national or international legal system, or U.S. leadership's legitimacy among national votership and the international state community.

Building on these assessments of a major conflict of norms between the secrutiy interests of the U.S. and the normative restrictions on state violence, I am particularly interested in the attempts at consolidation through the strategic use of legitimation by U.S. presidents. Thus, my driving motivation in this research project is to understand how legitimation is strategically performed by powerful actors in norm transformation processes. Finding out how U.S. leading politicians practically tried to gain legitimacy for the controversial application of violence in the war on terror is the aim of this study. These legitimation activities are considered efforts to not only legalize and justify detention and detainee treatment but also to permanently change detention norms and the normative framework on legitimate violence. The aim of this analysis is to answer the research question: How did the Presidents George W. Bush, Jr., and Barack Obama practice legitimation to foster the transformation of violence-regulating norms in the war on terror?

Proposing this question, I assume a two-fold strategic purpose of political legitimation. Firstly, the obvious one is that democratic politicians seek legitimacy for their policies, as they depend on public support. Secondly, the underlying, and in the context of norm research more important, purpose lies in the role legitimation plays regarding the formulation, use, and shaping of international law. Based on the practice conception of Adler and Pouliot (2011), I understand practices of legitimation to be competent performances of key political persons, which are aimed to make acts of state violence appear as legitimate, i.e. legal and just, to a defined audience.

In the empirical analysis, I search for patterns and routines in U.S. legalization and justification activities in relation to detention which work towards a transformation of violence-regulating norms. Rather than reconstructing government positions, the aim here is to reconstruct the complex legitimation strategy of government actors. Thus, I search for activities adding up to a state actor's practice of legitimation regarding two sub-questions: (1) Whether regularly repeated patterns occur in legitimacy-seeking activities over time *in deeds*; and (2) whether regularly repeated patterns occur in legitimacy-seeking *rhetoric* actions acts over time which add up to a strategic practice of legitimation.

Understanding state legitimation practices helps to enhance the conceptual understanding of how state actors can interact with and/or use the law to justify politics but also engage in politics to shape international law. The war on terror, I consider a security political discourse after the end of the Cold War during which rules on the use of force and application of violence are questioned, affirmed, and altered by the United State who claim a role of leadership in this process. In the specific case of detention law, the strategic use of legitimation practices is considered norm entrepreneurship, which aims to transform violence-containing norms into violence-enabling norms. Understanding the strategic legitimation practice U.S. political leaders use in this process helps understanding how the U.S. act as norm-entrepreneur in transforming norms on legitimate violence. In this process, I consider the U.S. presidents as representatives of an interest-driven state engaging in legitimation to actively shaping the normative order of legitimate violence in order to realize power political goals, strengthen the U.S. position in the international system, and to govern the possibilities of other state and non-state actors regarding the use of force and application of violence.

1.2 Theoretical Assumptions and Concepts

Finding out how, by which practices, U.S. government officials legitimize the use of force and application of violence which conflict with robust humanitarian protective norms in the war on terror is subject to the empirical analysis of this study. Common to the Bush and Obama administrations between 2001 and 2017 is, that they do not fundamentally question the normative order in place. Both presidents argue that their use of force is covered by the established normative framework of the international system. More precisely, both presidents interpret violence-regulating norms changing the scope of application, thus transforming violence-regulating norms and the normative order of legitimate violence. This research problem and approach build on theoretical assumptions on legitimacy in the international system, legitimate violence as a normative system, and conceptual understandings of norm transformation as a specific dynamic of norm change and legitimation as a specific set of strategic actions contributing to norm alterations.

Building on a conception of the international system as a power-structured, hierarchically ordered system of legitimate actors of sovereign states, I understand the United States as a powerful actor, seeking a leadership position in the determination of violence-regulating norms in the normative order of legitimate violence. By normative order or framework of legitimate violence, I refer to the body of robust norms, codified in international humanitarian law and customary international law as well as principles of domestic law, which regulate the use of force and violence of state actors in international and non-international armed conflict. As the critical legal and political debate in the war on terror show, U.S. policies regarding the use of force and application of violence in the war on terror are perceived as norm violations as well as productive attempts to change violence-containing norms.[2] This seems puzzling considering the U.S. reputation of setting good, violence-containing norms, as proved by the legal framework established after World War II (Reus-Smit 2007). Considering the historical development of the violence-regulating legal framework, institutionalized in the *UN Charter*, *Declaration of Human Rights*, and the *Geneva Conventions*, the U.S. have taken a leading role as norm-entrepreneur for violence-containing norms since World War II. Setting norms and dominantly interpreting the meaning and use of violence-regulating norms is a key feature of U.S. security politics serving the perception as global security power (Keating 2014). Likewise, the U.S. seek a defining role interpreting and setting regulations for violence in the war on terror, which apply to conflicts with non-state actors, especially to terrorist actors.

Considering that the legal framework, despite pressure on violence-regulating norms, remains in place and is still widely accepted and considered a robust prohibition of state violence, I propose a more nuanced perspective on norm conflicts during the war on terror. I consider the discussions on the detention norm, and similarly the argument over a possibly emerging new killing norm, as debates on the transformation of norms on legitimate violence. Examining the legal arguments brought forward in defense of terrorist treatment, several authors argued for the formation of a new (secret) detention law (Alexander 2013; Sall 2013; Hajjar 2014). Like the early discussion on the Bush administration's detention and interrogation policy, the CIA targeted killing program triggers debate on norms undergoing transformation. Senn and Troy (2017) as well as Hurd (2017) make a case for a transformation in the international legal order of violence regarding current U.S. practices of targeted killings.

[2] For a review of the relevant political and legal debates on norm conflicts in the war on terror see Chap. 2 and Chap. 3.

Norm transformation (Senn/Troy 2017; Pratt 2018) constitutes a promising concept for explaining the political events as opposed to approaches that argue for norm death or decline (McKeown 2009; Kutz 2014). Norm transformation accounts for what is often termed the double standard established in U.S. anti-terrorist politics (Greenberg/Dratel 2005; Greenberg et al. 2008; Hühnert 2016). Whereas the U.S. grant *Geneva* protection to regular forces and demand those rights for their own troops, the same protection is denied to terrorist suspects. Instead of applying a traditional reading of international law—which classifies terrorism as an act of crime and thus refers terrorists to the judicial system of their state of origin—the U.S. establish a new interpretation of the detention rights and set a new norm for terrorist detainees. Arguing that terrorist suspects qualify as *unlawful enemy combatants*, the U.S. exclude them from *Geneva* protections, legitimizing the imprisoning at Guantanamo Bay and the killing by drones (targeted killings) (Greenberg 2006; Greenberg et al. 2008; Hühnert 2016; Johns 2011; Keating 2014; Venzke 2009). Instead of understanding U.S. norm-interpretation merely as a breach of international law, as is claimed in the critical legal debate, I argue that the U.S. act as norm-entrepreneur in a complex norm transformation process. While violence-containing norms are affirmed, violence-enabling regulations are innovatively added by the United States and thus the original norm is transformed (Pratt 2018).

Norm transformation regards not only the stages in the development process of a norm's life cycle over time but also concerns the content and the quality of a norm. The main transformation of norms I am interested in is the transformation from violence-containing norms to violence-enabling norms regarding detention during the war on terror. This includes setting modalities on who qualifies for protection, which norm grants rights to whom, which kind of violence is prohibited, and where the limit of humane treatment is drawn.

In this process, the United States are norm-transforming entrepreneurs who shape the transformation discursively in several stages and lobby not necessarily for adoption of the altered norm but mainly for the acceptance of others. Likewise, Jose (2016) argues that the U.S. can best be considered norm-entrepreneurs framing a violence practice as legal, thus fostering the emergence of a new killing norm. While norm-transformation by the U.S. has been identified by norm research, this study goes beyond these findings by asking how the U.S. managed this transformation process through strategic legitimation practice. Acknowledging conceptual and qualifying contributions from norm research (Jose 2016; Jose 2017; Senn/Troy 2017; Hurd 2017; Pratt 2019), I want to add to this debate by proposing a practice-oriented approach. Although the U.S. have acted as norm-entrepreneur for violence-containing norms, in the war on terror they act as norm-entrepreneurs for violence-enabling norms and a towards the transformation of the normative order on legitimate violence. Adding to these theoretical considerations, the case study analysis provides a conception on legitimation practices used in the norm-transformation in violence-regulating norms. In the war on terror, I consider the U.S. a norm-entrepreneur acting out legitimation practices designed to work towards a transformation in violence-regulating norms. The U.S. I consider an international powerful actor actively shaping and adapting the normative framework based on a crisis-induced (new) threat perception to (re-) gain capacities and capabilities and engage in a fight against a diffuse (terrorist) enemy. Furthermore, they set precedent for the application of violence in the war on terror and by introducing normative regulations where they see a gap in the international legal order.

As norm-entrepreneurs for violence-enabling norms, the United States act within social and normative structures and need to strategically engage in legitimation activities to convince other political stakeholders nationally and internationally. Gaining legitimacy is not only a system requirement but also has power political advantages for the United States as a stabilizing factor in domestic politics and as a currency in international relations. Thus, legitimation activities are directed at audiences: to the inside, legitimation strategies need to convince the national public, and to the outside, legitimation strategies must convince the international state community, mainly allies, but also deter non-allied states.

By arguing for the legitimacy of these violent acts the United States engage in a process of transforming norms of legitimate violence to consolidate strategic wants and political activities on the one side and respect the violence-containing character of international law on the other side through strategic actions of legitimation. Legitimation is not only a necessary, system-immanent set of activities, which stabilizes expectations and signals compliance, but also a strategic political action because states gain privileges, power, and bargaining chips. By going forward in the fight against terrorism, the United States fill the constructed void of rules in waging war with terrorists by engaging in a complex process of precedent-setting, norm-violating, norm-stabilizing, and norm-innovating actions in the material world and by discursive actions. In this process, the U.S. are not only norm-takers but actively engage in the shaping of norms in meaning and use by precedent-setting actions of violence and by legitimation. Thus, I consider the U.S. as a powerful legitimacy-seeking actor who strategically chooses where to stay within the legal boundaries and where to exceed them. The U.S. also use the law for their strategic purposes, as they use the language of the law arguing for the legality of their use of force. These legitimation activities for norm transformation include reinterpreting the law, rephrasing legal texts and legitimizing state actions using force. Such changes trace in political actions and rhetoric presented in meaningful speech acts in which the new interpretation of the norm is practically acted out and justified. With this study, I seek to provide evidence for recurring justification activities that are used to implement changes in the dominant interpretation of the violence-containing norms, including the lasting alteration of legal provisions.

1.3 Research Design

The research design of this case study analysis builds on methodological assumptions combining interpretive and pragmatist approaches (Schwartz-Shea/Yanow 2012; Friedrichs/Kratochwil 2009). Following the guidelines of Eisenhardt's method to build theory from cases (Eisenhardt 1989; Eisenhardt 2021; Eisenhardt/Graebner 2007), I apply a practice-oriented research perspective based on the practice conception of Adler and Pouliot (2012). This appraoch provides procedures for examining processes thoroughly and for generating theory from a collection of rich empirical data, which I analyze using methods of qualitative content analysis to reconstruct activities leading to a conception of a practice of legitimation (Schwartz-Shea/Yanow 2012).

In this study, I analyze the terms of office of the two presidents Bush and Obama and trace the transformation of detention law considering the case of indefinite detention in Guantanamo Bay Detention Camp. Indefinite detention is here understood as the incarceration of men by U.S. security personnel at the designated area of the military base, Guantanamo Bay Detention Camp, for an unspecified amount of time, without charges, and with unclear purpose. Undoubtedly, detainee treatment includes a variety of measures like conditions of housing and humane treatment in captivity, status definition issues, and interrogation methods, through to torture and other forms of maltreatment. However, in this analysis, the focus is limited to indefinite detention as the defining feature of a set of norms in conflict with detention and detainee treatment at Guantanamo.

This case is chosen according to Eisenhardt's proposition to select cases based on the benefit for the advancement of theory (Eisenhardt 1989). Indefinite detention is a promising case for the advancement of the conceptual understanding of legitimation as a strategic political practice in norm transformation processes for several reasons. For one, the norm dynamic in this case qualifies as a norm transformation because political actions affirm the importance of the existing norm, while adding meaning to the norm by precedent-setting acts of violence and discursive actions of legalization and justification. Although several acts of norm dynamics in the war on terror—torture, extraordinary renditions, and targeted killings—share attributes qualifying as a norm transformation, the transformation of the detention norm in this case presents as a full cycle of norm transformation instead of a mere attempt (like in the case of torture). Thus, this case allows tracing legitimacy-seeking activities in a complete cycle of norm transformation from violence-containing to violence-enabling norms. For another, indefinite detention in Guantanamo is a well-documented case due to public attention in the media and of political actors, and therefore allows a thorough investigation and reconstruction of government actor legitimation activities based on a rich data basis (which is harder to accomplish in cases of political denial, reluctance of comments, or secret keeping like torture and targeted killings).

Thus, I consider the case of the transformation of detention law as one having considerable value for the advancement of theoretical assumptions on state legitimation practices for the use of force and the application of violence against non-state actors with transformative effects on single norms, the normative order of legitimate violence, and underlying ideas, values, and beliefs on legitimate violence.

Legitimation I understand as a strategic state practice in norm transformation processes using a pragmatist appraoch to the concept of practice as competent performances, proposed by Adler and Pouliot (2011). This understanding of practice has several advantages: it allows to view political actions as intended, discursively embedded, socially anchored doing. Thus, the concept of practice links structural factors that condition political action with discursive political acts. Norm contestation and its justification merge in this understanding of legitimation practices which are designed to work towards the transformation of the normative order of violence in favor of the expansion of a state's scope of action. Practices combine political actions in and on the material world and discursive, argumentative actions, promising a comprehensive actor-centered and action-focused conception of legitimation.

An approach based on practice theory allows for an advancement of existing theories on the formation, contestation, and rearrangement of and within international normative orders. Norms are in need of interpretation and the interpretations of rules on legitimate violence require legitimation. In the interplay of different legalizations and justifications, complex narratives and discourses emerge that are shared and commonly agreed or disputed and contested by state actors in political and legal actions, contextual framing, and rhetorical activities. I argue that the need for legitimation is especially high in cases where political actions contradict the agreed-upon interpretation of the protective norm. These debates raise issues wherever the administrations have challenged the normative framework of standards of legitimate violence. Challenges in this sense include activities that are called illegal or norm-breaking action; the interpretation of a norm in use and/or meaning that is contradictory to former applications of the norm; and the introduction of new terminology, phrases, and adding of new meaning to the norm's content. By violence-regulating norms, I refer to a specific set of security norms that fulfill humanitarian protective functions and restrict state violence to specific defense situations. Generally, those norms are understood as international humanitarian law codified in several legal documents mainly including *The Declaration of Human Rights* and the *Geneva Conventions (1949)*. The sum of these activities of legalization and justification, designed and strategically used to convince an audience of the transformation of violence-regulating norms, I call the practice of legitimation.

Consequently, I understand practices of legitimation to be competent performances of key political persons which are aimed at making acts of state violence appear as legitimate, i.e. legal and just, to a defined audience. In this sense, legitimation is understood as a complex set of political actions that are patterned and repeated in a similar matter over time. Political actors strategically perform practices of legitimation to reconcile politically favored actions with normative ideas about what is right and just in a given situation. As actors, political leaders function as the sender of legitimation efforts and the receiver of legitimation which can only be granted by the audience. The relevant audience in the cases examined here is on the one hand the U.S. people, and on the other hand, the international state community, especially states allied to the U.S. Examining the case, I look for the following activities, which add up to practices of legitimation, which may include but not be limited to denying; keeping secrets; characterizing the enemy as evil, unhuman, or unjust; arguing for political decisions with reference to the law; legalizing and legal arguing; innovatively interpreting robust norms; arguing for exceptions; and marginalizing atrocities.

The case study traces the main political and legal developments during the Bush and Obama administrations regarding indefinite detention in Guantanamo Bay Detention Camp. Therein, reconstructing legitimation activities includes two dimensions: one concerns the accounting for formal legalization activities used in transforming violence-regulating norms; the other concerns argumentative activities in legalizing and justifying the use of force and the change in the violence-regulating norms. Only the combination of those two spheres provides for a full account of legitimation as a strategic political practice.

Data collection in both dimensions of the analysis concerns the norm transformation process in both presidential terms of Bush and Obama. In the first step, I collect documents building a basis to reconstruct the governments' activities over time. Here, I gather as much evidence as needed for saturation to reconstruct the activities of both administrations concerning indefinite detention in Guantanamo. This includes documents from different sources and official government communication as well as news coverage. In the second step, the corpus for the in-depth analysis includes transcripts of specific speeches. For an in-depth analysis of argumentative legitimation activities, I analyze the transcripts of these speeches looking for legalization and justification activities with regard to detention related topics. These serve as key documents for the identification of patterns in argumentative legitimation activities. Searching for these activities includes checking for patterns and for repetitions in actions. I assume that each practice of legitimation is traceable as a set of actions performed over a period, and accompanied by a set of arguments, which is traceable in speeches. Based on this two-phased case study design, the analysis of actions adding up to the practice of legitimation consists of two reconstructive steps: for the reconstruction of the legitimation practices over time, and in addition, for the reconstruction of argumentative legitimation activities evaluated in a qualitative content analysis.

Evaluating the data in a first step, the analysis focuses on reconstructing relevant events and legalization activities for a detailed description of norm transforming efforts by the presidents over time. The second part of the analysis focuses on legalization and justification in speeches through interpreting presidential role, topic setting, issue framing, and rhetorical activities. With regard to these practice-building actions, both presidents shared some common ground despite great differences in strategic positioning in the war on terror. The evaluation of all activities in comparison adds to the final conceptualization of legitimation as a strategic state practice for norm transformation. Analyzing legitimacy-seeking activities adds to a more thorough understanding of the actions state leaders take to frame their use of force and application of violence as just and legal—thus legitimate.

1.4 Relevance and Contribution

Adding to debates in IR norm research, critical legal studies, and practice theory, the results of this research project seek to contribute to a deeper understanding of legitimation as a strategic practice of powerful state leaders in norm transformation processes. Thus, the results of the case study provide added value regarding the following aspects:

- *Offers a conceptualization of the practice of legitimation*: Focusing on the case of indefinite detention, the study provides an in-depth analysis of U.S. legitimation activities concerning the application of violence in the war on terror. The analysis results in a comprehensive list of actions providing an actor-centered and action-focused conception of legitimation as a practice.
- *Contributes to a deeper understanding of the strategic use of legitimation in U.S. foreign and security politics*: The empirical analysis adds to research on U.S. foreign and security politics, as it provides a detailed reconstruction of political legitimation activities accounting for legalization and justification in the war on terror. The results thus contribute to a deeper understanding of how U.S. foreign and security policies are strategically formed, acted out, and legitimized.
- *Provides an explanation for crisis management in states of emergency and the function of exceptionalism*: The findings of the analysis contribute to a deeper understanding of how crisis management functions within a democratic state. Moreover, the results help understanding how administrations communicate to convince the respective audience within a state and among states, concerning the legitimate use of force and application of violence. The findings thus contribute to a deeper understanding of strategic political communication and persuasion nationally and internationally bridging the gap between security interests in time-sensitive situations of crisis and prolonged states of emergency.
- *Adds to the conception of legitimation as a strategic means in foreign and security policies*: The war on terror characterizes through disputes on how much violence states are allowed to use. The case study offers insights as to how state leaders argue for the legitimate use of violence in a controversial case while affirming yet changing and eventually transforming norms on legitimate violence. The analysis contributes to a deeper understanding of how state officials act out legitimation to justify and legalize security political actions.
- *Adds to IR norm research on dynamic changes in meaning and use of robust norms through powerful actors*: This study contributes to norm research with a focus on norm transformation processes within the normative framework of legitimate violence. The findings of this study add to research on the norm life cycle and to the question as to how norms develop in terms of quality and content over time. Thus, the results contribute to ongoing debates on whether norms change in use, possibly die, or transform, and focus on the role of state actors in these processes. Conceptually clarifying practices of legitimation adds to the theoretical understanding of how powerful states can practically take an influence in norm transformation processes.

- *Adds a conceptual approach to the debate on practice theory and research methods*: On a theoretical and methodological level, the results of this research project add to practice theories. Following a practice-oriented approach, the study contributes to a deeper understanding of how states practically, in deeds and argumentatively, act towards the changing of norms by conceptualizing legitimation as a practice in norm transformation processes.

1.5 Chapter Overview

The first two chapters address theoretical issues building the ground for empirical analysis. In Chap. 2, I review approaches to legitimacy in IR and present my assumptions and conceptual understanding of the meaning of legitimacy of rule, through rulings, and with reference to rules regarding the research interests of this study. Based on different approaches to U.S. use of force and application of violence, I discuss norm conflicts with violence-containing norms and effects on the order of legitimate violence in the war on terror. Finally, I present my approach and theoretical assumptions on legitimation as a strategic political practice used by the United States to influence, gradually adapt, and eventually transform norms in the war on terror.

Similarly, Chap. 3 functions as the theoretical foundation for the empirical case analysis by featuring norm transformation as a complex concept to model norm dynamics. Reviewing current IR debates on norm dynamics in the war on terror, I discuss the advantages of norm transformation. This concept not only accounts for the change in norms and normative frameworks but allows adds features to existing models for norm life cycles and norm development over time. Acknowledging changes in the normative character, quality, and content of norms, I propose violence-regulating norms as an alternative wording instead of the qualifying terms good and bad. Further, I conceptualize the U.S. as norm-transforming entrepreneur in a complex process of dynamically changing the meaning and use of violence-regulating norms through strategic legitimation efforts.

Chapter 4 contains the research design, featuring methodological assumptions, a pragmatic approach to practice research, and the analytical appraoch for the empirical case study. Following the interpretive turn, the methodological approach combines elements from building theory with cases and practice-oriented research programs. Building on theoretical assumptions from Chaps. 2 and 3, I develop my conceptual understanding of legitimation as a practice. The research design explains the case selection in further detail and presents a detailed account of the analytical steps including data collection, evidence-gathering, and the evaluation in the qualitative content analysis.

The empirical case study in Chap. 5 contains a detailed description of the analytical results from fieldwork and deskwork. For one, I trace the norm transformation in detention law from an evidence-based evaluation of legalization and justification activities observable in events and official acts. For another, I analyze rhetorical activities of legalization and justification based on the evaluation of speeches through a qualitative content analysis of Bush and Obama. Presenting these analytical results, I reconstruct legitimation activities of both presidents in the stages of the transformation of detention law over time.

Building on the descriptive analysis over time, I analyze the presidential activities regarding repetitions, patterns, and routines in Chap. 6. Reviewing both president's activities, I evaluate role interpretations, topic setting, issue framing, and rhetorical activities of Bush and Obama in legalization and justification actions and compare the results. Consequently, I present the conceptualization of the practice of legitimation in norm transformation processes.

In Chap. 7, I discuss the findings regarding the theoretical debates on legitimation as a strategic political effort to realize a norm transformation in violence-regulating norms and possible effects on the normative order of legitimate violence. To this end, the seventh chapter draws back to Chaps. 2 and 3 and discusses the empirical findings of Chaps. 5 and 6 regarding the contribution to IR norm research. In addition to theoretical and conceptual contributions to fields of research, I discuss the relevance of the findings in view of the methodological and methodical limitations of the study and evaluate areas and issues for further research.

2 Legitimacy, Legitimate Violence, and Legitimation in the War on Terror

In this chapter, I present current debates in IR and legal scholarship on legitimation of the use of force and the application of violence in the war on terror. This chapter serves two functions. For one, reflecting the case selection of this research project as announced in the introduction, I want to place the research interest and envisaged aims in a wider debate on legitimate violence and norm conflicts in the war on terror to argue for the explanatory value of a practice-oriented appraoch on norm transformation. To this end, I discuss cases of U.S. conflicts with violence-containing norms in the war on terror, reviewing the critical legal debate and considering explanatory approaches in IR. For another, I present my positions on core meaning of conceptions, constitution of actors, and systemic structures regarding the use and function of legitimacy in the international system, international law as the normative order of legitimate violence, the state and state officials as strategic actors in social and interest-shaped international relations, and legitimation as a strategic political practice of state actors in norm transformation. This chapter builds the ground for the following theoretical considerations. The subsequent Chap. 3 reflects IR debates on norm dynamics during the war on terror and reveals my theoretical and conceptual understanding of norm transformation as the main analytical concept in this study.

2.1 Legitimacy and the Normative Order of Legitimate Violence

Tracing the transformation of violence-regulating norms, I build on a conceptual understanding of legitimate violence and the normative order of legitimate violence, as I search for legalization and justification activities adding up to a practice of legitimation of powerful state actors in norm transformation processes.

D. Hühnert-Hugendubel, *Between Rules of War and Rule of Law*,
https://doi.org/10.1007/978-3-658-49121-5_2

I understand legitimacy as a quality of being perceived as right and just. This quality has to be attributed to an actor (the constitution of a state or a power position of a state leader), a group of actors (the constitution of states, otherwise known as the international system), a system or a principle of order (the international state system or the relations between sovereign states in an anarchic, but power-structured hierarchic order), or a norm by a designated audience. In distinction, legitimation I consider a set of actions, as in meaningful and deliberate activities, competently performed by a legitimacy-seeking actor designed to convince a defined audience, that an action, norm, or norm interpretation is right and just.

While legitimacy traces back in a long philosophical tradition as an integral conceptual part of democratic research, International Relations scholarship focuses on the legitimacy of the global order of state and non-state actors regarding the presumption of an anarchic system and hierarchic structures, legitimacy in processes of global governance, and the legitimacy of international norms. Researchers are divided between those who see legitimacy and legitimation as necessary part and intrinsic practice in international relations, and those who find the lack of legitimacy or legitimation as problematic and search for suitable solutions (Clark 2005). Acknowledging that legitimation is observable as performances by state actors in competitive processes, I understand legitimation as a deliberate political choice and a social construction, aiming at gaining legitimacy (Goddard/Krebs 2015; Wajner 2019). As deficits of legitimacy and deficiencies in legitimation are as ubiquitous as unavoidable, this research project focuses on state attempts to gain legitimacy through acts of legitimation. The concepts and interconnections presented here form the basis of my understanding of the international system and the system of international norms and laws in which and with which legitimation is practiced, and legitimacy is sought. In distinction to legitimation, legitimacy is a quality attributed to an actor, an actor system, a norm or a set of norms. In this regard, I differentiate between (1) the legitimacy of *rule*, which is the perception of an actor, group of actors, or system of actors' use of and distribution of power as right and just, and (2) the legitimacy of *rules*, which is the perception of a norm or system of norms as right and just.

Legitimacy of Rule

Legitimacy of rule in the international system mainly concerns the quality of a state, or group of states to claim, use, or project power against other state actors and the residual hierarchic order which subsequently emerges from unequal distribution of power.[1] Although assuming an anarchic world, legitimacy is often reduced to a Weberian understanding of justification of rule, authority, a hierarchic system of order among political actors, and thus the use of power by elites (MacKay 2019; Weber 1925). In the sense of legitimacy of rule, legitimation, as the justification of authority of elites to project political power over others, is seen as a means in addition to the use force or coercion. To maintain rule and authority, powerful actors favor legitimation as the least costly option to gain an audience's support. Whereas the use of force and coercion in terms of repression of resistance are costly efforts, state leaders engage in legitimation as the most cost-efficient option to persuade a designated audience to intrinsically support a system of rule because it is perceived as right and just (Hurd 1999; Krebs/Jackson 2007).

Legitimacy of *rule* within states translates to the international level as legitimacy of power and authority among actors. Legitimacy as a product of social interaction and perception, must be gained. As legitimacy can only be granted by a respective audience, no actor can simply declare themselves legitimate, or at least without coercion or voluntary support by an audience any declaration would be effectless. While procedures for legitimation within states are formalized through constitutions, procedures, and institutions, legitimacy-granting processes are more diversified among the international community. For one, the international system is characterized by a multitude of actors who seek influence. For another, legitimacy-granting audiences are not limited to citizens but growing to a global audience due to technological advantages in media and communication.

Legitimacy of rule among states is based on mutual recognition. Regarding the use of force and application of violence, the legitimate monopoly lies with state actors. However, the international system is characterized by a multitude of actors who seek power by using force, i.e. non-state actors like private military and security companies (PMSCs), para-state militia, criminal organizations, terrorists, and terrorist networks are also part of armed conflict scenarios (Krahmann 2013). While I acknowledge the variety of actors, I also restrict the focus of this study to states as legitimate actors to use force and apply violence under the restriction of international treaty law and international customary law (ICRC 2024). In this regard, legitimacy of states in the international system has two socially constructed, legally formalized, and practically institutionalized sources among

[1] While legitimacy of rule, as presented here, focuses on legitimacy *of* a given social order (i.e. the government's), legitimacy *in* a social order is to be distinguished, which is mainly an issue in research focusing on global governance (Clark 2003).

states. On the one hand, sovereign states grant each other legitimacy through the diplomatic act of mutual recognition of statehood. On the other hand, states formally legalized sovereign statehood in mutually accepted treaties granting each other the right to use force and apply violence within the confinements of international war law. While states function as legitimacy-granting institutions for each other, this mainly concerns constitutional legitimacy of rule in terms of actor qualities. Regarding procedural legitimacy of state actions, legitimacy-granting audiences are more diversified. Legitimacy of security policies is dependent on the support of the inner state audience of citizens and voters; the international state community in terms of governments and officials in state organizations; and the international civil society in terms of national, transnational, and global audiences.

Legitimacy of Rules and Legitimate Violence
Based on these considerations, in this study I focus on the U.S. as a sovereign state, as subject to international law, and as legitimacy-seeking actor, practicing legitimation through and in foreign and security policies. In this actor-centered approach, legitimacy of rule accounts for the actor's constitution and status in the international system. While these considerations are essential to conceptualizing actor qualities, the research problem of this study is concerned with the perception of U.S. actions as being legitimate regarding the rules. Legitimacy of *rule* and legitimacy of *rules* are interconnected concerns. On the one hand, constitutional norms attribute legitimacy to actors, and on the other hand, legitimate actors establish legitimate rules. Moreover, norms have constitutional effects by defining actors' status, rights, and positions and have regulative effects by prescribing right and just behavior. Concerning the focus of this research project, rules on legitimate violence are not only the product of U.S. law-making and norm-setting actions, but also the U.S. commit to comply with these rules which allow and constrain the use of force and application of violence. U.S. legitimation of the use of force and application of violence takes place within a systemic framework of traditional, routinized, and recognized rules of procedures and actions, references the framework of legitimate violence, and is assessed against the normative framework of legitimate violence by audiences. The United States thus draw on the legitimacy of the rules on legitimate violence.

The rules referred to here are the sum of all norms on legitimate violence recognized as legal and just by the international state community which constitute the normative order of legitimate violence. The normative order of legitimate violence concerns the body of rules and accepted behavior regulating when to use force and how to apply means of violence appropriately and proportionately on the domestic as well as international level. Moreover, I understand the normative order of legitimate violence as complex discourse encompassing the codified system of rules (international war law), precedent-setting cases, and rhetorical legal and moral justifications for the use of force and application of violence. Thus formally, rules on the legitimate use of force and application of violence are codified in international war law as the main structure of the normative order of legitimate violence. International war law encompasses regulations on international and non-international armed conflict, regulations on international criminal forms of political violence, such as terrorism, and national regulations on state violence and political violence.

Legitimate violence I consider as standards, values, and beliefs codified in norms which are made by states for states and are also changed by state actors through security political actions in the material world (precedent-setting actions) or through rhetorical reinterpretation by state officials. This legal and normative framework spells out the principles for the legitimate use of violence and regulations on the use of force which include the ban of aggressive war and restraint of force to self-defense or in cases of crimes against humanity (*jus ad bellum*). The application of violence in warfare is also restricted by principles including necessity and proportionality as well as protective obligations for civilians (*jus in bello*) (Hurd 2017: 308). Violence-containing norms relevant in this study are mainly established after the Second World War and under U.S. leadership, including war law (*Geneva Conventions 1949*; *UN Charter*), humanitarian law (*Additional Protocols to the Geneva Conventions 1949*; *Declaration of Human Rights*; *Convention against Torture*), and *ius cogens* (ICRC 2024). These internationally agreed-upon norms are nationally rooted, as every state has its own system of rights and legal obligations in times of war. Mainly this body of law is understood as the attempt to contain state violence and thus limit the horrors of war and ban acts of violence that are considered especially cruel and evil and thus are defined as inhumane. Consequently, each legal or customary rule for the conduct of state violence is based on an idea of just use of force and application of violence.

This normative order of legitimate violence is to be seen in the context of the historical development of international law as contingent and prone to change over time depending on varying threat perceptions and changing security environments. The endeavor to limit the uses of force is subject to a philosophical debate that goes back centuries (Koskenniemi 2001). What is considered legitimate violence, thus content of the rules, is dependent on the dominant ideas, values, and beliefs and thus prone to change through state actors and the respective societies. States confirm, adapt, or change this normative order by precedent-setting actions, formal negotiations, or discursive challenges according to their security needs, threat perception, and safety requirements. Changes in the normative order of violence have occurred throughout the past centuries, triggered by paradigm-shifting events in threat perceptions affecting the security environment (Krahmann 2013). Some consider the history of international law as the expansion of colonial rule and consolidating power structures that create and reinforce inequality and secure Western power up until World War II (Donnelly 1998; Eberl 2008; Gong 1984; Gozzi 2007; Koskenniemi 2001). Current laws of war are the product of a political development after World War II, which is often described as one fostering the containment of violence through law (Dunne 2007; Gray 2004; Hurd 2016: 4). After the Second World War, the history of war law, featuring self-restraint and violence containment as driving motives for the establishment of the post-World War II normative framework on the regulation of violence, was mainly described as a development towards the containment of violence by the force of the law. Critically, Hurd examines state interpretations of the ban of war in the *UN Charter* and finds that "the illegality of war makes war harder to choose" (Hurd 2016: 15). Thus, the law spelling out right and wrong uses of force and applications of violence, changes "the terms of political legitimation for states engaging in war" (Hurd 2016: 15).

By agreeing to comply with standards of legitimate violence, states bind themselves to obeying rules which not only limit the amount of applicable violence but also define conditions under which the use of force is in order, legal, and legitimate (Hurd 2016; Hurd 2007a). In this regard, norms on violence have a special character as these are made by states to regulate the behavior of states in absence of an overriding, superior power. However, this understanding of legitimate violence is based on the Westphalian system featuring the state as the only legitimate actor holding the monopoly on violence. Thus, international law attributes qualities to the state and denies non-states certain qualities and rights regarding the use of force and application of violence (Hurd 2017; Krahmann 2013; Senn/Troy 2017). So, the normative order of all norms on legitimate violence functions as both the constitution of actors, their rights, and obligations, and a regulative prescription of when and how to use force for subjects to the law.

The legitimacy of *rules* concerns perception of rules, as in norms and laws, as right and just regarding their constitution, application, and effects as well as the question of sources for acceptance. Rules on legitimate violence draw legitimacy from several sources. Constitutional legitimacy is gained within states when rules on legitimate violence in terms of inner state laws are produced through legitimate institutions (legislative, input), in legitimate procedures (throughput) and accepted as legitimate products (output). Internationally, legitimacy of rules is formally produced through consensus among states, in fixed writing, and through national ratification of rules and recognition. Nationally and internationally, procedural legitimacy of rules is produced through acceptance, and commitment to the rules, compliance in behavior, and demand of obedience by others (Wajner 2019).

Legitimacy of Rule and Rulings with Rules
The above presented approaches, which are concerned with the constitutional aspects of legitimacy, are often based on a Weberian understanding of legitimacy as right to rule. This research project is more interested in the procedural aspects of legitimacy as the performed actions of legitimation by states through engaging with norms. Although the intent to limit the use of force and the horror of war is the driving motive of the makers of the post-1945 normative order of legitimate violence, these legal provisions are also in need of interpretation by state actors who seek legitimacy for their security political actions. In this regard, I define legitimation as the sum of all attempts by states to gain legitimacy of rule (power, status, and domination) and ruling (the use of force and application of violence) based on rules (norms and laws) (ICRC 2024).

The normative order of legitimate violence distinguishes between legitimate and illegitimate, legal and illegal forms of violence; yet, all rules are prone to interpretation of state actors, weighing circumstances and conditions as well as interests, consequences, and effects. States thus engage in legitimation including the interpretation of the rules on legitimate violence to gain legitimacy from a national and international audience. The normative order of legitimate violence and violence-regulating norms is a reflexive structure. On the one hand, laws and norms function as a stable structure enabling and limiting state actions (Reus-Smit 2004: 43). On the other hand, states can actively shape those structures to the advantage of interest-fulfilling politics, norms are thus changeable. State actors have an interest and an obligation to legitimize the use of force and application of violence with reference to regulatory norms on legitimate violence (Reus-Smit 2003).

Thus, I also understand states, and this includes powerful states, as embedded in a social system of expectations, rules, reputations, interests, and dependencies which guide and inform security political actions. State actors cannot act outside this social system. I consider legitimation as inscribed as a necessary activity especially when security interests pose a conflict with a violence-containing norm. In this regard, legitimate violence as subject to a set of norms is prone to political negotiation over the meaning and use of the normative order in the international state system. Thus, legitimation is seen as an inevitable state practice, where states have no choice but to gain legitimacy through legitimation (Reus-Smit

2003). Moreover, especially in democratic states, legitimacy is deeply rooted in the domestic political system. Legitimation works within the social framework of the international system towards the needs of two major audiences: to the inside, legitimation strategies need to convince the national public, and to the outside, legitimation strategies must convince the international state community, mainly allies, but also deter non-allied states. So, seeking legitimacy for foreign and security policies is not only inscribed in the international system but also domestically routinized towards domestic audiences and like-minded allies.

Acknowledging legitimation as a system inherent practice, I understand legitimation as a socially constructed state practice which is actively chosen and acted out strategically in deeds and rhetoric and as such a political instrument as a language between states to gain legitimacy, which is a currency between international state actors. Moreover, the international order of legitimate violence also provides states with certain incentives to gain legitimacy because legitimacy is associated with certain benefits like reliability in expectations, trust, mutual support, exchange, and recognition. Legitimation is mainly discussed as a language to consolidate actions with shared understandings or procedures, institutionalized norms, and international law (Finnemore/Sikkink 1998; Goddard/Krebs 2015; Levi et al. 2009; Wajner 2019). Hurd emphasizes the importance of legitimation as a justification for foreign and security politics as a form to ensure social control by persuading others of compliance and obedience to international law (Hurd 2017: 316; Hurd 2007b; Hurd 1999). In this study, I conceptualize legitimation, more comprehensively exceeding a language-limited appraoch, as a political practice of discursively fixing the meaning and use of norms on the use of force and the application of violence while realizing foreign and security political goals despite or against the interests of other stakeholders. Especially concerning international legitimacy, the legitimation strategy aims at the international state community to tacitly accept and actively share the proposed norm interpretation. Legitimation is thus a political activity which state leaders use to consolidate the use of force and application of violence with normative standards of legitimate violence.

In this regard, legitimation rhetoric references norms as sources for legality and justice. Whereas legalization of state actions uses norms to consolidate security political actions with prescriptions in norms and laws, justification consolidates state actions with underlying normative beliefs, ideas, and values. As legitimacy matters in international politics, legitimation is a necessary state activity in the struggle over legitimacy with norm transformation as a possible side-effect or intendet outcome.

2.2 Legitimate Violence in the War on Terror

This research project builds on a broad scientific debate on legitimate violence in the war on terror. The U.S. use of force and application of violence are subject to critical approaches dealing with the legality of the war on terror and the application of international law, the proclamation of a national emergency and the suspension of constitutional rights, the effects of norm violations in human rights for the international order of legitimate violence, and legitimation crisis within the United States. While scholarship seems unified on the finding that U.S. use of force and application of violence challenge the principles of legitimate violence after 9/11, the research interests, assumptions, and explanatory approaches vary greatly. The U.S. conflicts with norms on legitimate violence in the war on terror concern both the use of force, i.e. the question of when to go to war and for what reasons; and the application of violence in warfare, thus the choice of means and treatment of adversaries.

Critical legal scholarship discusses U.S. use of force and application of violence considering codified and customary law reviewing different aspects of the law. Most fundamentally, critics find puzzling that the U.S. have broken those international laws, they set themselves after the horrors of World War II originally intended to contain state violence in international conflict (Dunne 2007; Venzke 2009). Accounting for the unique character of international law and norms, international legal scholarship recognizes the politics of the United States choosing to voluntaryly comply or re-define situations, choose favorable law (O'Connell 2010), and legitimize political actions (Vernzke 2012; Venzke 2009).

Regarding specific cases, legal scholars discuss the legality of U.S. use of force and application of violence in warfare entertaining different arguments. Regarding legal provisions on the use of force, conflict determination, choice of law, and sovereignty rights are discussed regarding the concept of war and a terrorist adversary. Debated about the legality of detention is whether terrorism counts as crime or international armed conflict under and with consideration of status determination, regulations under sovereignty, and the law of other nations aspects (O'Connell 2010; Crawford 2010). Especially concerning the legality of the war in Iraq, the Bush administration's interpretation of self-defense and the pre-emption norm are discussed critically (Arend 2003; Freedman 2003).

The application of violence in the war on terror is also critically assessed considering rules on legitimate violence and the applicability of the *Geneva Conventions*, with regard to the debate on GTMO detainee status as *unlawful enemy combatant* (Dörmann 2003; Hühnert 2016; Maxwell/Watts 2007; Meisels 2007; Sassòli 2006; Zachary 2005). The legality of captivity in GTMO is questioned regarding the interpretation of the *Geneva Conventions* and *Common Article 3* in particular, as well as detainee treatment in captivity regarding CIA interrogation methods and the *Torture Convention* as well as national legal principles like *habeas corpus* and *due process* (Crawford 2010; Cronogue 2012; de Lonadras 2008; Paust 2003; Proulx 2005; Sassòli 2004). Detainee rights are also debated regarding extraordinary renditions and enhanced interrogation methods (Hajjar 2014; Johns 2013; Sadat 2007; Sadat 2006). Concerning the use of targeted killings, the legality of lethal force is debated with reference to the international ban on assassination and U.S. legal principles (Guiora 2011; O'Connell 2010) and considering issues of sovereignty (Ahmad 2014; Downes 2004) and U.S. legal provisions (Murphy/Radsan 2009).

Thus, the critical legal debate represents the view of the law and the application of the law to judge state actions as legal or unlawful but also recognizes productive aspects of law-interpretation by state actors and by state courts and the effects on legal institutions (Alston et al. 2008). The United States capacity to re-interpret regulations on legitimate violence is not only discussed concerning executive or legislative interventions (Frakt 2012) but also accounting for the effects of national litigation, and Supreme Court rulings, for instance on *habeas cases* (Sall 2013; Wittes et al. 2010). In this regard, Drumbl reviews federal courts' decisions and their influence on the development of detention law and discusses legal problems with prosecution (Drumbl 2005).

Consequently, the critical legal debate on violence in the war on terror features not only legal interpretations of U.S. politics and the production of law through U.S. policies, but also includes normative aspects of the law, developing recommendations up to moral appeals to the United States government on the use of force, application of violence, and interpretation of the law. For instance, Radsan and Murphy discuss legal and moral principles for CIA targeting procedures (Radsan/Murphy 2011). Likewise, Wachtel demands a clear legal definition of assassination and legislative regulations for the use of targeted killings from U.S. Congress (Wachtel 2005) and Young is concerned with principles on accountability, transparency, judicial and legislative overview, and regulations for *due process* in executive targeting decisions (Young 2014). By judging international policies and morally appealing to government officials, the international legal scholarship is not only an observer and examiner of security political discourse but also actively intervenes in security political discourse.

While the critical legal debate is concerned with applying the law to judge state actions in legal and moral terms, the debate on lawfare is concerned with the instrumentalization of protective legal provisions creating a strategic disadvantage for states, and for democracies in particular. The concept of lawfare conceptualizes governments' fear of strategic disadvantages legitimizing emergency rights and the temporary suspension of basic human rights (Stephens 2011).[2] The term lawfare was coined by U.S. Major General Charles Dunlap (2001) and means "the use of international law and litigation as a method of gaining military advantage" (Luban 2008: 2020). As Sadat and Geng argue, the term has been used in defense of *habeas cases* of GTMO detainees, torture cases, and cases of extraordinary renditions. Luban argues that the "lawfare hypothesis," which was adopted by the Bush administration, thus reflects a major fear in the war on terror. The United States could be defeated by their own compliance to the rule of law, as enemies, international terrorists, take advantage of the self-binding of the U.S. to the violence-containing and protective laws, causing a strategic disadvantage for the U.S. in an asymmetric warfare. The concept even appears in the *2005 National Defense Strategy* (Department of Defense 2005) and accuses the enemies of the U.S. of using, next to terrorist means, legal processes and access to international fora to weaken the U.S. (Luban 2008: 2020). However, as Luban states, the idea of lawfare is "fundamentally, a paranoid overreaction to perfectly legitimate legal challenges to Guantánamo detentions" (Luban 2008: 2021). Thus, albeit the explanatory value of lawfare for U.S. strategic actions in applying violence and arguing for the legality, Luban criticizes the concept of lawfare as an argument for avoiding legal engagement (Luban 2008: 2021). Sadat and Geng even condemn the concept of lawfare as a "fruitless—and even dangerous—rhetorical debate" (Sadat/Geng 2010).

While the critical legal debate and the debate on lawfare deal with the interpretations and possible instrumentalization of the law, research on states of emergency and exceptionalism in times of security crisis deals with the suspension and absence of the law. Steyn describes the problem of democratic governments that face events of crisis and manage them with means of force disproportionate to the crisis: "Executive branches of government, faced with a perceived emergency, often resort to excessive measures" (Steyn 2004:1). This body of literature is concerned with the dilemma in democracies, which are under massive and perceivably existential threat, between the rule of law restricting state violence and the permitted use of force and application of violence in self-defense. Facing security threats, democratic societies are more and more willing to suspend robust violence-constraining normative standards hoping to (re-)gain safety using massive force. The state of emergency declared by President Bush after 9/11, allowed for the temporary suspension of constitutional civil rights and

[2] For a critical assessment of the strategic use of 'lawfare' by states see Butler (2015).

the empowerment of the president. This was legally fixed with the passing of the *USA PATRIOT Act*, which allowed the Attorney General to imprison any alien suspect of terrorist activities and threatening national security. Additionally, the *Military Order of November 13, 2001*, allows for the indefinite detention of enemy combatants and the trial before a military commission. As Agamben concludes, these main legal changes situate detainees in the war on terror outside the standards of international law, as prisoners are not granted *Geneva Rights*, and outside U.S. legal provisions (Agamben 2004: 9–10; Butler 2006).

Throughout the war on terror, the argument of exceptionalism by the U.S. government is critically discussed by the literature concerning detainees regarding constitutional and procedural rights in Guantanamo Bay Detention Camp (Greenberg et al. 2008) and the use of torture and enhanced interrogation methods (Greenberg 2006; Greenberg/Dratel 2005). Research on states of emergency and exceptionalism as a political strategy is also concerned with the development and the effects of prolonged suspension and emergency regulations on the state legal system and order with negative consequences for civil rights (Esch 2010; Förster/Lemke 2016). In addition to these approaches which mainly deal with national law, scholars discuss the U.S. attempt to place Guantanamo detainees outside the scope of international law. As this cross-section of international law and international norms, scholars coining the term "the legal black hole" for Guantanamo discuss the creation of a law-free zone and the effects of U.S. legal exceptionalist arguments on international violence-containing norms and normative order (Steyn 2004; Wilde 2005; Wilson 2003). Next to the approach to the specific legal situation created by the United States based on territorial location and sovereign and treaty law (Gregory 2006; Kaplan 2005; Wilde 2005), Guantanamo is discussed with regard to the constitutional rights of prisoners based on international legal status on provisions on treatment in captivity as well as legal obligations of the United States in trying detainees (Alexander 2013; Fletcher 2004). The state of emergency is thus considered a territorial space and a discursive space for the construction of the absence of the law (Aradau 2007; Aradau/Van Munster 2009). Neocleous challenges the idea of a permanent state of emergency and the notion of normalization of exception in law. He questions whether legal emergency categories, such as extraordinary renditions or enemy combatants, have become the new rule and whether exceptionalism has transformed the world into a lawless one (Neocleous 2006: 193–194). Similarly, rejecting the idea of a law-free zone, Johns argues that Guantanamo Bay Detention Camp is a zone in which new regulations are made as an exception to discarded rules and by practical procedures. The permanence of the structures installed over the years on the leased territory are proof to a political effort that enabled, prolonged, and consolidated indefinite detention as a violent act of the U.S. in the war on terror (Johns 2005; Johns 2013: 70–108).

IR norm research is mainly concerned with how state activities of making and breaking international law have shaped and changed the normative order of violence. Norm research in international relations also recognizes a conflict of U.S. security politics with international war law and violence-containing norms. Reflecting on the policies of the Bush administration after 9/11, Dunne, Hurd, and Reus-Smit discuss whether the policies implemented after 9/11 caused "a legitimacy crisis" (Dunne 2007: 270). They argue that since 9/11 state leaders have increasingly questioned norms that used to be considered robust international rules for containing violence and limiting the horrors of war in efforts to counter terrorism. According to Dunne, since 9/11 fundamental rights have been in danger of being sacrificed to short-term security interests and U.S. policies question "fundamental human rights commitments" (Dunne 2007: 270). Especially regarding detention and torture, Dunne sees a legitimacy crisis of human rights triggered by U.S. security politics in the war on terror (Dunne 2007; Reus-Smit 2007). Likewise, Hurd argues that U.S. use of force in the war on terror undermines norms on legitimate violence, causing a crisis of legitimacy for U.S. power, norms on legitimate violence, and the U.S. hegemonic position in the international system (Hurd 2007b). The intent of norms on legitimate violence, which was to contain state violence, is thus in conflict with the interest-shaped war on terror strategy of the United States.

In the war on terror, several cases of norm conflicts occurred concerning torture (Greenberg 2006; Liese 2009), indefinite detention (Maran 2006), targeted killings (Banka/Quinn 2018; Senn/Troy 2017), and extraordinary renditions (Sadat 2007; Sadat 2006). Although international law on international and non-international armed conflict remains in effect, the question of its effectiveness in containing state violence has been raised in the light of U.S. counterterrorism activities. Normative approaches on U.S. conflicts with norms on legitimate violence deal with: contradictions to a norm and breaches or non-compliance (Drumbl 2003; Hurd 2007b; Keating 2014; Liese 2009; Venzke 2009); dissociation from a norm or its transgression (Evers 2017); decreasing adherence to norms (McKeown 2009; Rosert/Schirmbeck 2007; Shannon/Keller 2007); the end of a norm's life (Kutz 2014); and with the emergence and diffusion of alternating ('bad') norms (Heller/Kahl 2013; Jose 2016; Pratt 2018).

Building on these debates on legitimate violence in the U.S. war on terror, I propose a comprehensive approach accounting for the complexity of the process of state legitimation activities to secure power in times of (prolonged) crisis—thus I propose norm transformation to understand norm dynamics and strategic understanding of legitimation as political practice, which I discuss in more detail in Chap. 3. In this regard, I understand 9/11 as an event with far-reaching consequences for national and international security political decisions. Not only did the attacks trigger a violent reaction by the United States, but also 9/11 constitutes a security political caesura concerning the legitimate use of force and permitted amount of violence questioning the global normative order of legitimate violence. Security crises I consider as politically constructed situations of emergency. Security crises are not only discursively constructed but also politically used as an argumentative basis and reference for political issue framing and legitimation narratives through strategic political rhetoric. As such, I consider 9/11 a security political event which was referred to as causal for a national emergency and security crisis in the United States. As event I consider 9/11 and the immediately following state of emergency a window of opportunity and motor for the transformation of violence-regulating norms. Overall, I argue that the modalities of international law on legitimate state violence—the scope of application, the conflict determination, the status definitions—are under transformation. In this study, I examine the case of indefinite detention as a norm conflict in the war on terror. Indefinite detention[3] is the incarceration of men by U.S. security personnel at the designated area of the military base, Guantanamo Bay Detention Camp, for an unspecified amount of time, without charges, and with unclear purpose. In this regard, the case of indefinite detention constitutes a case of norm transformation in U.S. detention law and international law which is practically legitimized by U.S. presidents. The *Geneva Convention* is the main international legal provision questioned in application by the United States after 9/11. However, the *Geneva law* is not dead, as the U.S. still claim protections for regular forces; yet the *Geneva Conventions* might be less and less seen fit to meet the realities of conflict scenarios and state interests. In this understanding, I consider the war on terror a security political discursive era, during which the normative framework of legitimate violence is re-negotiated and norms on violence as well as underlying conceptions of the right and just application of violence are changed in the process. While these norm dynamics play out in a complex system of actors, norms, and relationships, I argue that the U.S. strategically engage in legitimation fostering norm transformation, as I explain in more detail in the following. Building on the debates discussed, I understand legitimation as a complex strategic process consisting of a series of government actions designed to

[3] The terminology of 'detention' and 'detainee' is deliberately used by the U.S. in order to avoid the term 'prisoner' which is clearly regulated in the *Geneva Conventions of 1949*. In this thesis, I adopt the U.S. terminology for analytical reasons, however this does not signify agreement with U.S. detention policies.

gain legitimacy for the use of force and application of violence with reference to legal and normative prescriptions in a social setting.

2.3 Legitimation as a Strategic Political Practice for Norm Transformation

As the critical legal debate shows, arguing for the legality and justice of U.S. security policies is a strategic government practice. Legitimation is thus used by U.S. government actors to manage norm conflicts and gain support for foreign and security policies not only concerning the national public but also addressing the international state community. Hence, political actors follow legitimation strategies while acting out legitimation as a political practice to gain support for a political course of action and foster norm transformation. In this regard, the practice of legitimation in norm transformation processes consists of several patterned and routinized actions, which are based on a shared conception of background knowledge and are performed competently, experienceable to an audience, and observable in the material world and in discourse (Adler/Pouliot 2011).[4] In distinction to the practice of legitimation, a legitimation strategy concerns the content of the legitimation practice, and as powerful state actors perform a practice of legitimation, the political strategy conveyed through this practice may differ greatly.

Strategic positioning starts on the national level with political actors shaping national interest, identifying threats, choosing means to the defined end, and align national and international audiences as well as strategic allies in support (Goddard/Krebs 2015: 9–12; Goddard 2006). All actors practicing legitimation are embedded in social and cultural relationships formed in the international system and no one can just realize personal interests (Reus-Smit 2003). Especially state leaders, although acting as one person, are bound to the social and security cultural ties that brought them to this powerful position and keep them in a powerful position. Thus, legitimation as a strategy is the product of national interest-forming processes, consensus-finding and deliberation, as well as social and cultural factors (Goddard/Krebs 2015: 15; Finnemore 1996: 2). As Goddard and Krebs argue, legitimation is the attribution of meaning to events and actions in the world through explaining, sense-making, and framing of issues

[4] See Chapter 3 and Chapter 4 for a detailed discussion of theoretical assumptions and development of a conceptual understanding of norm transformation and the practice of legitimation.

and actions and thus a strategy through which "[t]hreats are constructed, not merely revealed" (Goddard/Krebs 2015: 16; Esch 2010). Legitimation matters for state actors depending on the visibility of security policies and the government's need for mobilizing the public for support (Goddard/Krebs 2015: 18–19). On the national level, legitimation is mainly concerned with consolidation and unification for a common cause to use force and apply violence. So, political actors are driven by the need to gain support from a designated audience by using persuasive language, and breach gaps between politically favored actions and diverging normative understandings. In this regard, legitimation strategies are tailor-made for audiences and thus practiced in a competitive contest over dominant positions, meanings, convictions, and beliefs (Goddard/Krebs 2015: 18–26).

In international power politics, legitimation is a performative act which is strategically used unilaterally to secure power (Hurd 2007b: 210; MacKay 2019; Reus-Smit 2004). In this sense, legitimation concerns state strategies to define, maintain, or advance their power position within the international hierarchy of the international state system or with reference to a single adversary (MacKay 2019).[5] Contrary to such strategies for the legitimation of rule, authority, and power, legitimation can also be used to strategically argue for the legality and justice of actions. As Goddard and Krebs argue, legitimacy-seeking activities which are developed by elites as part of "grand strategies" can be used in competitive situations by state actors as an expression of power to gain advantages over others (Goddard/Krebs 2015: 8–9). Emphasizing the importance of rhetoric and global advancements in multi-media communication, Wajner argues that state actors are "battling for legitimacy" in international conflicts to win the support of international audiences (Wajner 2019: 1037). In this regard, legitimation is a performance in international power politics and strategically used in international conflicts to justify the use of force and the application of violence with reference to norms on legitimate violence. Repeated use of legitimation strategies to consolidate political actions with normative prescriptions ultimately has effects on the normative structure (Wajner 2019: 1037; Krebs/Jackson 2007; Payne 2001).

Legitimation is necessary wherever the administrations have challenged the normative framework of standards of legitimate violence, i.e. a single or a set of violence containing norms. Challenges and norm conflicts in this sense include state activities that are considered in breach with the norm, thus are called illegal or norm-breaking actions; the interpretation of a norm in use and/or meaning that is contradictory to former applications of the norm; and the introduction

[5] On a comprehensive conception of hierarchies in international relations accounting for different logics of hierarchy see: Bially Mattern/Zarakol 2016.

of new terminology, phrases and adding of new meaning to the norm's content (Hurd 2007b; Keating 2014: 6). As discussed in the previous section, the legal points of conflict show the demand for legitimation, which the U.S. are facing, concerning the use of force and the application of violence in the war on terror. To consolidate strategic wants and favored political activities on the one side and respect the violence-containing character of international war law on the other side, legitimation is necessary. That is, the U.S. need a strategy that plausibly argues for the rightfulness of their actions and the lawfulness of the use of force and application of violence. As Hurd argues, the U.S. operate in a "dual dynamic in the use of norms by states, where states are constituted to seek legitimacy for their actions by associating them with existing norms while also behaving strategically to reconstruct the norms in ways that they believe will serve their interests" (Hurd 2007b: 209).

As norm-takers, states use interpretive legitimation actions to consolidate security political actions with normative prescriptions (Keating 2014). In this regard, norms on legitimate violence may be interpreted as containing violence or as permitting violence (Hurd 2016; Krahmann 2013). However, legitimation is also a strategic tool to gain and to keep control over dominant interpretation and stabilize state power through norm shaping. Thus, legitimation can either have an empowering or a delegitimizing effect (Hurd 2016: 2; Hurd 2007b). Although states move within given normative structures, they are also capable of changing and creating new normative structures to their liking. Thus, state actors are the creators of norms and the actors who induce change, making powerful state actors both norm-takers and norm-makers.

Although states may not always abide by the traditional interpretation of the rules due to strategic reasons, they argue that their violent actions are legal and just and thus legitimate (Hurd 2007a). While security political decisions are often framed as acting within the margins of the laws, maximizing state interests often entails bending the law by creatively interpreting the normative framework (Shannon 2000). In these cases of norm conflict, the need for legitimation is especially high, as the use of force and application of violence fundamentally contradict the common interpretation of the protective norm. These legitimation arguments need to convince not only the international community—convince allies and deter foes—but also need to be convincing towards the national people. However, at times these interpretations are so far off the original norm's intent, that the interpretation is perceived as undermining or innovating the norm, changing the legal understanding by setting precedent and introducing altered readings (Hühnert 2016). Thus, states act as norm-shapers and norm-makers by applying legitimacy-seeking actions which shape law by setting precedent and function as a point of legitimatcy-seeking references in similar or different future cases. As Hurd argues in this regard, "[c]hanges in norms and in state power have consequences for the underlying structures of international society, and so American behaviour is part of the broader process of changing and remaking the social foundations of the international system" (Hurd 2007b: 198). Finally, legitimation thus serves to foster normative innovations for single norms with effects on the normative order.

Norms on legitimate violence, and war law in particular, are both a resource of legitimacy-seeking rhetoric and a subject of dispute in interpretation, contestation, or redefinition of violence-regulating norms. Legitimacy-seeking actors refer to the law as normative framework and reference point legally consolidating and justifying the use of force and application of violence. While the law is used as language and reference in legitimation strategies, the law is also subject to change through legitimacy-seeking activities. International law is fixed in meaning in text but prone to change not so much by negotiation and contract-making diplomacy but more by interpretation of states and the legitimation practice (Hurd 2007a; Hurd 2007b). Thus, international law is in constant flux in an inner state and interstate discourse of competing interpretations over the meaning and use of norms. The meaning of the law is generated and altered by spoken interpretation and unchallenged acts of violence, active and tacit, which may set precedent and be used as justification by imitators. Interpretation of international law in deeds and arguments is a strategic political choice. The choice of law and the legal framing of a conflict are political decisions which are made by powerful state actors balancing state interests, costs, benefits, and situational options (Reus-Smit 2004; Wajner 2019).

As the legal debate shows, the counterterrorism policies of the U.S. use acts of violence which contradict the violence-containing character of international norms. The interpretation of a given norm in meaning and use lacks legitimacy, if the interpretation and actions taken accordingly are not in line with the commonly agreed-upon understanding of the norm, thus demanding state actions of legitimation. As Hurd finds "that US norm breaking is inescapably connected to efforts to legitimate new norms, and that the process is a continuation of the political struggle over legitimation in international relations" (Hurd 2007b: 194). Moreover, the United States not only use legitimation to consolidate violent actions with commonly shared normative understandings but also use legitimacy-seeking activities to shape violence-regulating norms to realize political goals and to govern others. In this process, the United States thus act as norm-taker and strategic norm-maker. As norm-taker, the U.S. act within given normative structures. Yet, they are strategically choosing where to stay within the legal boundaries and where to exceed them. However, the United States' use of force and application of violence constitute a norm conflict, which may have negative consequences both domestically and internationally. As the United States do not operate in a political vacuum but are dependent on others to agree with their policies, especially when sensitive regulations on state violence are at stake, state actors engage in strategic legitimation. All these activities combined I understand as the practice of legitimation designed to change the meaning and use of violence-containing norms, eventually inducing transformation, which ultimately has an effect (intended or not) on the international legal and normative order of violence.

Conceptualizing legitimation mainly as a political practice, which is designed to realize security political interests and adapt the normative order by working towards a change in single norms or the normative understanding of provisions on violence, I reconstruct the political actions involved in legalization and justification of norm transformation. While the discussed approaches cover partial aspects of legitimacy and legitimation, such as strategies, rhetorical means, functions, subjects of justification, or legalization, the debate lacks a complex approach that encompasses the different elements of legitimation and explains state actions and effects on norms and normative structures considering strategic alignments. With this comprehensive practice-oriented appraoch, I want to provide an approach to legitimation which accounts for the complexity of actions in the material world and rhetoric of powerful state actors. I discuss how legitimation can be used to foster norm transformation in the case of violence-regulating norms in Chap. 3. Furthermore, I develop a conceptual understanding of legitimation as a practice in Chap. 4 and conduct an empirical analysis on legitimacy-seeking activities adding up to the practice of legitimation by U.S. Presidents Bush and Obama in Chaps. 5 and 6.

3 Transformation of Violence-Regulating Norms

As this study seeks to contribute to norm research in International Relations by providing insights to the practices of legitimation of powerful states, in this chapter, I focus on how states can induce norm change and act as norm entrepreneurs for violence-enabling norms. The theory-guided considerations serve the development of my conceptual understanding of practices of legitimation in norm transformation processes in the subsequent chapters.[1] Following Friedrichs and Kratochwil's approach of pragmatism and abduction, I favor working with concepts rather than theory (Friedrichs/Kratochwil 2009).[2] The concepts presented in the following build the ground for the development of analytical categories for the case study. As the major concept to explain norm dynamics in the normative order of legitimate violence[3] in the war on terror, I propose norm transformation because it allows for a detailed account of norm change which combines the stability of an established norm with the emergence of a new or rather adapted norm.

In the following, I develop my understanding of norm transformation drawing on IR research. In the first step, I discuss approaches to norm conflicts in the war on terror, conceptual considerations on norms, and the models for norm dynamics. In a second step, I focus on conceptual aspects of norm transformation.

---

[1] For a detailed development of the conception of practices and legitimation see Chap. 4, and for the analytical use of the concepts see Chap. 5. For a critical discussion of the concepts and usability in further research see Chap. 6.

[2] See Chap. 4 for further details on the methodological approach, the research design, and further presuppositions for the case study.

[3] See Chap. 2 on the conception of legitimation and the normative order of legitimate violence.

D. Hühnert-Hugendubel, *Between Rules of War and Rule of Law*,
https://doi.org/10.1007/978-3-658-49121-5_3

Building on existing definitions of norm transformation, I propose a comprehensive conception of norm transformation as a complex model to understand and analyze norm change in international relations. With respect to the criticism of the 'good norm bias,' I discuss the idea of 'bad norms' and propose an alternative wording. Adopting and modifying the concept of norm entrepreneurship, I reflect the United States' role as norm entrepreneur in the transformation of violence-regulating norms.

3.1 Norms and Norm Dynamics

Norm transformation is but one concept to model a dynamic process of change in a single norm or a normative order. To develop a comprehensive model of norm transformation, I reflect International Relations scholarship on norms and lay out my understanding of norms regarding violence-regulating norms. Drawing on research on norm dynamics, I review the norm life cycle and its adaptations to develop a procedural but non-linear understanding of norm dynamics. Furthermore, I discuss various conceptions of norm change arguing why I favor norm transformation as the main conception to model U.S.-driven norm dynamics after 9/11.

3.1.1 Norms and Norm Dynamics in the War on Terror

The war on terror shows a qualitative change in the use of violence and in the interpretation of violence-regulating norms.[4] Countering terrorism, the United States have used an excessive amount of force and types of violence which are prohibited by established violence-containing norms, namely, torture, indefinite detention (Greenberg/Dratel 2005; Greenberg et al. 2008; Rose 2004; Walen/Venzke 2007), targeted killings (assassinations, leadership decapitations) (Hurd 2017; Price 2012; Senn/Troy 2017), and extraordinary renditions (Sadat 2007). As discussed in Chap. 2 from a legal point of view, U.S. actions were widely considered in breach with national and international law. Likewise, in IR scholarship the violent acts in the war on terror raised doubts concerning the stability of violence-regulating norms. In this section, I review approaches for norm change and concepts for norm dynamics dealing with violence in the war on terror to

[4] In the following, I use the term violence-regulating norms not as a synonym but as an upper category for both terms: violence-containing and violence-enabling norms.

explain my conceptual focus on norm transformation as the main concept to model norm dynamics and the U.S. role in these processes in the subsequent section.

In the war on terror the United States engaged in a couple of norm conflicts all sharing the same pattern: while adherence to the core norm is emphasized, a new regulation is favored for dealing with terrorists. As Keating describes, the norm conflicts seem to also follow the same stages: secrecy, overt violation, justification, and innovation (Keating 2014: 6). Secrecy entails state efforts to keep the violent actions from other actors' knowledge to avoid sanctions and reputational losses. Once illegitimate actions are public, states turn to open violations, breaching violence-containing norms without legitimation efforts. As Keating argues, this strategy may not prove effective for long when dealing with robust norms because the norm deviance will not go unsanctioned. Then, justification will be necessary, which entails the claim to comply with given rules. For instance, the Bush administration argued that violent actions are legal according to the proposed interpretation of the rules. The final step in this sequence amounts to introducing norm innovations which cover the preferred violent act (Keating 2014: 6). Considering the conflicts with violence-containing norms in the war on terror, they all have in common, that the United States emphasize the importance of the initial, robust norm and repeatedly affirm their commitment to the norm. However, as the violence-containing norm remains, the described four-step sequence is not completed in all cases. In the case of extraordinary renditions clandestine actions seem to prevail (Sadat 2006); in the case of torture innovations failed (Deitelhoff/Zimmermann 2020); but in the cases of detention and targeted killings new regulations were introduced (Alexander 2013; Banka/Quinn 2018; Sall 2013).

In contrast to most legal scholars who are interested in determining the (il-) legality of a state's actions, norm scholars seek to explain norm conflicts, as in non-compliant behavior. To this end, scholars of norms in IR have developed various explanations for the U.S. use of violence in the war on terror. Approaches dealing with norm dynamics seek to understand and explain the use of extreme violence and thus the failure of violence-containing norms: contradictions to a norm and breaches or non-compliance (contestation, non-compliance, violation); dissociation from a norm or its transgression (norm dissociation, norm transgression); decreasing adherence to norms (erosion, regress, decay/decline); the end of a norm's life (norm disappearance, norm death); and with the emergence and diffusion of alternating ('bad') norms (norm emergence, norm diffusion, norm transformation).

Contradictions to a norm and breaches or breaking are mainly considered as (legal) contestation (Keating 2014; Liese 2009; Venzke 2009), non-compliance[5], transgression[6] (Evers 2017), or violation (Drumbl 2003; Hurd 2007b)[7]. A norm violation or contestation occurs when a state acts to pursue an interest that conflicts with the prescription of the norm. As not every norm violation automatically causes instability of the contested norm, the question remains how contestation affects norms especially in cases of reoccurring non-compliance of many or powerful actors or challenges of robust norms and grave violations. Like most critical legal scholars, many norm researchers interpret the U.S. security politics in the war on terror as norm violation leading to the erosion of protective norms (Keating 2014; Shannon/Keller 2007). For many IR scholars, contestation of violence-regulating norms or the failure of norms to prevent extreme acts of violence question the robustness of violence-regulating norms. As Deitelhoff and Zimmermann (2020) argue "robustness is high when a norm enjoys widespread acceptance by norm addressees and when its claims guide the actions of addressees by and large" (Deitelhoff/Zimmermann 2020: 53). While the application of violence clearly changed, indicating applicatory contestation of violence-regulating norms, the original norms' validity was also in danger (Deitelhoff/Zimmermann 2020: 70). Possibly, U.S. efforts to emphasize the applicability of protective norms for regular troops even strengthened protective norms (Kutz 2014). Yet, the scope of application of protective and violence-restricting norms changed in U.S. interpretation, no longer including suspected terrorists and collaborators. Furthermore, adapted wording in U.S. legitimation excludes certain violent acts from the restrictive normative scope. Enhanced interrogation, *unlawful enemy combatants*, and targeted killings are all not subject to protective norms and normative bans, according to U.S. arguing.

However, norm conflicts are very complex and depend on various factors. As Shannon and Keller argue, leadership style matters regarding political decision-making and norm adherence. Investigating the reasons for norm violations, Shannon and Keller examine political decision-making focusing on leadership characteristics. In the case of the Bush administration's decision to go to war in Iraq they find the sensitivity to the political context and universal view of the international system as influential factors for norm compliance or deviation.

---

[5] On conceptual considerations on contestation and compliance see: Lantis/Wunderlich2018, Wiener 2004, Wiener 2007, Wiener 2017, Wiener/Pütter 2009, and Zimmermann 2016.

[6] Evers argues that states deliberately violate norms and commit "intentional and purposeful violations of international law" which he calls norm transgression (Evers 2017: 786).

[7] On the conception of norm violation see: Shannon 2000.

They thus find that contestation is dependent on specific individuals, their beliefs, values, and world views (Shannon/Keller 2007: 80).

Likewise, Hurd points to the productive or destructive power options available to state leaders who engage in norms and possibly induce change. Hurd analyzes the U.S. attempt to change the meaning of the preemption norm by examining how the United States proposes a new interpretation of the norm, and the impact this has on the U.S. position of power, the norm, and the normative order of legitimate violence (Hurd 2007b: 198). Hurd argues that legitimation matters in states' engagement with norms. Regarding U.S. attempts to change the meaning of violence-regulating norms, Hurd mentions two factors. On the one hand, norm violation may indicate a loss of the norm's power to guide behavior. On the other hand, repeated violation might indicate an attempt to delegitimize and destabilize the norm (Hurd 2007b: 197).

Another interpretation is to consider U.S. norm conflicts as revisionist activities and cases of decreasing adherence to norms as in erosion (Banka/Quinn 2018; Rosert/Schirmbeck 2007) or regress (McKeown 2009). Rosert and Schirmbeck examine the weakening of the ban on torture and argue that even robust norms can lose adherence over time (Rosert/Schirmbeck 2007). Similarly, McKeown examines the case of torture and argues that the United States act as a norm revisionist, reversing the norm life cycle by fostering a regress in the torture norm. The re-framing of violent actions as not amounting to torture is considered an issue-framing strategy of the Bush administration in a degenerative sense (McKeown 2009: 10). Banka and Quinn use the revisionist life cycle proposed by McKeown to analyze the normative shift in the assassination norm in the case of U.S. targeted killings. Especially regarding the torture and assassination norms, the conceptions of norm death (Kutz 2014; McKeown 2009) and norm disappearance (Panke/Petersohn 2012; Panke/Petersohn 2016) are discussed (critically Pratt 2018). According to Pratt, death of a norm means "that the prohibition has disappeared" (Pratt 2018: 4). While violent acts continue to be applied, it is no longer considered normatively wrong. Reasons for norm death or disappearance may be historically changing conditions, or the norm ceases to be applied. Another reason may be the deliberate non-use and erosion of the norm by active politics working towards the death of the norm and fostering an alternative norm. "The end result is that a norm that did regulate, constitute, or otherwise dispose actors in significant ways ceases to exist" (Pratt 2018: 4). Likewise, addressing not only the breach with robust norms but also the innovation and introduction of new regulations, authors discuss the emergence and diffusion of 'bad' norms (Heller/Kahl 2013) such as the new detention or the new killing norm. In this regard, Jose examines the unconventional case of human rights organizations suppressing the emergence of the targeted killing norm fostered by the United States (Jose 2017).

However, these approaches often underestimate the stabilizing effect of deviant actions and overlook the definition of new conditions for a norms scope of application. While contestation questions the meaning and usefulness of a norm, however, in the given norm conflicts, contestation only applies to distinct sections of the norm's scope of application. For example, whereas the Bush administration denies applying POW status to terrorist fighters, the U.S. adherence to the *Geneva Conventions* is emphasized. This also negates the death or disappearance of detention norms, as these regulations continue to be applied. For the same reason, dissociation or regress do not fully describe the U.S. engagement with detention norms. While the United States continue to claim the validity of war law and protective norms for regular participants in armed conflict, they deny declared terrorists the comfort of protective rights. Thus, the U.S. use of violence in the war on terror shows not only norm failure to prevent state violence but also shows the importance of norms as source for state legitimation efforts (Keating 2014; Shannon 2000). This example shows that the United States factor norms into their strategy to legitimize the use of force and application of violence.

The approaches capture two points in state actions. First, the approaches emphasize the importance of power politics of interest-driven actors who may deliberately choose non-compliance and violate a norm to realize security political goals. Second, the approaches capture the importance of legitimation in speech acts. The significance of norms and the normative system to U.S. politics moreover shows in the legitimation efforts, which the United States undertook transforming violence-regulating norms to match their needs (Hurd 2007b; Hurd 2017).

Yet, the mentioned approaches do not capture the change in the detention norm. By establishing specific rules for the treatment of terrorists, the U.S. politics strengthen the core norm but also contribute to creating a new norm understanding applicable to the adversary. Also, the concept of norm death does not fully capture the phenomenon, as the POW norm or the torture norm do not seize to exist or be used. Violence-regulating norms did not die, nor did they lose importance. I conclude that the phenomenon of discarding some parts of robust norms while establishing new regulations for declared exceptions or new situations is captured by the concept of norm transformation (Pratt 2018).

While the above-mentioned approaches are generally fit to conceptually grasp norm deviations, the phenomenon in the war on terror is best captured by the concept of norm transformation. The idea of transformation applies on several levels. I understand the war on terror as a short-term trend in a larger cyclical development of social negotiation over violence-regulating norms.[8] Assuming that detention norms are but one area of norm transformation in the war on terror (other norms regarding the ban on assassinations and torture), I suppose that several single norm transformations taken together affect the complex normative structure of legitimate violence. I understand the overall development in the war on terror as a transformation from violence-containing norms to violence-enabling norms (Jose 2017; Senn/Troy 2017). In cases of indefinite detention, I argue that the transformative process occurs in violent acts and in normative arguing. I assume that the change in norm interpretation led to the emergence of new, violence-enabling norms fostered by the U.S. legitimation efforts to gain support for the security politics applied in the war on terror. This I understand as a specific norm dynamic, namely a norm transformation process. In the following, I display in more detail my conceptual understanding of norms, norm life cycles, and the specific dynamics of transformation into violence-regulating norms.

3.1.2 Norms: Concepts and Definitions

As discussed in the previous section, research on the war on terror has dealt with norm failure to contain violence. In the following sections, I develop my understanding of violence-regulating norms based on different approaches to norms in security politics. Thereby, I reflect on differing norm conceptions and approaches ranging from rationalist and sociologically influenced approaches to constructivist discursive conceptions and present my understanding of norms, specifically violence-regulating norms in the war on terror. Then, I further discuss cyclical models to explain norm dynamics leading up to the conception of norm transformation in more detail.

International Relations research has shown great effort to explain norm dynamics using different approaches to norms. Although many scholars use the term 'norm,' the conceptions vary widely from defining norms as regularized behavior to understanding norms as discourses representing actor interests and moral and ethical beliefs (Björkdahl 2002). Up to the 1990's a rationalist conception prevailed, defining norms as stabilizing factors, which contribute to stable mutual expectations (Axelrod 1986; Florini 1996; Goertz/Diehl 1992; Raymond 1997). Whereas realists (Axelrod 1986; Keohane 1986) mainly reject norms or regard norms as dependent variables, rationalist-institutionalists see norms as intervening

[8] See Chap. 2 on cyclical developments of international law and especially war law over the past centuries.

variables (Wunderlich 2013). Rationalists-institutionalists consider norms "standards of behavior, defined in terms of rights and obligations" (Krasner 1983: 2). Similarly, Goertz and Diehl emphasize the "regularity and consistency of behavior" as characteristic of norms (Goertz/Diehl 1992: 636). As such, norms are a vital part of regimes, which combine "sets of implicit or explicit principles, norms, rules, and decision-making procedures around which actors' expectations converge in a given area of international relations" (Krasner 1983: 2). Norms are "generalized standards of conduct that delineate the scope of a state's entitlements, the extent of its obligations, and the range of its jurisdiction" (Raymond 1997: 128). In this sense, norms are guarantors of stable expectations over time in a given issue area (Björkdahl 2002: 13).

Although realists never denied the existence of norms, norms were not assigned explanatory value. While a certain stabilizing function and effect is attributed to norms, they are not focal points in explanations but rather dependent or intervening variables. Following the *logic of consequence*, these approaches further share the assumption that states, as actors who seek to maximize their own benefit, only comply with norms when it suits their interest, or when they are forced to do so (reputational loss, social pressure, coercion, or sanctions)[9] (Goertz/Diehl 1992: 637–638; Wunderlich 2013: 21). In this regard, Goertz and Diehl stress the "the importance of sanctions" to ensure compliance (Goertz/Diehl 1992: 638). Regime theory, for instance, uses norms to explain cooperation of states. However, cooperation and the emergence of international institutions were often researched in issue areas with high cooperation benefits and low costs and risks for states, like in social projects (the environment, health) or economic cooperation (Krasner 1983). The value of norms in security politics was thus long underestimated by IR scholarship.

Since the 1990 s, norm theory has advanced to an established section in IR scholarship, positioning norms at the center of research (Finnemore 1996; Kratochwil 1989; March/Olsen 1998). While constructivists emphasize the guidance function of norms regulating behavior in complex social situations, they also attest a constitutive function to norms ascribing identities and interests. As Finnemore and Sikkink define, a norm is "a standard of behavior for actors with a given identity" (Finnemore/Sikkink 1998: 891). Distinguishing between regulative and constitutive norms, Finnemore and Sikkink conceptualize norms and international law in terms of content, function, and intent. Norms are *regulative* as

[9] In this regard, Goertz and Diehl distinguish cooperative, hegemonic, and decentralized norms, which differ in the degree of conflict between compliance with rules and realization of state interests (Goertz/Diehl 1992: 640).

they "order and constrain behavior" (Finnemore/Sikkink 1998: 891) prescribing desirable behavior (how an actor ought to behave). To the contrary, *constitutive* norms "create new actors, interests, or categories" (Finnemore/Sikkink 1998: 891). Norms not only regulate behavior but also reflect socially shared values, ideas, and interests. Norms are "a set of intersubjective understandings and collective expectations regarding the proper behavior of states and other actors in a given context or identity" (Björkdahl 2002: 15). Norms are embedded in communicative structures. As such, norms are constantly in flux as any norm's meaning is prone to interpretation (Finnemore/Sikkink 1998; Jose 2017). Interpretation of norms' meaning is a communicative process. Since the 1990's, IR scholars have focused on norms as research subject and developed various norm definitions reflecting differing ideas, theoretical assumptions, and philosophical beliefs (Björkdahl 2002: 13). Understandings of norms vary from behavioral concepts emphasizing regularity and normality to normative moral and ethical legitimacy claims for "standards of behavior" (Florini 1996: 364).

Moreover, constructivist norm research approaches emphasize the normative character of norms.[10] In such an understanding, states adhere to norms following a *logic of appropriateness*. As Björkdahl states, "norms prompt justification for action and leave a trail of communication that can be studied" (Björkdahl 2002: 13). As Goertz and Diehl highlight, "norms are *normative*, [...] there are issues of justice and rights of a moral or ethical character" (Goertz/Diehl 1992: 638–639). In a constructivist understanding norm adherence results from internal obligation and conviction of appropriate behavior, norms prescribe how states "ought" to act (Wunderlich 2013: 21–22). As many authors claim, norms prescribe desirable behavior, and thus prescribe how actors are supposed to, 'ought' to behave. Some argue that this *logic of appropriateness* is based on ethical and moral ideas, beliefs, and convictions. As Björkdahl argues, the normative is the distinctive character of prescriptive norms. Norms, interests, and ideas should not be separated. Since norms describe how behavior ought to be, they also express actor's interests and represent values.

However, norms are not to be confused with actual behavior, which may deviate from the norm. "The manner in which states talk about norms is often just as important, if not more so, than how they act. Hence, an exclusive focus on action

[10] By contrast, a sociological perspective on norms entails "normal, customary and usual practices in the international system" (Björkdahl 2002: 14). Such definitions emphasize regularity, normality, and uniformity in behavior but neglect the normative character of norms (Finnemore 1996). Clearly, not all norms need to have a moral component; however, the norms considered in this study are highly normative, as they are based on moral and ethical understandings of how to use force and how to apply violence.

would recognise norms only after states decided to adhere to the norm in question or act upon it" (Björkdahl 2002: 13). This poses a problem, as many norm researchers analyze actors' behavior to trace norms. As Björkdahl defines, norms are "intersubjective understandings that constitute actors' interests and identities, and create expectations as well as prescribe what appropriate behaviour ought to be" (Björkdahl 2002: 21). In addition, Bull argues that defining appropriate behavior lies upon the respective community (Bull 2012: 27–30).

Despite a large research base offering a multitude of approaches, according to Krahmann, most norm definitions share four attributes (Krahmann 2013: 55). (1) Norms express collective social expectations (Payne 2001). Individuals may support a norm or feel obliged to follow it. Yet only groups can establish or change norms, as they express collective social understandings. Changes in collective understandings of ideas, values, and beliefs translate into changes in the norm or its interpretation. (2) Norms are "generalized standards of behavior" (Krahmann 2013: 55; Krasner 1983). Hence, the collective expects that members of the group follow the norm. Sanctions are in place to ensure compliance. (3) Norms are normative. This normative element constitutes the main difference to a rule—which only prescribes a certain behavior (like stopping in front of a red traffic light) without moral engagement. A norm prescribes how the behavior ought to be. In this regard, norms reflect ethical or moral ideas, beliefs, and convictions of a given identity. (4) The "power of a norm" may vary in strength and influence on behavior (Krahmann 2013: 55).

Based on these considerations, the conception of norms used in this study includes the following attributes. Norms I define as generally accepted standards for behavior which a group with a given identity consider appropriate due to a shared understanding of appropriateness. Norms are thus collective. Although individuals may follow or disobey a norm, only groups can establish and enforce norms, with sanctions if necessary. Although individuals may act as norm entrepreneurs, a norm needs collective acceptance and adherence to cascade and become internalized. Norms express the interests of actors containing moral and ethical ideas, values, and beliefs. As such, norms reflect traditions and stabilize expectations. Norms may differ in the degree of institutionalization. Whereas some are highly codified in international law and organizations, others are customary. Norms are regulative prescribing desirable behavior (how an actor ought to behave) and constitutive ascribing attributes to actors. Norms are context specific and embedded in intersubjective communicative structures and discourses. As such, norms are subject to public debate, in which actors discursively produce, question, and negotiate intersubjective meaning of norms. In this regard, norms are the source and point of reference for legitimation. Norm change, even though it may occur event-induced, evolves over long spans of time. As short-term change may show in singular dominant interpretations, permanent norm alterations show in collective agreement which is rather stable over time.

Using this conception, I adopt a constructivist normative conception of norms stressing the moral and ethical routing of norms as standards for behavior based on a socially shared understanding of appropriateness. Acknowledging that this study covers a specific issue area in security politics, I define violence-regulating norms as normative and discursive. I focus on violence-regulating norms as a specific kind of prescriptive norms, which are considered robust and thus less prone to change but instead stable over long periods of time.[11] Such prescriptive norms express rights, define obligations, and establish justice. Regulations on violence are normative, as they are based on ethical and moral ideas, beliefs, and values, on how to apply violence humanely if necessary. Violence-regulating norms are codified in law, institutionalized, and generally are expected to be robust. Violence-regulating norms encompass all codified regulations on legitimate violence and customary regulations on legitimate violence.[12] In this regard, I distinguish between violence-containing and violence-enabling norms. Violence-containing norms express bans and prohibit certain kinds of violence, setting restrictions on state violence, and thus limiting the horrors of war regarding all participants in armed conflict. On the contrary, violence-enabling norms permit state violence intending to grant permission to states to help realize security political goals of single or small groups despite the disadvantages of others (the de-humanized enemy). I consider violence-regulating norms as the product of long-term discursive processes to regulate state violence in which powerful states take active roles in setting, shaping, and changing normative understandings and eventually norms.

Both the individual norms as well as the normative structure of legitimate violence are generally considered robust and less prone to change over time. Even though, many violence-regulating norms are codified in international law and are considered robust and stable, these legal texts need to be interpreted by actors and hence, norms are prone to change which may be triggered by events that challenge ideas, values, and beliefs. Yet, I understand violence-regulating

[11] In the context of this study, violence-regulating norms refer to the codified and customary regulations on violence relevant to the cases treated in the empirical case study of this thesis as developed in Chap. 2.

[12] Violence-regulating norms and legal provisions are here limited to the relevant acts of violence as developed in Chap. 2.

norms[13] as a specific set of norms, which is of high interest for powerful actors to be altered catering security political needs. Assuming self-interest maximizing actors in security politics, taking influence on the shaping and interpretation of regulations on violence is a high priority in violence use and legitimation politics. Thus, powerful actors not only benefit from guiding regulations as they stabilize mutual expectations but also are interested in actively shaping regulations on violence to realize security needs and govern others.

Considering states' engagement with norm interpretation and change, I am interested in norms as subjects to state efforts to legitimize the use of violence and norms as a subject to change through states' legitimation. Understanding norms as source of legitimation means that actors try to frame security political actions as legal (conform to norms and legal provisions) and just (in a generally shared moral understanding), thus legitimate. In this regard, Florini emphasizes the connection between norms and legitimacy, arguing that no norm can exist without being perceived as a "*legitimate* behavioral claim" (Florini 1996: 365). Thus, Florini argues that norm compliance is more dependent on a norm being perceived as legitimate than on enforcement, like through sanctioning (Florini 1996: 364–365). While both factors seem relevant to the lasting implementation of a norm, legitimacy is clearly a decisive factor to norm obedience and thus a relevant factor in states' engagement with norms and in norm transformation processes. Thus, framing security policy in accordance with norm prescriptions is a vital part of communicative processes justifying politics in the international system (Hurd 1999; Hurd 2007a). However, I argue that legitimacy works in two ways: on the one hand, norms can confer legitimacy, but on the other hand, the normative structure pressures actors into justifying their behavior with respect to a norm or a set of norms.[14] As international regulations are always the product of state conduct and negotiation, the law and norms are in flux. Acknowledging different approaches to norm dynamics, I explain my understanding of cyclical development of norms in the following section.

---

[13] As defined in Chap. 2, the normative order of legitimate violence I understand as a complex normative structure consisting of non-codified (customary international law) and codified norms (international law) designed to regulate violence among the various actors in the international system.

[14] The nexus of norms and legitimation is further explained in Chap. 4 on legitimation practices.

3.1.3 Norm Life Cycle or the Cycle of Norm Change

Building on conceptions of norm life cycle and cycle of norm change, in this section, I develop a comprehensive process-oriented model for procedures of norm dynamics including actors, power structures, norms, norm structures, events and situational conditions, and legitimation. Norm dynamics I conceptualize as a complex process that is not necessarily structured linearly, but rather cyclical. Then, I discuss the advantages of the cycle of norm change model with expansions to include the pre-emerging stage and the possibility of norm erosion or even death.

Conceptualizing norm dynamics, I adopt Sandholtz's model of cycle of norm change (Sandholtz 2008). In essence, this model is based on Finnemore and Sikkink's norm life cycle (Finnemore/Sikkink 1998). According to Finnemore and Sikkink, a norm life cycle consists of three stages: norm emergence, norm cascade, and internalization. In the first stage, norm entrepreneurs set the agenda for a given issue area. Norm emergence is fostered by campaigns to persuade as many states as possible to adopt the norm. Once the critical mass is convinced, the cascading phase of a norm's life is reached where more and more states adopt the norm. Internalization is complete when the norm is no longer questioned but taken for granted (Finnemore/Sikkink 1998: 896).

This concept of a linear process of norm life cycle applies to a prominent example in violence-regulating norms. Finnemore and Sikkink examine the development of the *Geneva Conventions* as a case initiated by a civil society norm entrepreneur, who convinced states to engage in a law-making process.[15] The *Geneva Conventions* work as a case in which norms on violence-containment were codified and adopted by many states up to the point where violence-containment is considered a stable and robust norm in international relations.

In this model, norms are treated as things, transitioning from one life stage to another while their content remains unchanged (Krook/True 2010: 104). Norm emergence is conceptualized as a linear bottom-up process. Norm entrepreneurs are mainly actors from civil society, individuals, activist groups, and NGOs, trying to convince states to change their beliefs and actions and to adopt a new norm (Finnemore/Sikkink 1998). Contrary to these main assumptions, norm research on the war on terror has focused on states as motors of change or norm entrepreneurs

[15] Finnemore and Sikkink report that the norm entrepreneur in the case of the subsequently developed *Geneva Conventions* was Henry Dunant, a banker from Switzerland (Finnemore/Sikkink 1998: 897).

instead of viewing states mainly as norm takers (Dunne 2007; Hurd 2007b; Jose 2016; Reus-Smit 2007; Venzke 2009). Concerning the norm conflicts in the war on terror some authors argue that many violence-regulating norms were considered robust and stable over time but eroded or even died during the war on terror (Kutz 2014; McKeown 2009; Panke/Petersohn 2016). While the model of norm life cycle explains how norms come to life and spread, the model does extend to what happens after a norm is well established and how changes in norm content can be explained.

Filling this void, authors who define norms as processes are interested in understanding and explaining the changing contents of norms. Building on the, by now classical, conception by Finnemore and Sikkink model of the norm life cycle, further norm research has since produced a great number of additions, adaptations, and further insights exploring norm emergence, life, dynamic change, and possible death (Finnemore/Sikkink 1998; Krook/True 2010; Kutz 2014; Rosert 2019; Sandholtz 2008). The question 'do norms matter' seemed to be answered with a final 'yes.' IR research especially explored the instability and dynamic changes of norms, which have been described using different conceptions like contestation, norm regress, norm dissociation, or norm death. Studies concern norm diffusion on the international, regional, and national level (Acharya 2004; Zimmermann 2016). Extensions of the model among others include a pre-emergence stage and norm death (Jose 2017; Kutz 2014). Jose criticizes that the model allows dynamics but only within the stages of a norm's life cycle. The content of a norm is assumed to remain untouched (Jose 2016: 2). Similarly, Krook and True argue that norms in such approaches are seen as things, when norms should be viewed as processes following a discursive approach (Krook/True 2010: 104). Instead of modelling norm life cycles as linear processes, norms should be modelled as a complex dynamic of negotiation, contestation, and competition over meaning, use, and scope of application (Krook/True 2010: 106). Such a model allows for an understanding of norm life cycles, which accounts for the adaptability of norm content vulnerable to changing interests and changing possibilities due to upcoming technologies or security-relevant events.

An approach accounting for more complexity is provided by Sandholtz's model of cyclical effects of norm change over long time. According to Sandholtz, norms are constantly in flux because they are permanently contested and compete with other norms, since the system of all norms can never be free of contradiction (Sandholtz 2008: 103). As defined, norms are context specific and need interpretation and subject to negotiation. A norm's content and scope of application, despite a high degree of fixation in legal text, is constantly in need of interpretation without clear or pre-determined outcome: a norm can be confirmed or rejected. Special situations, like security relevant events—the terrorist attacks of 9/11—can open windows of opportunity for actor-induced norm change. Thus, norms do not necessarily lead a linear life but are prone to change which powerful states can induce and shape to their liking.

Building on Sandholtz's conception for cycles of norm change (Sandholtz 2008: 104–110), I develop a comprehensive model for norm dynamics as further specified as the cycle of norm transformation. The model shows four phases of norm tranformation: (1) normative structures limit and allow actions; (2) actions and precedents conflict with normative prescriptions; (3) rhetorical actions confirm and add to norms; and lead to (4) transformation in single norms which affect norm structures (see Fig. 3.1).

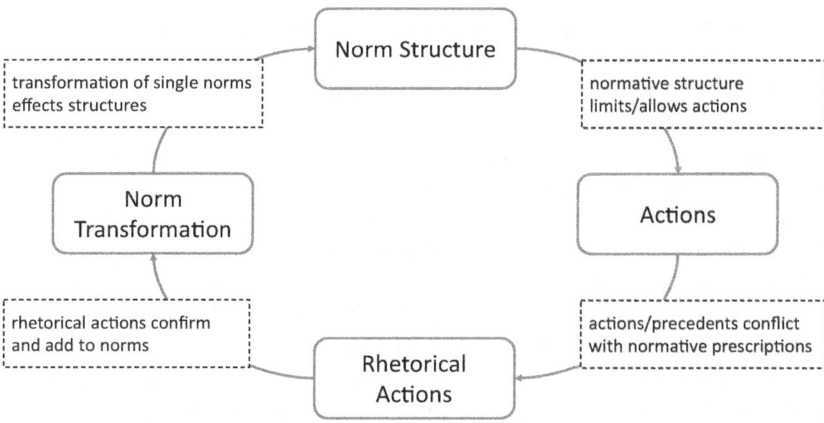

Fig. 3.1 The Cycle of Norm Transformation

Like Sandholtz, I assume strategic actors, who are rationally acting, interest driven, utility maximizing, and egoistic, yet not blind or in total ignorance of social rules and appropriate behavior but also calculate losses in terms of possible sanctions. Following rules is part of state rationality because actors weigh their interests against social disadvantages (i.e. reputational losses, disputes with allies). Like Sandholtz, I seek to connect international law and norm research. Adopting the idea that norms cycle through phases, I want to focus on norm change, including the emergence of new or adapted norms as a form of change, during a norm's life span. Analytically, I focus on the pre-emergence stage, as Jose, or pre-norm stage, as Ben-Joseph Hirsch, add to the norm life cycle (Ben-Joseph Hirsch 2014; Jose 2016; Jose 2017). This additional stage refers to the stage where the behavoirs are already practiced but are not yet considered a norm.

However, elaborating Sandholtz's model, (pre-)emergence can happen as a form of dynamic norm change, i.e. norm transformation.

This model allows for conceptualizing a state norm entrepreneur that is a rational strategic actor. The model acknowledges that actors act in given structures and such structures guide actor's choices and actions. However, no one actor can change a norm or a normative system unilaterally, but change may be induced by a powerful state. Even though no actor exists outside given structures, states are able to shape normative structures. Powerful states are in a position to structure especially sensitive security-related issues areas to their liking. The model also factors in the capacities and capabilities of states with limited resources of time and material to choose those rules worth following and to act according to egoistic, rational, utility maximizing interests. Strategic calculations include the risks and costs of rule breaking (i.e. sanctions or reputational losses). However, states do argue to legitimize their actions with reference to restrictive norms, especially those actions, which cause disagreement with others (Sandholtz 2008: 104–105). Arguments brought forward in order to legitimize actions consequently modify the norms and the normative system.

Whereas in Sandholzt's model rule change is inevitable, I propose a more nuanced idea of norm change with the idea of norm transformation. Norms do not necessarily die or disappear because actors act against the prescribed behavior. On the contrary, secrecy or exception may have strengthening effects for norms. In the cases of robust violence-regulating norms, I argue that the core norms continue to apply—but the United States changed the conditions for the application, keeping the initial norm for the benefit of the own troops and creating new rules for the application of violence, grating strategic advantages over the declared enemy. Using the concept of norm transformation, this case can be modeled. The original norm stays in effect while a new understanding of a once banned action emerges introducing a new norm to be established in the respective group. In this process, norm entrepreneurs—a powerful state or group of powerful states—persuade others to accept the disputed behavior as legitimate action under given circumstances and the new rule as a generally agreed-upon standard of legitimate behavior. Any change in single norms affects the structure of norms, which again influences actors' motives and choices. Sandholtz emphasizes precedent-setting events as an influence on actors' arguments posing reference points for the legitimation of exceptions and the need for adapted standards of appropriate behavior. In this regard, I argue that further argumentative strategies are applied in legitimizing violent actions through discursive practices, like framing and other persuasive strategies, which I further develop in the upcoming chapters. In this sense, norm dynamics are understood as lengthy cyclical processes of norms changing in life stages and content backwards (decline) or forward (gaining adherence). While some norms remain stable in content over long periods, modes of application may change up to the point where new interpretations create new norms. In the following, I focus on norm dynamics and explain my understanding of norm transformation as the main concept for norm change used in this study.

3.2 Norm Transformation

This section serves as the background for conceptualizing legitimation practices for norm transformation in the following chapters, i.e. how powerful states act and engage in legitimation to work towards the transformation of violence-regulating norms and the normative order. Based on the discussion in Chap. 2, I understand the war on terror as a phase of norm transformation in violence-regulating norms showing a trend from demanding the privileges of violence-containing for state forces while favoring violence-enabling norms for terrorist enemies. As discussed, several norms on violence are affected in the war on terror adding up to a change in the normative structure of legitimate violence. This transformation process applies on several levels: the norm level (single norms on legitimate violence) and the systemic level (the normative order of legitimate violence). The number of single changes in violence-regulating norms (torture, detention and status of conflict participants, state monopoly on violence, etc.) eventually affects the global order of legitimate violence. Conceptually zooming in, I understand norm transformation as a complex process encompassing actors, violent actions, norms, and the normative structures on the state levels and on the international level. Norm transformation allows for a detailed view on activities powerful states undertake to induce norm change or argue for the legitimacy of their actions, implicitly inducing possible norm emergence. As change occurs in the acts of violence, the normative interpretation and use of single norms on the legitimate use of violence follows. The concept, I apply as a complex model to conceptualize norm dynamics in the war on terror because it captures the U.S. use of violence and engagement with norms in legitimacy-seeking activities.

In the following, I lay out my understanding of transformation as a concept to model norm dynamics on several levels. Conceptualizing transformation, I draw on IR literature on norms and explain why and how I feature the idea of norm transformation rather than one of the discussed conceptions like, for instance, contestation, norm regress, or norm death. Building on existing conceptions of norm transformation, I seek to come to a comprehensive conception of norm transformation exceeding definitions by encompassing all levels of change which are relevant to norm transformation processes. Acknowledging the criticism concerning the good norm bias of IR norm scholarship, I discuss the idea of bad norms regarding the observable trend towards violence-enabling norms. Finally, I develop my understanding of the powerful states' possibilities to act as norm-transforming entrepreneurs, changing single norms and the normative order to realize their strategic interests and to govern others.

3.2.1 Transformation as Concept for Norm Dynamics

In a general sense of the word, 'transformation' describes a process of change. In a military or political context, the term means a fundamental change of strategy or a political system. According to the *Oxford Learners Dictionary*, 'to transform' means to change the form of something or a change in the appearance or character (Oxford Learner's Dictionary 2023). Similarly, IR scholars have used the term 'transformation' for more or less fundamental (processes of) change in practices, norms, regimes, institutions, or the normative order (Finnemore/Sikkink 1998; Krasner 1983; Krook/True 2010). Rarely, scholars conceptualize transformation as dynamic process but rather use the term as a synonym to indicate change of any sort, without further specifying the kind or amount of change. Yet, some scholars have used the term transformation in connection with norm dynamics (Krahmann 2013; Pratt 2018).

In such conceptions, norm transformation describes a process in which observable changes in state behavior respective to the norm go along with changed interpretations of the initial norm. For example, Pratt applies concept of norm transformation in the case of U.S. targeted killing policies. While the assassination ban stays in effects, U.S. officials no longer consider targeted killings to qualify as assassination. Pratt uses the concept of norm transformation as opposed to norm death or norm dissociation. Whereas norm death signifies erosion or disappearance of the (torture or the assassination) norm (Kutz 2014), norm dissociation means that the prohibition "never meaningfully existed in the first place for the actors in question" (Pratt 2018: 2). In distinction, norm transformation entails that the initial norm remains in force as well as its interpretation. What changes is the political view on violent acts. Consequently, the initial norm does not include the violent action any longer so that action and norm no longer (have to) correspond. In the case of targeted killing this means that assassination, as violent act, remains illegal while targeted killings are no longer considered as assassinations. According to Pratt, norm transformation occurs when the "relevant norms persisted in name but came to define or extend to different practices over time. They transformed" (Pratt 2018: 6). Norm transformation in this understanding means that the initial prohibition norm "still exists but has changed in form" (Pratt 2018: 3).

In thid regard, three factors cause norm change: "technology, rhetorical contestation, and bureaucratic politics" (Pratt 2018: 3). Technical development is not a necessary factor for norm transformation in general but indeed facilitates the use of targeted killings in large numbers.[16] In a wider understanding, technology could be conceptually understood as the general emergence of an opportunity to realize a policy which may not be limited to technological advancements in weapons. In the case of indefinite detention, the military base in Guantanamo provided the opportunity of a special place for holding detainees (Kaplan 2005; Maran 2006). In the case of torture, advancements in physical and psychological treatment provided the grounds for the enhanced interrogation debate (Greenberg/ Dratel 2005).[17] Next to the opportunity, rhetorical contestation, and bureaucratic politics are equally important factors in initializing norm transformation. Prerequisites in this regard are political willingness to change the use of violence and to find persuasive arguments legitimizing the change.

While Pratt's study is limited to the case of U.S. security policies in targeted killing, the nexus of the violent act and the violence-regulating norm well captures the general problem in the war on terror. Nevertheless, the conception of norm transformation is extendable to other cases of conflicted violence-regulating norms: the deviations from the prisoner of war regulations or the re-interpretation of the torture convention to name only the most prominent ones. However, since Pratt conducts a single case study focused on the U.S. application of the assassination norm to the practice of targeted killings, the study does not address long-term effects or systemic repercussions of single norm transformations on the systemic level of normative structures regulating violence. This concept does not include attempts to establish competing or additional norms but remains focused on the changed meaning of the norm. The possibility of emerging parallel, adapted violence-enabling norms thus remains underdeveloped. Norm transformation as conceptualized by Pratt lacks a systemic explanation including effects

---

[16] For instance, bin Laden's killing can be considered as a targeted killing, yet not one committed by a drone. However, the availability of drone technology facilitated and accelerated the the extended use of targeted killings in the war on terror by the U.S.

[17] See also Chap. 2.

of single norm changes and remains unclear as to the role of states in fostering the emergence of alternative and/or additional norms in the transformation process.

Another approach provides Krahmann who analyzes long-term norm transformation processes. Her approach includes changing state behavior, i.e. changing security interests and use of violence, as well as changing interpretations of security norms[18] (Krahmann 2013). Krahmann examines the development of the norm on the state's monopoly on legitimate violence and the development of the norm concerning mercenaries and private military and security companies in the timeframe of several centuries and under the changing conditions of evolving security environments. In her understanding "the transformation, development or evolution of norms thus refers to long-term variations in the strength and understanding of a norm" (Krahmann 2013: 55).[19]

In addition to observing changes in the use of violence and in the interpretation of norms, Krahmann considers the repercussions in the state community and on the structural level of the normative system. A contestation of a norm, even though committed by a powerful state, does not secure a permanent change in the norm's shared meaning. Norm transformation will only be successful if the new meaning of the norm becomes generally agreed-upon and is reproduced by states traceable in enactment and rhetorical reference. In this sense, a transformation process shows in the following activities: a change in interpretation and a new understanding of the norm; the formalizing of this new understanding in international institutions (regimes, treaties, codified norms); the passing of domestic legislation in several countries; the fixation of moral principles in support of the new interpretation of the norm; and the formalization in international agreements (Krahmann 2013: 59). According to Krahmann's understanding, Pratt's analysis can be seen as a case of a powerful state contesting robust security norms and can thus display an early stage in the transformation process and a case of norm-transforming entrepreneurship (Pratt 2018). Whether and how a newly introduced norm understanding or an additionally introduced norm then cascades or is internalized can only be studied over long periods of time.

---

[18] Krahmann works on the example of the norm of the state monopoly on the use of force. She explores how the interpretation of this norm has changed over the centuries from the restriction of non-state armed groups to the banning of non-state armed groups and the formation of institutions like *Kellogg-Briand Pact*, the *UN Charter*, or the *Geneva Conventions of 1949* (*Additional Protocol I*). She focuses on the historical role of non-state armed groups and the contemporary increasing commissioning of Private Military and Security Companies (PMSCs).

[19] On the evolution of norms see also Nadelmann (1990).

Krahmann provides a practical and broadly applicable approach for analyzing norm transformation. According to Krahmann, an analysis of transformation should include practices, responses to norm violations, changes in laws and regulations, and discourses (Krahmann 2013: 60–65). The analysis of practices may include changes in behavior of governments, adoption of the behavior by other states, open praise for the behavior, and/or acceptance of the new behavior. States can act towards norm transformation by setting precedent or influencing discourse (Krahmann 2013: 56). Krahmann situates the transformation process in the model of the norm life cycle as proposed by Finnemore and Sikkink (1998). Surely, the war on terror is rather a short- to medium-term period compared to world history. The U.S. efforts to legitimize the use of violence and legitimize new understandings of violence-containing norms in the war on terror can thus at least be understood as norm entrepreneurship in the initial phase of a transformation process with open outcome. Using Krahmann's conception, the United States did not stop at the initial point of introducing alternating interpretations but followed with national legislation formalizing the proposed legitimation of the violence conduct. How this affects the normative order on legitimate violence in the international system in the long run remains to be seen. For now, attestable is a short-term transformation which may be completed through the adoption by other states or reversed due to ignorance of others.

Krahmann identifies three factors, which foster the transformation and emergence of new norms: prominence, precedent setting, and coherence. Prominence means that the enactment of a norm is observed by a large enough number of powerful states who copy the changed interpretation of the norm. Precedent setting means the reinterpretation and alternated enactment of a norm, so that this behavior becomes a point of reference for other actors, especially, when enacted by powerful states who remain uncontested (Krahmann 2013: 56–57). Coherence means conformity with an existing norm. This factor is given when the new interpretation shows similarity to an established norm and resembles it in meaning and wording.

Both Pratt and Krahmann examine the nexus of changing use of violence and the interpretation of violence-regulating norms in effect. In both empirical approaches the United States are the main actor, a powerful state in a leading role in the interpretation of violence-regulating norms. The approaches show that norm transformation can be observed on the single norm level in short-term changes, however, to evaluate effects on the systemic level, long-term observations are necessary including actor interests, the use of force in the field, and the security environment.

Another approach to norm transformation focusing on the systemic level is provided by Senn and Troy (2017). Addressing the broader effects of norm transformation, they offer a conception linking single norm changes to alterations withing the international order of states and the normative order of legitimate violence, thus conceptualizing single norm changes and changes in the normative order. Reviewing scholarship on targeted killing the authors find that research has largely investigated how the violent act compares to existing norms. However, Senn and Troy criticize that little research deals with the question "*whether and how the current transformation of targeted killing is transforming the global international order*" (Senn/Troy 2017: 176). Senn and Troy argue that a transformation of targeted killing is taking place, as the violent act is used by an increasing number of states in an increasing number of instances and is no longer denied but openly used. An increasing proliferation of armed drones facilitates this development (Haas/Fischer 2017). Acknowledging that these changes occur "against the background of ideas, norms, and rules" Senn and Troy focus on effects of this transformation of the international order of legitimate violence (Senn/Troy 2017: 176). The international order signifies the Westphalian system of the 19th and 20th century. To explain the maintenance and change of the systemic order Senn and Troy "use a theoretical framework that conceives the interplay between violence and discursive processes as the behavioral dimension of an international order and ideas, norms, and rules as its institutional dimension" (Senn/Troy 2017: 176).

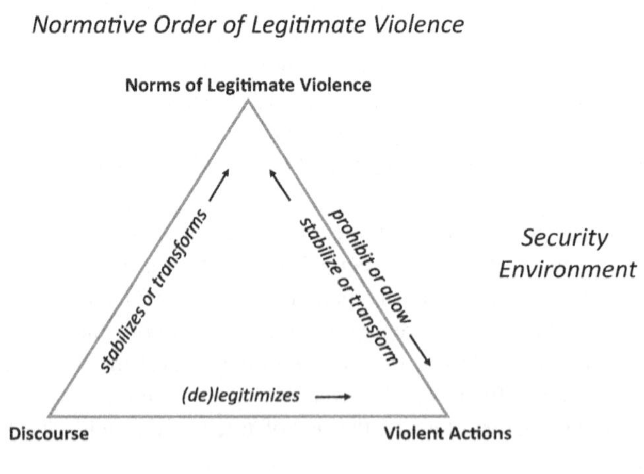

Fig. 3.2 The Stability and Transformation of Order

Figure 3.2 shows the relationship between discourse, violent actions, and norms of legitimate violence with regard to the influence of stabilizing and transforming activities in the context of a dynamically changing security environment. Based on the conception of Senn and Troy, 'order' is present in two dimensions: the body of rules on the institutional level and the rule-conform or rule-breaking actions on the behavioral level. Discursive and violent actions are equally important in either stabilizing or initiating transformation. Discourse is a means to actively legitimize (or delegitimize) violent actions. "Agents (de)legitimize the use of violence and (re)interpret the existing ideas, norms, and rules of an order in view of changing threats, technologies, and military doctrines" (Senn/Troy 2017: 177). Norms on legitimate violence are prohibitive or allow for the use of violence but can be changed through discursive actions. On the one hand, norm transformation may be triggered by the need to interpret norms and resolve contradictions within a given normative system (Sandholtz 2008; Senn/Troy 2017: 185). On the other hand, contextual factors in the security environment, like technologic advancement or upcoming events of crisis, may trigger or influence the dynamic of normative transformation (Senn/Troy 2017: 185).

Concluding from these conceptual considerations, norm transformation traces in changes in state acts of violence, the interpretation of respective norms, and in rhetoric legitimizing the use of force with respect to a violence-regulating norm. Norm transformation entails that a norm is used and/or codified in an adapted or new understanding and possibly institutionalized in an adapted or new legal document (nationally and/or internationally). In the following, I present the conceptional understanding of norm transformation for the case study.

3.2.2 Transformation as a Complex Process of Norm Dynamics on Several Levels

As a theoretical background I use the concept of norm transformation to describe the process of norm change in the case of indefinite detention. After 9/11 and due to a changed threat perception, U.S. legitimation activities can be understood as attempts to make the use of violence seem norm conform, thereby changing normative meaning and adding regulations to the existing body of violence-regulating norms. Norm transformation here is understood as a complex process in which state actors actively work towards changing the normative structures they operate in, to gain advantages for themselves and govern the possibilities of others by adhering to the existing normative framework while adapting norms and adding regulations to the framework. Norm transformation processes follow and/

or accompany changes in violence committed by state actors. Building on the discussed conceptions above, in this subsection I conceptualize[20] the transformation of a norm and consequently the normative order as used in this study.

Norm transformation means that the initial norm remains in its scope of application while a new, adapted norm is introduced and established for a different scope of application. To meet security interests and limit the violence ambitions of others in new security environments, state actors change the interpretation of violence-regulating norms. These changes in interpretation may be limited to a single norm or encompass several security related norms. Such attempts to reframe the norm are initial activities to induce norm transformation. Declaring exceptions to the widely accepted rule may strengthen the existing norm and open an opportunity to establish a new, similar norm that addresses the exception. Whereas torture remains forbidden, 'enhanced interrogation' is argued to be a necessary and legal method for the questioning of suspected terrorists. Although the assassination ban remains in effect, targeted killings of terrorists are exempt from the prohibition.

In this sense, state actors support the transformation throughout the different stages of the process. In the initial phase, state actors function as norm entrepreneurs, arguing for the need for this new normative interpretation, framing the violent act as legitimate, and trying to persuade others to accept and adopt this new interpretation. State agents may then strive for legalization on the national level (the norm becomes domestic law) to enhance legitimacy of the violent action thereby advancing the transformation process. On the international level, referring to the life cycle model, activities to legitimize violent acts may induce a cascading process. A norm cascade occurs when other state actors engage in discourse about the interpretation, accept the new interpretation or the emerging alternating norm, and adopt the interpretation in meaning and use. In addition to acceptance and reproduction, a legalization process on the international level would also be a sign of progressing transformation: changes in institutions, international law, and decision-making processes in organizations. The process would be finalized by internalization which is complete when no one even questions the new norm anymore.

[20] The conceptualization of transformation consists of three components: the definition of the term, the intension including elements which characterize and specify the term, and the extension which hints to the correspondent empirical cases of the term (Senn/Troy 2017: 180). On conceptualization see also: Goertz 2006.

Adopting Pratt's definition, norm transformation occurs when norms persist for a specific issue area and scope of application while new norms are introduced for the same issue area but with a changed scope of application (Pratt 2018). So, robust norms on legitimate violence continue to remain in force for conventional forces, and new norms are developed to meet the security challenges of global terrorism. The conception of transformation does not only address the altering of the meaning or use of a single norm but addresses changes in the whole structure of a set of norms on legitimate state violence. Norm transformation is a holistic process of fundamental event- or crisis-induced change encompassing in this case the use of violence, the interpretation of norms, and the normative order on the domestic state level and on the international state level over time.

Drawing on the presented research and conceptions, several exogenous factors foster norm transformation: change in threat perception (terrorism, 9/11), perceived change in conflict formation and actor constellation (war on terror as a new kind of war), and technology or (windows of) opportunities offering new possibilities (development of UAVs and armed drones for the execution of targeted killings). All these factors may trigger the change in the use of state violence. The change in violent acts goes along with a transformation on the single norm level: certain norms and norm interpretations are added and/or altered. These modifications on the single norm level have repercussions on the normative structural level: single norm transformations eventually lead to a transformation of the pre-existing overall normative structure (international order of legitimate violence).

In addition to these structural transformations on the global level (the overall structure changes due to several single norm changes), transformation on the single norm level is actor driven. On the single state level, one powerful state may change the norm interpretation with repercussions on the domestic level and for the interactions on the international level. In foreign and security politics, a state must address both audiences, the national public and the international state community. This includes inducing change in the domestic legal system and the international legal system.

Assuming the adapted norm life cycle model as discussed above, one single state can only attempt to transform a norm and the normative order of legitimate violence. A new norm may be proposed but unless actively accepted or adopted by other states, no permanent change occurs neither in the norm nor in the normative order. Hence, for a norm transformation to be successful, acceptance by many states is a necessary condition, a cascading effect up to a tipping point leading to internalization is another success-indicating factor. Similarly, Jose argues when she states that the United States are norm entrepreneurs in the case of targeted killings, but whether and how others adopt the violent act and refer to the same normative legitimation remains to be seen (Jose 2016). Likewise, in this study the focus lies on the initial process of the transformation, where a norm contestation or diversion leads to an alternate interpretation and a new norm proposition—the entrepreneurship phase of the transformation.

Although covering more than a decade, the following case study must be considered a short-term observation with respect to cycles of change in the regulation of violence. As Krahmann pointed out, violence-regulating norms are a subject to be studied over centuries regarding the normative structures, the institutions, and surrounding environmental factors. The trend of containing violence as it showed up until WWII, may have been reversed especially after the fall of the iron curtain. As Hurd argues, U.S. security politics, especially in Latin America and after the end of the Cold War have shown a tendency towards the permission of violence rather than violence containment (Hurd 2016). Adding to these propositions, I argue that violence-regulating norms are transformed whenever a change in the security paradigm occurs, like after WWII, after the end of the Cold War, and after 9/11. Events which have an impact on threat perceptions trigger the need for a change in the use of violence and may initiate a norm transformation process. However, norm transformation can always be reversed, this process does not need to be linear towards norm establishment and internalization; cascades may never happen or stop entirely. As cycles of change become visible in the long run, a short-term observation, like this study, is not fit to make claims on success or permanence of the effects of norm transformation processes. Yet, the study provides insights as to how norm transformation may be initiated and fostered by the deliberate use of legitimation activities by state actors in powerful positions. The following sections provide more detail on the transformed norm and the participating actors.

3.2.3 Transformation in Violence Regulating Norms—From 'Good' to 'Bad' Norms?

In the proposed conception, norm transformation addresses changes on several levels. However, this concept does not judge the nature of the change or the quality of the norm. In the cases of norm transformation during the war on terror, a qualitative trend is visible concerning the qualitative core and content of the norm, what is often termed the 'oughtness' or logic of appropriateness. Whereas the end of World War II is often described as the motor for a normative development intending the containment of violence, 9/11 triggered a development toward the unleashing of violence (Hurd 2016). The war on terror seems to be a period, during which especially the United States have actively worked towards norm interpretations that enable violence and allow for the use of force. Concerning the qualitative content of the norm, transformation in these cases describes a change in the set of norms of legitimate violence from containment to permission of state violence (single norm) and from the general intention for containment of state violence to the permission of state violence in the war on terror (systemic).

Addressing the use of violence and change in violence-regulating norms in the war on terror, IR scholars criticize the 'good-norm bias' of norm research and call for the consideration of 'bad' norms (Jose 2016) or 'bad' norm dynamics (Heller/Kahl 2013; Heller et al. 2012).[21] The criticism includes two main points: (1) per definition norms cannot be bad; (2) despite being aware of 'bad' norms, norm research has mainly focused on 'good' norms. Particularly norm research on the war on terror has focused on upcoming bad norms, like the emerging preventive war norm (Dombrowski/Payne 2006; Fisk/Ramos 2014), the speading of state-directed cyberspace controls restricting civil liberties (Deibert/Crete-Nishihata 2012), or the emerging of a targeted killing norm (Jose 2016). As Jose distinguishes 'good' norms are considered norms, which "advance human rights and/or prohibit certain behavior" (Jose 2016: 2). Adopting Jose's definition, I understand 'good' norms as norms which advance human rights or contain and restrict state violence. Concerning the specific area of violence-regulating norms, good norms are violence-containing norms, banning state violence, like the ban of landmines, the ban of torture, of small arms, of weapons of mass destruction, and assassinations, to name a few, or such that grant protection, like the *Geneva Conventions* (1949) or the *Declaration on Human Rights*. I also argue that the idea of 'good' norms furthermore encompasses a good intention to limit the horrors of war for humankind. In the war on terror, we enter a world political era in which the idea of protecting one's own people from terrorist threat (thus an actor, who is perceived as not playing by the rules) is the driving force in security politics. In this regard, some authors criticize the United States who once put violence-containing norms in place for now undermining the normative system of legitimate violence (Dunne 2007; Reus-Smit 2007). Assuming an understanding of norms not only as expectable standardized behavior but rather as prescription for appropriate behavior, the idea of a killing norm or a detention norm is rather disturbing.

[21] For an initial debate on the terminology of 'good' and 'bad' norms see Finnemore and Sikkink (1998: 892).

At first glance, the idea of 'bad' norms seems compelling, as the qualifier signals a conflict with underlying values, ideas, and possibly moral understandings, like the conflict between targeted killings and the human rights convention. Thus, the term 'bad norm' would solve one of the problems addressed by the critics, which is that a 'bad' norm is excluded by definition. As Florini states, among others, by the end of the 1990's, norm research defines norms not only as standard behavior (as rules) but also as normative standard implicating an oughtness (Florini 1996: 364). Likewise, Finnemore and Sikkink argue that "one logical corollary to the prescriptive quality of a norm is that, by definition, there are no bad norms from the vantage point of those who promote the norm" (Finnemore/Sikkink 1998: 892). As Jose criticizes, in a strict reading, Finnemore and Sikkink's norm definition allows for targeted killing to become a 'good' norm, as long as the norm is based on a shared understanding that the violent practice is appropriate (Jose 2016: 2). However, in the war on terror, the problem is that the emerging norms stand in stark contrast to the existing violence-containing norms, which are based on the understanding of the equality prescribed by human rights. Finnemore and Sikkink's conception assumes consistency between the norm content and the underlying value system (what is perceived as appropriateness). This concept does not help resolve the case of norm conflict between emerging and existing value sets but rather explains historical change of values, ideas, and norms.

This view leaves a blind spot on those norms that prescribe behavior which is not in line with liberal democratic principles or more importantly the core idea of human rights prescribing equality of all humankind. Consequently, the second point of criticism is that despite the knowledge of so-called 'bad' norms, norm research has mainly focused on 'good' norms, i.e. such norms which do not conflict with liberal democratic principles or human rights. As Großklaus states, norm research has a western liberal democratic bias towards those 'good norms' containing violence or contributing to the idea of human rights (Großklaus 2017). Filling this void, research on 'bad' norms well captures the parallel structure—often criticized as double standard—that is established in the war on terror: while violence-containing norms are still in place for equal sovereign states, violence-enabling norms are proposed for dealing with terrorists (Großklaus 2017; Jose 2016; Jose 2017; Kutz 2014). In the war on terror, values and norms are contradictory. Assuming an understanding of equality as promoted by the *Declaration of Human Rights*, the targeted killing of suspected terrorists without trial or with trial *in absentia* is hard to be judged as normatively right, good, and appropriate, which has been widely criticized by the legal debate as discussed in Chap. 2. While principles of equality remain, the U.S. attempt to establish inequality for terrorists as a normative principle and to elevate the permission to indefinitely capture, torture, or killing as the norm.

The distinction of norms in 'good' and 'bad' seems compelling to illustrate the norm conflict in the war on terror; however, it is not useful as an analytical or conceptual category. Proposing a good-norms-only approach, Finnemore and Sikkink conclude that slavery was once considered a norm because it was considered right by a large enough group. The norm was dropped with the change in perception that slavery was no longer considered appropriate conduct. Following this line of argument, anything becomes a norm in terms of appropriate behavior given enough supporters. If the norm corresponds to the socially shared view that the behavior is good and right, then enhanced interrogation and lethal actions can also be presented as a 'good' norm. As the criticism shows, such a reading is rather unsettling, as it enables justifying human rights violations as necessary, right, and—good. As compelling as the idea of emerging 'bad' norms may seem, the expression mirrors the problem, as it is still an arbitrary category that relies on the judgement of the spectator or a large enough crowd without a clear point of reference. As compelling as both arguments are, as problematic is the distinction between 'good' and 'bad' when speaking about norms and normative quality—for the lack of analytical value.

As an alternative, I propose to differentiate by function. In the case of violence-regulating norms (such as torture, targeted killing, or detention) alterations to the norm should be distinguished in violence-containing and violence-enabling norms. Hence, I propose categorizing norms regarding their effect, intention, and purpose, supposing a norm set which is based on democratic values and human rights. Looking at the cases of violence in the war on terror, the question is whether the emerging norm prohibits or permits state violence. Using such criteria, the normative character remains with the norm, but the purpose changes from 'ought not to' to 'ought to be allowed to.' The transforming norms in question all trend from the containment of violence to the enabling of violence. Judging norms by their effect makes it possible to analyze the quality of the norm transformation and separately discuss whether this development is in line with other prescriptive norms and whether the behavior is morally and ethically desirable. For the cases at hand, I explore the U.S. use of legitimation in transforming violence-regulating norms towards violence-enabling norms.[22] In

[22] Similar tendencies are observable in the state monopoly on the use of force and the permission for PMSCs (Krahmann 2013), in the in the field of asymmetric warfare and in the field of maritime law (piracy, refugee issues, and migration), where deprivations of rights also occur (terrorists, illegal migrants, and refugees).

the following, I further explore the role of the U.S. as transformation-fostering entrepreneur for violence-enabling norms.

3.2.4 Norm-Transforming Entrepreneurship

In this section, I focus on the role of state actors as norm entrepreneurs for violence-enabling norms in norm transformation processes. Comprehending norm transformation as an actor-driven process, I argue that the United States act as a norm-transforming entrepreneur regarding violence-regulating norms in the war on terror. By engaging in legitimation practices, the United States not only try to frame their violent acts as legitimate, but they also propose transformed ideas of legitimate violence and violence-enabling norms. In this regard, I consider norm transformation as an actively induced process in action and speech acts (transformative and legitimacy-seeking actions). In the following, I look at norm entrepreneurship and state possibilities to engage with norm transformation in the different phases of the process.

Whereas I feature a state actor as norm entrepreneur initiating a top-down process, norm entrepreneurship is often conceptualized as a bottom-up process mainly driven by civil society actors, like NGOs. Finnemore and Sikkink understand norm entrepreneurs as social agents of change (Finnemore/Sikkink 1998). In the cases they describe, norm entrepreneurs are usually individuals or civil society actors who try to influence states and persuade state officials to add a certain issue to the agenda. Such issues often included the advancement of human rights or the limitation of state powers creating a distinctive framework of regulations, like women suffrage or the *Geneva Conventions of 1949* (Jose 2016). In this conception, states are the actors that need to be influenced. In the cascading phase, norm entrepreneurs from civil society take up the role of parading the new norm to influence many state actors to adopt the new norm up until the tipping point is reached and finally internalization is complete (Finnemore/Sikkink 1998: 901–905). Although research on civil society entrepreneurship covers the normative advancements in human rights, the conceptual focus on non-state actors underestimates the role of the state actors in top-down norm-setting or norm-altering processes which is especially relevant in security-related norms.

Considering states as norm entrepreneurs, I focus on norm emergence as a top-down process, including the use of power[23] in its various dimensions as a factor in the deliberate shaping of the normative structures to meet security political goals and govern the possibilities of others (creating a favorable framework of regulations or non-codified regulations). Whereas in bottom-up approaches states are the addressee of norm entrepreneurship activities, in this top-down approach the state actively fosters the norm-transformation (Nadelmann 1990). Thus, state actors engage in norm-entrepreneurship activities, like issue framing and agenda setting, prior to and during norm emergence, norm cascading, and norm-institutionalizing processes.

Regardless of the actor's constitution, I assume that the strategies of norm entrepreneurs are similar. States may act as norm entrepreneurs in the same sense that non-state actors do. For example, Ingebritsen analyzes Scandinavia, as a small group of states, who influence normative processes in certain issue areas on the international level (Ingebritsen 2002). This group mainly engages in agenda setting in issue areas like environment and diplomacy, acting like many NGOs do. For one, the issue areas (environmental issues) are alike and for another, the group of states functions as an expert—especially in the field of diplomacy. Here, norm entrepreneurship shows in the introduction of competing norms, the development of norms, and the strengthening of norms (Ingebritsen 2002). Ingebritsen shows how the group of states works in different fields of expertise: they act as good example in national politics and already implement the norm that is to be implemented on the international level; they act as diplomatic advocates of the norm in international fora, promote the norm, and diplomatically encourage others to follow the norm; they act as facilitator in terms of bridge-building, group-gathering, and fostering the negotiation of treaties; they offer expertise on certain issue areas in order to facilitate rule-making and legalization processes; and they help organize international events (UN initiatives) to promote the norm.

Having established the possibility of state actors acting as top-down norm entrepreneurs, the cases of norm entrepreneurship in the war on terror come with a distinguishing feature. Norm entrepreneurship is usually associated with the aim of persuading others to follow suit, aiming for a cascading process and eventually internalization of the proposed norm. In the case of the war on terror, the concept of the reluctant norm entrepreneur factors in that the main aim of the U.S. norm-transforming activities is to gain support for the violent use, while detering others from imitation. Evaluating U.S. norm entrepreneurship in the case

[23] I understand power following the conception of Barnett and Duvall (2005) who conceptualize four dimensions of power: compulsory, institutional, structural, and productive.

of targeted killings, Jose argues that the United States act as a reluctant norm entrepreneur, with the main aim to prevent sanctions by justifying the violent actions with reference to a transformed norm understanding. Hence, the aim of the norm transformation is not to induce active proliferation of the violent actions but rather the legitimation of the own violent acts.[24] However, as Jose states, even reluctant norm entrepreneurship affects the norm and the normative structure, since the violent action is not only legitimized for the United States, but the sense of appropriateness may change internationally. The development of a norm to regulate targeted killings for all states is secondary, thus reluctantly the United States aim for a targeted killing norm (Jose 2016; Jose 2017).

As IR scholarship analyzes, norm entrepreneurs use a variety of strategies to introduce new understandings of appropriateness, create new norms, or use similar tools to establish changed interpretations as a norm or transform a norm's meaning. I argue that states, when acting as norm-transforming entrepreneurs, use similar strategies. From research on individual or non-state norm entrepreneurs, we know that such strategies include framing, persuasion, interpretation, and advocacy (Finnemore/Sikkink 1998: 897; Krook/True 2010). Furthermore, I argue that transformative effects on protective norms are systematically induced by political action. The transformative processes considered in the cases at hand in state use of violence demand legitimation from state elites, as they contradict the established violence regulating norms. As such, both the violent acts as well as the U.S. interpretation of established violence-regulating norms have caused complicated public and scientific debate in legal, political, normative, moral, and ethic terms. How U.S. political elites engage in practices of legitimation and transformation of norms, dealing with the conception of legitimacy and state actors' capabilities to engage in norm transformation processes, is explained in more detail in the research design in Chap. 4.

As states may act as norm entrepreneurs like non-state actors and the strategies may be alike, the motives of state actors differ from NGOs, however. NGOs are motivated by altruism, empathy and idealism (Finnemore/Sikkink 1998: 898). States, especially in the sensitive issue area of security, are more concerned with survival and the pursuit of security interests. Moreover, state norm entrepreneurship is an expression and demonstration of power in the international system. Often a handful of states shape security-relevant norms and are capable of inducing transformation (Jose 2016: 4–5). The aim of such norm entrepreneurship is

[24] In this regard, Jose analyzes the activities of NGOs (Jose 2017). Civil society actors try to suppress U.S. efforts to introduce and promote a targeted killing norm. Hence, the roles are inversed here: the United States act as agents for change, the NGOs act as norm suppressors and thus as agents for stability of the established violence-containing norms.

shaping international order to the own linking, securing one's own power position among the international state community, and securing one's own people despite the rights of others. This is especially relevant in the issue area of security regulations. Concerning violence-regulating norms, the role of states is to regulate the use of force and set rules for interstate conflicts. Especially norm-setting, norm-reshaping, norm-transforming efforts address the rules for the use of violence against non-state aggressors.

Consequently, I argue that norm transformation is a process that is initially driven by a powerful state, the United States in this case, that take up a leading role in shaping the norms in the security relevant area of violence-regulating norms and transformation processes. The United States as a powerful state took a lead role in the making of the post-World War II normative order of legitimate violence. On the one hand, it is thus surprising that the Unites States establish exceptions to the application of these robust norms after 9/11. On the other hand, it is not surprising that the United States strive for a leading role in dominating the discourse on how to deal with terrorism in terms of the use of force and violence and to take the lead in the shaping of the normative framework. In this regard, I focus on U.S. efforts in seeking legitimacy for the violence in the war on terror. Considering the historical process of norm emergence and the normative changes that have taken place since World War II, I argue that the normative order of violence established after 1945 has undergone significant changes and continues to evolve with the war on terror as a specific period in foreign and security policies after the era of the Cold War. Whereas the norm advancement up to the establishment of the humanitarian legal framework including the *Geneva Conventions of 1949* is considered as one that generated a far-reaching protective framework, the development since shows growing tendencies towards the development of violence-enabling norms.

Conceptualizing the United States as norm-transforming entrepreneur, state actors work through interpretation, justification, and legalization towards the legitimation of the use of violence thereby transforming violence-regulating norms. Assuming the United States as the leading actor in an actor-driven norm transformation process, I adopt the idea of a reluctant norm entrepreneur (Jose 2016). This understanding entails that the United States did not primarily design norm-transforming activities to change norms by fostering other state's imitation but foremost to seek support for the violence applied by U.S. forces in the war on terror. Rather national and international audiences are supposed to be persuaded that violence is necessary, good, right, and in line with the normative system. Yet, single changes induced by U.S. norm entrepreneurship may have long lasting effects on the normative order of legitimate violence. The same holds for institutionalizing, as legalization efforts, which mainly take place on the national level, strengthen legitimacy but do not necessarily cascade into legalization or violence-regulating initiatives on the international level. Hence, norm transformation is foremost a legitimacy-seeking strategy aiming for national security, acceptance, recognition, and consensus on the international level but not for adoption, cascading, or internalization of violence used in the war on terror. Thus, I understand the United States as norm entrepreneur in the issue area of security-relevant norms and as a dominant interpreter of violence-regulating norms, especially in rapidly changing security environments.

Research Design: Building Theory from Cases

4

"Research design is about making choices and articulating a rationale for the choices one has made" (Schwartz-Shea/Yanow 2012: 2). Following this understanding, this chapter lays out the research design of this study as a carefully formulated plan for the research exercise including the systematic analytical approach. This research design is based on what Langley and Abdallah coined as "The 'Eisenhardt Method'"[1] (Langley/Abdallah 2016; Eisenhardt 1989; Eisenhardt 2021). According to the Eisenhardt[2], the case selection is made depending on the expected added explanatory value of the cases regarding theory advancement. Investigations in the single-case study include the evaluation of a rich body of data, which I analyze using qualitative interpretative methods. Before I outline the steps in the research process guided by the Eisenhardt method, I unfold my methodological perspective placing this research project in a qualitative interpretive logic of inquiry.

[1] The term was introduced by Langley and Abdallah (2016) and further specified by Eisenhardt (2021). For the sake of reading flow, I refer to the term as in the original article's main writing: the Eisenhardt method (Langley/Abdallah 2016).

[2] Eisenhardt (1989; 2021) and Graebner (Eisenhardt/Graebner 2007) further developed grounded theory as proposed by Glaser and Strauss (1967) offering a qualitative, interpretive method as opposed to strictly positivist and quantitative methods. In terms of inductive research, this approach further develops the general idea of grounded theory (Glaser/Strauss 1967). Whereas Glaser and Strauss are foremost interested in understanding the perception of the involved actors, Eisenhardt and Graebner propose a broader empirical approach accounting for the actors involved as well as the institutional structures and the processes.

Supplementary Information The online version contains supplementary material available at https://doi.org/10.1007/978-3-658-49121-5_4.

D. Hühnert-Hugendubel, *Between Rules of War and Rule of Law*,
https://doi.org/10.1007/978-3-658-49121-5_4

4.1 Methodological Approach and Case Study Design

Aiming at theory development on state legitimation practices, this study takes a pragmatist, abductive approach consistent with the guidelines of Schwartz-Shea and Yanow (2012) and Friedrichs and Kratochwil (2009; Büger/Gadinger 2008; Kelly/Cordeiro 2020). As Schwartz-Shea and Yanow point out, in many positivistic research designs, methodological[3] presuppositions are rarely discussed. Rather the presupposition of the material world as objectively researchable almost like in a laboratory situation is taken for granted. In interpretive, qualitative, abductive designs discussing the researchers' worldview and assumptions, concerning meaning-making processes, actor perceptions, and ideas, is stressed to contribute to transparency and thus ensure the quality of empirical research. Unfolding presuppositions helps to understand what a researcher finds puzzling, what led to a research question, and how analytical approaches were shaped (Schwartz-Shea/Yanow 2012). Consequently, the aim of this subchapter on methodology—as in a "logic of inquiry"—is to clearly state the assumptions and presuppositions behind the methods used in the research design—as in "the particular tools"—to contribute to this design's scientific rigor and validity (Schwartz-Shea/Yanow 2012: 4).

Serving the demand for a closer exchange between theory and empiricism, research in International Relations has undergone several turns in recent decades. As positivistic research designs continue to be relevant in designated areas, this methodology is not fit to answer every research question. Qualitative and interpretive approaches drawing on methods established in social sciences like sociology, anthropology, and ethnography have made their way into IR research, contributing to a greater variety in research designs and in research opportunities. Such approaches share the idea of choosing the design catering the needs of the research interests instead of asking research questions that fit the method. In line with this perspective, the research design in this study is chosen to fit the research interest, in a pragmatist, qualitative, and interpretive logic of inquiry and with the following presuppositions in mind.

The design pursues a pragmatist approach based on a social constructivist mindset (Friedrichs/Kratochwil 2009). Sharing a constructivist worldview, I assume a socially constructed world in which meaning is produced intersubjectively in performative action and meaning is conveyed in and through speech.

[3] Following Schwartz-Shea and Yanow, I understand methodology as the "presuppositions concerning ontology—the reality status of the 'thing' being studied—and epistemology—its 'know-ability'—which inform a set of methods" (Schwartz-Shea/Yanow 2012: 4).

This assumption entails that facts[4] need to be interpreted and those interpretations are prone to change over time and influenced by an actor's ideas, beliefs, and normative understandings. Consequently, I understand knowledge as generally accepted and shared by a social entity at a given point in time and as socially and historically contingent (Münch 2016: 9). As I am mainly interested in how powerful actors accomplish the construction of dominant meaning, I reconstruct this meaning from qualitative data (news reports, official government documents, and speech transcripts) and analyze this data using interpretive means.

This research design follows a pragmatist approach using an abductive[5] research logic[6] (Friedrichs/Kratochwil 2009). A pragmatist abductive strategy acknowledges the researcher's learning process which takes place during a case study. Abduction allows for admitting and accepting that researching social phenomena follows a non-linear process of constant matching of theory and empirical case data. By acknowledging that researchers are always part of the world they examine, the researcher's prior knowledge is factored into the research process. This sum of social experiences and theoretical knowledge naturally influences the research process and possibly the outcome. Hence, an abductive research procedure not only acknowledges but also benefits from the researcher's constant exchange between theoretical and conceptual knowledge while learning more

[4] A social constructivist perspective acknowledges the existence of an event or phenomenon in the material world but holds that more than one reading is possible due to interpretation. Concerning the war on terror, constructivists acknowledge that evidence on the attacks confirms Al Qaida's responsibility. However, a constructivist perspective would also understand that the framing of 9/11 as an act of war and not as an international crime is a deliberate political choice. From a constructivist point of view, problem framing and the interpretation of a phenomenon are part of discursive actions shaping generally accepted knowledge, and powerful actors are capable of making their interpretation the dominant one in a given political discourse.

[5] Abduction can be understood as the middle ground between inductive research where theoretical hypotheses are generated from empirical data or deductive approaches where assumptions are drawn from existing theory to be tested on empirical cases (Friedrichs/Kratochwil 2009).

[6] According to Friedrichs and Kratochwil seven pragmatic principles should be considered: "1. The purpose of research, including personal motivation, must be stated in public. 2. Orientation in a relevant field is more important than causal theorizing. 3. Pragmatic research is constituted more by concepts than by theory. 4. Conceptual distinctions should elicit patterns of similarity and difference. 5. Case sampling may follow a 'most important' or a 'most typical' case scenario.

6. Complexity can be reduced by appropriate formal tools. 7. Abduction is eventually compatible with causal theorizing" (Friedrichs/Kratochwil 2009: 716).

about empirical case data. This constant back and forth between theory and data characterizes pragmatist abductive research processes.

As Schwartz-Shea and Yanow stress, the choice of a qualitative, interpretive, pragmatist approach also implies taking measures to secure scientific quality like "rigor, validity, and reliability" (Dooley 2002: 338; Schwartz-Shea/Yanow 2012). Living up to these standards, I elaborate on the six criteria listed by Dooley: "Determine and define the research questions, select the cases and determine data-gathering and analysis techniques, prepare to collect data, collect data in the field, evaluate and analyze the data, prepare the report" (Dooley 2002: 338–339). With a detailed description of these points in the research design and procedures, I want to contribute to comprehensibility and transparency. Serving this aim, I also reflect on my role as a researcher in assembling the data by reflecting selection criteria for data and the analytical proceedings. In the following, I explain the steps of the research design guided by Eisenhardt's method (1989; 2021) with respect to the above-mentioned transparency criteria.

4.1.1 Building Theory from Cases

My analytical approach is based on the Eisenhardt method of building theory from cases.[7] Eisenhardt offers methodical guidelines to answer how-questions, aimed at the reconstruction of processes which then allow for further developing theoretical and conceptual knowledge. Since methods are often applied like baking recipes, I take Eisenhardt seriously when she states that her method is to be understood as a path and should be adapted to cater the needs of one's own research project. Although the method suits many of this project's demands, I will not copy the method as a template[8] but use it as a guideline and adapt it to fit the research interest wherever necessary. In the following, I lay open how my methodological presuppositions translate into distinct design choices to contribute to transparency. Guided by the approach of theory building from cases, I explain the design choices concerning case selection, data assembling, and analytical tools based on the research question and the pursued research interest (Eisenhardt 1989; Eisenhardt 2021; Eisenhardt/Graebner 2007; Schwartz-Shea/Yanow 2012).

---

[7] The following literature provides further guidelines on theory building from cases: Lynham (2002) offers a five-step method on theory building, on design and methods for case study research compare Yin (2009, 1981).

[8] On how to explore multiple research opportunities using the Eisenhardt method see: Eisenhardt 2021.

The Role of A-priori Knowledge and a Puzzle

According to Schwartz-Shea and Yanow (2012) research questions usually result from puzzles. In the designing process of a research project, prior knowledge constitutes the basis for finding puzzles and asking questions. This research project builds on prior knowledge gained in my previous study on the development of the term *unlawful enemy combatant* in memoranda exchanged by members of the Bush administration and legal advisors (Greenberg/Dratel 2005; Hühnert 2016). This legal construct, which was formally legalized with the *Military Commissions Act 2006*, served the Bush administration to argue for the legality of indefinite detention and enhanced interrogation[9] techniques used in Guantanamo Bay Detention Camp. This preceding research project was driven by the puzzling question of how the Bush administration argued for the legality and legitimacy of detainee maltreatment in the Camp depriving detainees of domestic, international, and most basic human rights which represent core democratic and constitutional values of the United States (Hühnert 2016).

Building on insights from this project, I wanted to dig deeper into the legitimation strategies for extreme acts of violence applied in the war on terror and the effects on the normative order of legitimate violence. Especially puzzling remains the fact, that the U.S. as a democratic state started to apply means of violence (torture, indefinite detention, targeted killings, extraordinary renditions etc.) that are internationally banned and fundamentally contradict democratic and constitutional principles, mainly the rule of law. Hence, the puzzle guiding my research remains: how did U.S. administrations manage to legitimize (justify and legalize) the use of force and application of violence during the war on terror?

The use of force in the war on terror is widely perceived as norm breaking and legal violation of international and national law. This is not only a legal dispute for courts to solve but also a political puzzle IR scholarship has tried to solve with norm research. As argued in Chap. 3, norm transformation provides a suitable conceptual approach to explain the emergence of violence-enabling norms for the treatment of terrorists while further strengthening violence-containing norms for state armed forces.

---

[9] The Bush administration coined the term 'enhanced interrogation' for methods to apply violence which are considered as torture by critics. The CIA interrogation program was developed under Defense Secretary Rumsfeld and applied at Guantanamo and later at other detention facilities in Iraq (Abu Ghraib) and Afghanistan. Alberto Gonzales argued in two memoranda, known as the *Torture Memos*, for the legality of enhanced interrogation and supplies the arguments for the impunity of the interrogators (Greenberg/Dratel 2005).

As argued, norm transformation is a strong concept to explain norm change and stability during the war on terror. Yet, norm theory still lacks a deeper understanding of how such transformative processes function. The following study seeks to fill this void by contributing an in-depth analysis on the legitimation activities of a norm-transforming entrepreneur. Since a single-case study cannot claim a high degree of generalizability, delivering a full theory is surely a goal set too high. However, as Eisenhardt proposes, a theory consists of "a set of constructs linked together in relationships that are supported by theoretical arguments (i.e. mechanisms) that seek to explain a focal phenomenon" (Eisenhardt 2021: 148).[10] In this sense, I search for legitimation activities that link together forming repeated patterns adding up to practices of legitimation as a comprehensive set of constructs. Providing helpful constructs, the case study intends to contribute to the advancement of a norm transformation theory providing insights to the capabilities and capacities of powerful actors in shaping these processes.

The Research Question

According to Eisenhardt and Graebner "the research question is *tightly* scoped within the context of an existing theory and the justification rests heavily on the ability of qualitative data to offer insights into complex social processes" (Eisenhardt/Graebner 2007: 26). As argued, norm transformation constitutes the conceptual and theoretical ground for the research question which explores the black box of how a powerful norm entrepreneur acts to fuel the norm transformation process. Thus, the research question asks: Which legitimation practices have the Presidents George W. Bush, Jr., and Barack Obama exercised to foster the transformation of violence-regulating norms in the war on terror? The research question aims to find legitimation practices which were applied by both presidents designed to support the norm transformation process in violence-regulating norms during the war on terror.

The research interest of this question is to come to an understanding of how legitimation is sought in presidential practice. By answering this question, I expect to find repeated patterns in presidential legitimacy-seeking activities in the material world and in rhetorical activities transmitted in speeches. Further, I want to find out whether and how legalization and justification activities occur in repeated patterns adding up to practices of legitimation. Such practices would have to be informed by background knowledge and embedded in security political discourse, designed to influence the meaning and use of violence-regulating

[10] For a deeper understanding of the background of the Eisenhardt method and theory-building approaches based on case evaluations see Lynham (2002) and Yin (2009, 1981).

norms. By reconstructing these legitimation practices, I seek to contribute to the conceptual development of norm transformation by adding practices of legitimation. Searching for legitimation practices in norm transformation processes in the war on terror, I engage in an iterative process based on the defined legitimation practices looking for confirming evidence to solidify chains of action. The aim is to reconstruct legitimation practices, i.e. condense and detailed descriptions of actions or chains of actions, acted out by both presidents to legitimize the use of force and the application of violence.

The research question sets the margins for the reesarch design in which I take a close look at norm transformation processes and legitimation activities. Both require an interpretive approach analyzing qualitative data, as I further explain in the following. This question and the research interest both result from an intensive literature review on the legal debate which emerged over the use of violence during the war on terror.[11] Consequently, for one, the number of cases for norm transformation is limited to this scene of conflict. For another, the choice of cases is also the result of a constant back and forth between theoretical and conceptual study and empirical case material. As stated above, the research interest is to shed more light on the proceedings in norm transformation on a conceptual level. Additionally, the research interest also lies in understanding empirical cases better from a perspective that allows for a deeper understanding of legitimation of violence.

Theoretical Sampling

As proposed by Eisenhardt and Graebner, the case selection is based on the benefit for theory advancement and the explanatory value for the phenomenon in question rather than based on statistical, randomized criteria (Eisenhardt 1989; Eisenhardt/Graebner/Sonenshein 2016; Eisenhardt/Graebner 2007).[12] The research interest thus provides criteria for the case selection. Some criteria are conceptually specific: norm transformation should be recognizable, as the accepted norm prevails while a new normative understanding develops; a norm conflict should be visible (the use of violence conflicts with commonly accepted normative restrictions); and a development in the performance of violence towards less restrictive use is recognizable. Some criteria concern research practicability: a sufficient database and public interest should be given. As my research

[11] Compare discussions reviewed in Chap. 2.

[12] For a contrasting approach see Gerring (2004) who describes a step-by-step overview on a positivist case selection. Also, Seawright and Gerring (2008) provide an overview of techniques for case selection, referring to common types of cases and choosing techniques for small-N case study designs.

interest lies in security politics, secrecy is an issue. Hence, I choose a case with sufficient public debate, media coverage (including legal measures to ensure access to information), and public attention (nationally and internationally) to trigger the need for political legitimation. Based on these considerations, a single-case study is conducted on indefinite detention of terrorists at Guantanamo Bay Detention Camp.

This case is especially suited for the advancement of norm transformation in theory, as political actions challenge robust norms on the containment of violence causing major criticism of the U.S. application of violence and legal reasoning. Opponents see this case as a violation of violence-containing norms, both domestically and internationally. Despite clear criticism of detainee treatment as illegitimate and illegal by the critical legal community, U.S. administrations did not fully stop the violent acts. Rather, both Bush and Obama have continued to engage in questionable actions openly or clandestinely. Due to this gap between the commonly agreed upon interpretations of violence-containing norms and the political actions of the United States, a high need for legitimation results.[13] Moreover, both presidents accompanied these security politics with legitimacy-seeking activities in political actions and rhetoric to seek legitimacy (legality and justification) for the violent acts. As the case received much public attention, a rich database allows for the tracing of legitimation activities and consequently for the reconstruction of legitimation practices. The case promises results speaking to both international and national law, as indefinite detention entails foreign and security policies during the state of emergency regulations after 9/11 in the United States. Thus, indefinite detention concerns both domestic and international norms and legal interpretations. Furthermore, the case lies at a cross section of the normative order, as it touches upon several different norms which aim to contain violence and thus promise to deliver results speaking to a multitude of regulations.

In the selected case, political actions contradict the prevailing interpretation of the norm, causing complex legal disputes, which concern a series of norms, constituting a norm conflict. The detention norm is among the ones which drew most attention in public debate, along with the torture norm and the assassination norm (targeted killings). The case of indefinite detention is chosen for analysis here due to the high prominence in public debate which also provides a rich and well documented database for analysis. In the case of indefinite detention in Guantanamo the norm transformation occurs with a new national detention law and a

[13] On a discussion of the legal issues and the violence-regulating norms in question see Chap. 2.

changed interpretation of international law. On the national level, constitutional issues concerning detainee rights and legal procedural issues are addressed in the new detention law (Alexander 2013; Sall 2013). On the international level, the change in interpretation concerns the *Geneva Conventions* (1949) regarding status, rights in captivity, regulations for legal prosecution, duration of incarceration, and modalities of release.

Exclusion of Alternative Cases

Other cases suitable for reconstructing legitimation practices concern torture, targeted killings, and extraordinary renditions. Surely, the listed violent actions match the discussed normative contradictions; yet, these cases lack certain features vital to the research interest and/or disqualify for research practical reasons. In the case of torture[14], norm transformation remains at best an attempt made by members of the Bush administration. Despite his knowledge of enhanced interrogation methods which have been criticized as torturous, President Bush publicly denied torture and a formal legalization process which would finalize a norm transformation did not occur.[15] The Obama administration strongly condemned torture. Enhanced interrogation methods applied at Guantanamo were banned and Obama took measures to improve detainee treatment.[16] If anything, both administrations tried to hide the exact use of methods instead of publicly defending or legitimizing interrogation techniques. Thus, the debate on the torture norm is rather a case of a failed norm transformation.[17] Whereas the new detention law (Alexander 2013; Sall 2013) and the new killing norm are discussed (Banka/Quinn 2018; Jose 2017; Pratt 2018), no new torture norm is debated in norm literature, but rather the damage to the ban on torture is evaluated (Kutz 2014; McKeown 2009; Rosert/Schirmbeck 2007). Nevertheless, the case of torture in the war on terror provides ample data for testing the findings of this study.

[14] The torture scandal occurred when pictures of tortured prisoners in Abu Ghraib were made public by the media in 2004 and 2006. For an overview of the political debate among government officials and legal advisors concerning the treatment of detainees in interrogations not constituting torture during the Bush administration see: Greenberg/Dratel 2005.

[15] President Bush publicly denied torture on numerous occasions, like in "Remarks on the War on Terror" on September 6, 2006 (Bush, Remarks on 2006–09-06: 1617) and "Message to the House of Representatives Returning Without Approval the 'Intelligence Authorization Act for Fiscal Year 2008" (Bush, Message to 2008–03-08: 338).

[16] On his first day in office, Obama signed three executive orders promising lawful interrogations (Executive Order 13491), the closure of Guantanamo Bay Detention Camp (Executive Order 13492), and to review the detention policy (Executive Order 13493).

[17] On norm transformation see Chap. 3.

Similarly to the debate on a new detention norm, norm transformation is discussed regarding the U.S. use of targeted killings (Senn/Troy 2017; Großklaus 2017; Kasher/Yadlin 2005; Pratt 2018). The debate on targeted killings encompasses not only the use of drones to realize military operations in remote areas but also military scenarios such as the operation to find and capture or kill Usama bin Laden. Like indefinite detention, targeted killing has a normative history and was considered as normatively and morally wrong and a robust ban under international and national law (Senn/Troy 2017). The increased use and proliferation of targeted killings by drones during the war on terror sparked a new discussion on the legality of targeted killings (Haas/Fischer 2017; Gregory 2017). Whereas some see in targeted killings a clear violation of the ban on assassination (Alston et al. 2008; Banks/Raven-Hansen 2003), others argue for the legality of U.S. targeted killings (Kretzmer 2005; Pratt 2015; Yoo 2011). On the national level, the new killing norm stands in contrast to constitutional issues such as *due process* and procedural legal issues (Murphy/Radsan 2009). On the international level, targeted killings pose a norm conflict with the assassination norm and factors into a newly arisen debate on the regulations of drones as weapon systems (Alston et al. 2008; Downes 2004). Based on these arguments, the case of targeted killings fulfills the theoretical requirements of my research interest. However, for a lack of accessibility to sufficient data, the case is dismissed for this study. Nevertheless, the findings of this study should be tested on the case of targeted killings.

In the case of extraordinary renditions, which were committed under both administrations, the norm transformation did not reach the extent of formal legalization. Furthermore, a core principle is that targeted killings are committed in secret. As a result, this act of violence is perceived less critically by the public and there is less pressure to legitimize it, so that access to sufficient quality data remains a practical research problem (Sadat 2007; Sadat 2006).

Organization of the Research Process: Data Assembling and Analytical Approach
The research process I divided into several phases, which Schwartz-Shea and Yanow distinguish in "fieldwork," "deskwork," and "textwork" (Schwartz-Shea/Yanow 2012). Following these guidelines, the first step for generating theory is to collect and analyze a rich set of empirical data. Since no field research in the classical sense took place, fieldwork in this regard refers to what Schwartz-Shea and Yanow call "archival work" (Schwartz-Shea/Yanow 2012: 7).

In the context of this research project, material was researched using databases and internet searches. In terms of data accessibility, the case has raised great attention from critics and supporters, leading to a massive output in various genres: documented political speeches and decision-making documents, media coverage, legal reasoning, and court rulings. This archival field access takes into account that, for one, the legitimacy-seeking activities in this case are in the past and no other form of access is possible without a time machine. For another, a great amount of material documenting the legitimation efforts of the time despite being made public in this period still needs systematic evaluation. Moreover, the time of the war on terror is a period of documentary overflow. The systematic collection of data and information is a significant characteristic of government activities in this time, a lot of government documents were leaked but have not yet been subject to research. The added value of this research project thus lies in the processing of existing data and their evaluation. Deskwork in the context of this research process means the interpretive analytical work of making sense of the material. The theory development is based on a thorough case investigation creating "rich, empirical descriptions of particular instances of a phenomenon that are typically based on a variety of data sources" (Eisenhardt/Graebner 2007: 25). Finally, textwork refers to the step of text production and the writing of the research report presented in Chap. 5. All three steps are further explained in the subsection on the analytical approach of this chapter.

Generalizability and Representability

Conducting a single in-depth case study for theory advancement triggers the question of generalizability. These methodological considerations entail for the researcher to abstract from the in-depth analysis of only a few cases, which promise a high degree of generalization. As a reminder, generalizability is not the top goal in a qualitative, interpretive research setting, but gaining knowledge on specific cases is. Rather, generalizability refers to the selection of cases with a grounded database that allow the researcher to find constructs which again can be tested (Eisenhardt 1989; Eisenhardt 2021; Eisenhardt/Graebner 2007). In this research project, the aim is to find conceptually detailed practices of legitimation which can then be tested in further research. Hence, instead of presenting a complete theory, the results of the study should present starting points for further inquiry into generalizable constructs that eventually form theory.

The selected case is considered a crucial or extreme case which is also sometimes referred to as a "talking pig" (Eisenhardt 2021: 149; Eisenhardt/Graebner/Sonenshein 2016: 1118). Although the phenomenon may be extremely rare and hard to find elsewhere, this does not mean that we should not examine unique cases. Even though the transferability to other cases is expectably low, the availability of data is especially rich, since the phenomenon draws a lot of public attention producing output that can be analyzed qualitatively and interpretatively. Regarding this research project, I argue that analyzing the selected case presents a value. Moreover, I argue with reference to Eisenhardt that the results in form of specific constructs—the practices of legitimation—will be testable in many areas in and outside of the security political realm (Eisenhardt 1991). As such, this study is to be seen as a starting point for theory advancement that should be strengthened by further testing research. For instance, the analysis generates insights concerning U.S. treatment of norms in situations of security crises. The practices found in these cases can be searched for in other cases of norm conflict. Furthermore, the results can be tested in other democracies or non-democracies in similar security crises or cases of norm conflict. Results from legitimation practices in violence-regulating norms could also be tested in other policies.

However, debatable remains to what extent a single-case study is representative in terms of generalizable results. This refers to the question whether those legitimation practices can be found in other state actors' strategies. A common argument for the singularity of U.S. politics is that very few states are capable to act as the United States do, especially when it comes to disputed areas of the use of force and the applicability of violence. In that sense, I agree that the United States have a very privileged position among the international state community which does not lightly translate into acceptable behavior for other states. However, I argue that the U.S. practices of legitimation provide a case worth analyzing also with the aim of generalizing results. In the issue areas considered in the in-depth analysis, observable is that U.S. politics concerning international law often call for imitators of the argumentative patterns among other states' leaders. Thus, concerning disputed security policies, the likelihood that other states (democracies or not) refer to or use similar arguments is high. In this regard, I consider the U.S. acts of violence cases of legitimation practices with considerable value for the advancement of theoretical assumptions on states' legitimation practices for the use of force and the application of violence against non-state actors. I would assume that legitimation practices resulting from this study also show in non-related issue areas of political legitimation. In this sense, testing legitimation practices understood as defined concepts and scripts of political action should prove fruitful.

4.1.2 Analytical Approach to Reconstructing Legitimation Practices

Focusing on the transformation of violence-regulating norms, this study answers the research question which legitimation practices have the Presidents George W.

Bush, Jr., and Barack Obama exercised to foster the transformation of violence-regulating norms. The aim of this research project lies in the reconstruction of political practices of legitimation in the case of detention-related norm transformation. Empirically, I examine the case regarding legitimacy-seeking activities focusing on the interpreted meaning and use of violence-regulating norms. The analysis divides into two sections evaluating rich evidence generated over the legislations of both Bush's and Obama's time in office regarding indefinite detention in Guantanamo Bay Detention Camp.

The empirical analysis focuses on two dimensions of legitimation: (1) reconstructing the legitimation practices over time and accounting for conflict developments (which practice of legitimation for norm transformation was used when, by whom, and how), (2) reconstructing the rhetorical and argumentative legitimation practices used to foster the norm transformation towards violence-enabling norms. The first step concerns the reconstruction of legitimation practices over time (legitimation practices in political activities and speech over time) based on a dense description and serves to trace the formal legalization process and the development of justification activities over time. The case reconstruction is based on the evidence of a rich data collection from investigative journalism, critical research (legal and political science), leaked government documents, official government documents, and legal case rulings. The second step reconstructs legitimation practices from an in-depth content analysis of presidential speeches on the case topic (argumentative legitimation practices). This includes an in-depth rhetorical analysis of statements justifying the use of force and the application of violence in detention-related speeches. In addition to the evidence-based analysis of the first part, I analyze presidential speeches searching for repeated argumentative patterns in the second part.

Concluding the empirical analysis, I present the resulting list and conceptualization of norm-transforming legitimation practices that trace in performative actions and rhetorical speech actions. The expected list of legitimation practices includes but is not limited to secrecy, denial, marginalization, newness and exceptionality, necessity and self-defense, and barbarization of the enemy. Chapter 6 discusses the findings and possible reasons as to why these practices are used and what they are aimed at. Furthermore, I discuss similarities and differences in the strategies of applying violence and legitimation strategies used by Presidents Bush and Obama.

4.2 Conceptual Approach: Practices of Legitimation

Having outlined the methodological approach of this study, I turn to the conceptual approach to practices of legitimation. Reconstructing legitimation practices contributes to a deeper understanding of how states or state leaders try to foster norm transformation processes. Regarding the theory-building aim, those state practices of acting out and rhetoric framing are of concern that question the violence-containing function of international humanitarian law and the inscribed standards of legitimate violence.[18] Legitimation becomes an issue when one or more actors question a norm's meaning and/or use. As conceptualized in Chap. 3, norms provide for behavioral rules reflecting collectively shared ideas, beliefs, and moral convictions. Norms are always in need of interpretation. Usually, interpretation is shared and mutually accepted, even more so when norms are considered stable and robust in meaning and use over a long time. Actors cannot arbitrarily and unilaterally change the meaning of norms—this meaning must be accepted by the respective social group. Thus, powerful actors who wish to alter a norm's meaning must argue and act to change not only the meaning in terms of the acted-out rule but also the reading of the rule, not necessarily in writing but the commonly agreed upon interpretation—the reading—of the rule. Otherwise, norm-transforming entrepreneurs risk sanctions, resistance, or other high social, political, and material costs (loss of reputation or cooperation benefits). Norm transformation requires legal changes and interpretive changes which require legitimation in terms of legal reasoning and (moral) justification. The research aim of this study is to reconstruct how this norm transformation is practically fostered by powerful actors.

In the context of this study, I base my conception of legitimation practices mainly on the approach presented by Adler and Pouliot. Both argue for a comprehensive approach: "An IR practice-oriented theoretical approach comprises a fairly vast array of analytical frameworks that privilege practice as the key entry point to the study of social and political life" (Adler/Pouliot 2011: 3). The advantage of this approach is that instead of providing a full theoretical framework which is to be applied, practice theory offers a conceptual framework that is rather to be seen as a research perspective. Thus, a practice-oriented approach allows for an all-encompassing analysis of political processes by combining actions of actors and the resulting effects in and on the material world (Adler/Pouliot 2011).

[18] By standards of legitimate violence, I mean specific security norms that fulfill humanitarian protective functions and contain violence as defined in Chap. 2 on legal issues and Chap. 3 on norm transformation.

In the case study, I analyze actions of norm interpretation and norm-based justification of foreign policy as a complex process of dealing with and attempting to change the normative order (international law). These are understood as a complex process involving a multitude of actors engaging in a dynamic normative transformation. A conceptual approach featuring practices in International Relations allows for the reconstruction of shared knowledge on how legitimation in norm transformation processes is done. The advantage of practices, as Reckwitz states, is that the concept offers a vocabulary, which can be used to understand and describe the world (Reckwitz 2002: 257). Following this perspective, this study focuses on the conceptual advantages practice theory offers combining a focus on actions with discursive analytical elements (Büger/Gadinger 2008: 275). Like in works on diplomacy, negotiations, or deterrence[19] (Neumann 2005; Adler 2008; Adler-Nissen/Pouliot 2014; Pouliot 2010), the aim of this study is to deduce a kind of manual—a 'how to'—on legitimation (legalization and justification) practiced in order to foster norm transformation processes. By reconstructing practices of legitimation from observations of legalization activities and justification in presidential speeches, I aim to contribute to a deeper, more practical, understanding of political legitimation of violence and state interaction with violence-regulating norms. In the following, I explain how the concept of practice is understood and used in this study.

4.2.1 Practice Turn and Conceptual Approach to Practices

The empirical analysis prominently relies on the concept of practices. In the past decades, IR scholars have largely debated the conception and theoretical contribution of a practice perspective to the field. The *practice turn* in International Relations refers to the increasing conceptual use of practices to analyze and describe phenomena in international politics.[20] As Bueger and Gadinger point out, "[p]ractice theories are a heterogeneous family" (Bueger/Gadinger 2015:

[19] What these research projects have in common is that they provide a practice-informed concept specification. For instance, diplomacy requires a certain set of actions that is performed following a script based on mutually known and accepted normative ideas on how a diplomat is to behave. While diplomacy is visible on the level of a person's actions, the foreign policy practice of deterrence is observable in the interaction between states as acting entities. The practice of deterrence is a conceptual container including a multitude of actions performed by military personnel, political decision-makers, and diplomats.

[20] For a detailed discussion on practice theory approaches and recent developments in the field see: Büger/Gadinger 2008.

1). The emerging field of practice theories divides into approaches reaching from sociological and post-structuralist to actor-network approaches.[21] Although the theories doubtlessly share common ground, understandings of 'practice' vary greatly, especially concerning the ontological and epistemological prerequisites. While I acknowledge the variety in practice theories, I feature a pragmatic use of the concept in this study. The term 'practice' as developed by Adler and Pouliot (2011) I adopt because of the conceptual advantages their practice-conception offers regarding the research interest of reconstructing political legitimacy-seeking activities as competent performances to foster norm transformation processes. Like Reckwitz (2002), I appreciate that practice theory offers a vocabulary that allows for combining political actions in specific social settings. Similarly to the approaches on diplomacy or deterrence (Neumann 2005; Adler-Nissen/Pouliot 2014; Pouliot 2010), the main conceptual advantage of a practice approach in this study is that a practice-perspective allows for the reconstruction of a manual on how to legitimize norm transformation. With this analytical purpose in mind, I focus on clarifying my conceptual use of terminology in the following.

Although the everyday understanding and use of the term practice suggests that any human activity can be a practice, practice theorists (Büger/Gadinger 2008; Bueger/Gadinger 2018; Adler/Pouliot 2011) clearly distinguish practices from other forms of human 'doing.'[22] Reckwitz refers to practice (singular; the German word *Praxis*) as the entity of human activities, contrasting practices (plural; the German word *Praktiken*) as a certain kind of social and socially recognizable action (Reckwitz 2002: 249, 253). This distinction points to the claim of practice theorists that practices (*Praktiken*) stand for a specific kind of action: "A 'practice' (*Praktik*) is a routinized type of behaviour which consists of several elements, interconnected to one other: forms of bodily activities, forms of mental activities, 'things' and their use, a background knowledge in the form of understanding, know-how, states of emotion and motivational knowledge" (Reckwitz 2002: 249).[23] A practice thus differs from other forms of doing, action, or

[21] On the emergence, development, and formation of competing approaches in the field of practice research see: Adler/Pouliot 2011, Adler-Nissen/Pouliot 2014, Bueger 2016, Bueger/Gadinger 2018, Büger/Gadinger 2008, Reckwitz 2002.

[22] For a deeper understanding of the foundations of social practice theory see: Bourdieu 1990, Bourdieu 1977, and Bourdieu 1976.

[23] For more conceptual insights concerning the differences between *Praxis* and *Praktiken* as well as an elaboration on practices and the meaning of body, mind, and things in terms of performative dimensions see Reckwitz (2002: 250–257).

behavior, as it is not just some form of doing but a set of meaningful actions that is recognizable as a certain practice.

Why do practice researchers feature the term practice over other forms of doing? A 'social practice' distinguishes from other forms of 'doing' in that it combines meaningful actions in and on the material world and the discursive component that enhances socially attributed meaning to such actions. In this sense, the definition offered by Adler and Pouliot (2011) provides a conceptual distinction between behavior, action, and practice. According to Adler and Pouliot behavior encompasses all doing that is without specific meaning, whereas action is meaningful behavior. A social practice can be understood as a container for several actions, as actions are observable in time and space. Practices are not only meaningful behavior, thus actions, but are also characterized by occurring in repeated patterns (Adler/Pouliot 2011: 5). A single action does not constitute a practice, but a practice consists of a certain combination of patterned actions which are performed repeatedly in a similar sequence or occurrence. As Reckwitz states: "A practice is thus a routinized way in which bodies are moved, objects are handled, subjects are treated, are described and the world is understood" (Reckwitz 2002: 250). Adler and Pouliot further specify practices as "competent performances" which "simultaneously embody, act out, and possibly reify background knowledge and discourse in and on the material world" (Adler/Pouliot 2011: 4).

A practice defines by showing specific features (Adler/Pouliot 2011: 4–8; Reckwitz 2002: 249–250):

- It is a performance. As such, it can be observed as an action performed by a socially meaningful actor in a public place in a certain amount of time.
- It is a patterned and routinized (set of) action(s) and can thus be recognized by others as a specific practice.
- It is performed competently (as opposed to incompetently) and thus can be judged by members of a social group as properly acted out or falsely done.
- It is based on background knowledge and can only be understood and recognized by those actors who are privy to this background knowledge.
- It combines actions in and on the material world with discursive actions, merging layers of meaning from doing something and speaking about it or in addition to it, framing the actions in a specific interpretation.

While many authors focus on social understanding, Adler and Pouliot take on an IR perspective on practices. Political actions are thus understood as meaningful behavior which aims to create and fix meaning (Adler/Pouliot 2011: 15–17). IR practices are acted out in an international political arena and by fixing political meanings for a politically relevant audience. Adler and Pouliot state that practice theory seeks to explain how "most political dynamics come to rest on the fixation of meanings—a hard work in which practices play a prominent role" (Adler/Pouliot 2011: 3). Commonly referred to examples from the realm of international relations are the practices of (coercive) diplomacy, nuclear proliferation, or deterrence (Neumann 2005; Adler-Nissen/Pouliot 2014; Adler/Pouliot 2011). A practice does not signify a specific action but can be understood as a container for specific foreign policy actions or IR-related discursive and material actions, which, taken together as a whole, represent repeated and patterned competent performances.

Building on this conceptual understanding, this study searches for legitimation practices which influence (change, interpret, and eventually alter and fix) the meaning of violence-regulating norms. Powerful actors foster norm transformation, as I argue, through legitimation practices. To transform a normative understanding, legitimation practices must be formed in a competent way observable to a respective audience. These legitimation practices I understand as the container for all those politically meaningful actions in deeds and rhetoric that aim to convince the respective audience of the norm transformation. Whereas practice and interpretive research often take a very close look at individuals, the research focus in this study is on collective actions, i.e. political practices which are in the above cited examples (deterrence, nuclear proliferation) state actions.[24] By referring to state actions which consist of actions by institutions and elected officials, I distinguish performing actors regarding the person, their role, the office, and institution. Legitimacy-seeking actions may be acted out by an individual, i.e. the president, but are representative for the state's actions. As legitimation is analyzed by looking at the actions of the person in the office, clearly these actions are performed in the role of the office and not by a private individual. As such, presidents are the representatives of a government institution and thus representatives of a state's people. Most actions performed are acted out

[24] The term 'state' actor or practice here may deviate from the use of 'collective practice' as described by Adler and Pouliot. In many practice theory articles, the notion of collective refers to corporate practices which are understood as communities of practice. I see my understanding partially in line with this terminology, yet, to avoid misleading usage, I refrain from including the term corporate practices in my design. Furthermore, I am not interested in researching a community of practice—like the G8 as a joint group of states or the United States as joint group of federal states and people. Rather, I want to research impulses given by a specific actor performing actions in the role of a norm entrepreneur to induce a complex process of norm transformation.

within the margins of the role and practice of being the president of the United States which already follows its own set of rules and routines and are in each incident the product of a strategic process which included a multitude of consultants and influences behind the scenes. Consequently, although it appears as though analyzing individual performances, the analysis mainly studies a collective, as in state practice of legitimation.

Methodologically, Adler and Pouliot point out that the "level of aggregation" for actions and actors depends on the research interest (see Adler/Pouliot 2011: 8). Taking this seriously, I determine the levels of aggregation for actors and activities in the following step, further explaining the conceptual and operational understanding of legitimation practices in this study. This conceptual understanding of practices has several advantages: it allows viewing political actions as intended, discursively embedded, and socially anchored performances. The concept of practices combines structural factors such as political actions aiming at normative change and the discursive legitimation of such actions. Norms, their contestation, and change, as well as the justification of these actions, merge into an understanding of practices as state actions that aim to change the normative order of violence in favor of a state's preferred course of action. In the interplay of different justifications, complex justification narratives, and social discourses emerge that are shared and commonly agreed or disputed and contested by state actors in political actions, executive output, and speeches. Overall, the actions that contribute to the discourse of legitimation can be summarized under the concept of legitimation practices. Analyzing state actions to legalize and justify the use of force and application of violence results in the reconstruction of a manual of political actions—how to practice legitimation to foster norm transformation.

4.2.2 Practices and Methods—How to Research Practices of Legitimation

In addition to the conceptual use of practices in this study some clarifications need to be made regarding the methods used in this study. The growing field of practice researchers has developed practice-specific methodological guidelines. Similarly to the interpretive approaches described earlier, methods for practice research are generally open to a variety of methodological approaches. Bueger calls "the methodology of practice theory [...] *praxiography*" (Bueger 2016: 332; Bueger 2014), which is understood as a (research) practice itself. This approach often entails fieldwork using ethnographic methods like participant observation and interviews with practitioners for reconstructing practices by analyzing competent everyday individualist performances. As Bueger and Gadinger clarify, "there is no universal recipe for how to do practice research" (Bueger/Gadinger 2014: 77). Thus, practice research offers a certain freedom for the researcher to choose methods tailored to the study's research interest. Yet, practice research designs share common ground when it comes to the choice of methods which is generally described as creative, undogmatic, and parsimonious regarding theoretical presumptions (Bueger 2016; Bueger/Gadinger 2018; Pouliot 2013). Practice research shares with interpretive approaches that research designs are closely guided by the needs of the research question and interest and seek a detailed reconstruction of empirical cases (Büger/Gadinger 2008: 295–296). Following guidelines from interpretive and practice research, I describe the choice of methods in terms of tools to research practices of legitimation in the following.

In this case study, I apply the method of "reading practices" from text. Bueger presents four methods to the study practices: "(1) observing practices, (2) learning practices, (3) talking about practices and (4) reading practices" (Bueger 2016: 333). For the purposes of my study, not all four methods are applicable. All four methods serve the purpose of reconstructing practices from closely studying everyday performances and the individual sense-making as well as meaning attribution of the performing actors. In this sense, reconstructing practices often means discovering background knowledge. Understanding practices as competent performances, this kind of knowledge reconstruction thus leads to quasi manuals, like in the research on how to be a diplomat. Reconstructing the practice of diplomacy means to reconstruct the hidden knowledge, rules, and behaviors which all make a person a diplomat—so one can learn the practice by learning the background knowledge—how to be a diplomat and how to perform the practice of diplomacy (Neumann 2005).

The first three methods all heavily rely on the possibility to join in situations of everyday life, to learn from observation or from participation, or to learn from the direct interviewing of practitioners. Although the idea is compelling to find practices where they are practiced (this would regard methods one through three described by Bueger), often in research projects witnessing performance is not possible due to a lack of access to the field or the people (Pouliot 2013: 48–49). The aim of research here is to reconstruct routines in performances and argumentative patterns from political positioning with reference to a specific political goal (i.e. transforming a norm's meaning). For the purposes of this empirical study, these three methods are not applicable, as the political processes I am interested in state actions. For one, data collection through interviews with practitioners would not serve the research goal, as I am not interested in retrieving personal reflections on meaning attribution through actions. For another, all actions lie in the past, thus the performances cannot be attended and observed firsthand. Thus, the fourth method of reading practices offers an approach that allows for reconstructing political practices performed by state agents in the past which can only be reconstructed from documentation of past performances (Bueger 2016; Pouliot 2013).

Reading practices has two distinct meanings. The first dimension concerns the situational reading of practices. This is closely connected to the conceptual idea that practices are performances in and on the material world, which are observable, placed in a geographical limited area or a distinct room, and are socially meaningful, including rhetorical performances and meaning in a given situation. Context matters for the meaning of social situations. The same line of words can take on very different meanings depending on the social setting and mood of the situation. In political performances status factors mainly attribute to the meaning of a statement—who said what, to whom, and in which function or position—as well as time and place—when was it said, in which situational context (after an attack, before an expiring deadline, in the midst of a public scandal) and even in which outfit the statement was delivered (in uniform, suit, or jeans). All these factors add meaning to the statements made and help reconstruct practices. Reading practices in this sense means reading the room, observing the situation, with all its settings and actions, and applying background knowledge to attribute meaning.

The second dimension of reading practice concerns the actual process of research activity to read up on documented actions in transcripts of events and spoken words. Meaning-attributing factors must be considered while reading about texts, as the text may contain rhetorical statements but may yet fail to deliver situational factors. For a full reconstruction of practices which accounts for all conceptual aspects (the worldly, bodily performance and the rhetorical performance) both—the situational and the text-based—readings are necessary research methods. The design for this case study thus includes the reconstruction of practices in terms of observable performances in time and space (course of action), the historical and geographical positioning of these performances in social rooms (situational reconstruction), and the attribution of meaning and dominant normative framing of political activities (meaning-production and sense-making in political spheres).

In the case considered in this empirical analysis a couple more characteristic factors for legitimation practices need clarification, distinguishing this design from other approaches to practice research. Legitimation practices are:

- *State practices rather than private practices*: Although legitimation practices are often individually performed (as in one person acting or speaking), I understand these individuals as representatives of a state, and thus as performing state action. So, I consider legitimation as a competent performance of a powerful political actor representing a group of (elected) government actors and being perceived as an (elected) government official or a country representative.
- *Based on background knowledge*, which is essential to perform and understand state actions. Background knowledge is necessary to identify state practices. Background knowledge does not necessarily have to be reported by the performing actor but can also be read from situational and cultural context.
- *Political, event-related, situational, past performances rather than an everyday routine, or daily observable performances*. Like deterrence, I understand legitimation practices as performances of domestic, foreign, or international politics with reference to specific events and issues, which makes them observable on an ad hoc or occasion-related basis rather than on a periodical (like daily or monthly) basis.
- *Occur in connection with norm conflicts and situations of security crisis*. Situational settings need to be considered in searching for legitimation practices, as those are the situational trigger points for legitimation activities or the absence thereof points to clandestine actions, denial, or hiding.

Acknowledging the specific characteristics of legitimation practices and the limited access to the field in the selected case, a couple of practical research issues need addressing. Pouliot suggests looking for proxies to overcome field research limitations (Pouliot 2013: 48–49). Likewise, I use the understanding of 'field' provided in interpretive research as in archival research (Schwartz-Shea/Yanow 2012: 7). This kind of fieldwork entails that 'getting access' does not signify entering a room full of practitioners to participate and observe. Rather access to the field means seeking a sufficient (in terms of leading to saturation, as Eisenhardt proposes) collection of data that encompasses all conceptual aspects and to follow an analytical strategy that accounts for those conceptual aspects. Archival research includes all evidence of the legitimation actions which have been recorded in collectable data sources: news coverage, documentation of government activities, bureaucratic documentation, and documentation of legal proceedings.

As with legitimation, which is especially present where norm conflicts occur, Bueger and Gadinger argue that analyzing political crises and controversies has productive value for the reconstruction of practices (Büger/Gadinger 2008: 294). Crises, they argue, reveal individual deviations from the practiced routine and by spotlighting the fault reveal the original pattern of action. Instead, I argue that crisis management is a political practice worth analyzing. In terms of legitimation, norm conflicts trigger political action and pose value for the analysis. Thus, turning to situations of crisis reveals practices of legitimation as the common order is challenged. I seek to analyze those situations and practices of legitimation which are either designed to reconcile the political course of action with the normative framework or aim for change in the common interpretation of the framework up to the point of altering the norm.

Concerning the data approach, the idea is "to 'read' practices from texts, documents, and visual and material artefacts" (Bueger 2016: 334). Naturally, the selection of documents is key to successful practice reconstruction. As reading material anything qualifies that suitably documents the performance of key actors. Valuable text categories include but are not limited to: "memoirs, personal diaries and written correspondence" which are summarized in the category of "'ego-documents'"; "handbooks, court cases, annual reports, diplomatic cables, meeting minutes, recordings and transcripts," and "visual and material artefacts" (Bueger 2016: 334). Wheras interpretive designs using qualitative content analysis or discourse analysis most often rely on written or transcribed documents (i.e. political correspondence, written and/or transcribed news coverage), practice theorists are open to including visual and material artefacts to analytical data. As Bueger further specifies "[v]isual artefacts can include, for instance paintings of everyday scenes, or videos, such as the rich repertoire of documents we find on YouTube. [...] Material artefacts might further include technologies, but also architecture and buildings" (Bueger 2016: 334). Following these guidelines, I explain in more detail the choice of documents and corpus building in the section on the analytical approach.

4.2.3 Legitimation as a Practice—Conceptual and Operational Understanding

Relying on practice conceptions and practice-oriented research approaches, I conceptualize and operationalize[25] legitimation as a practice. Legitimation practices I understand as consisting of a complex set of political actions that are patterned

[25] 'Operationalize' here does not mean a numerical positivist method in terms of countable entities. Rather the term here means to lay out how I know that doings or sayings qualify as 'legitimation.' Following interpretive guidelines of revealing research strategies, I seek to achieve transparency by spelling out my conceptual understanding and by providing examples for legitimation expressions and account for each research step.

and repeated in a similar way over time and are observable in actions and in rhetoric by a state actor (a single representative or a group actor). Political actors perform practices of legitimation to reconcile politically favored actions with normative ideas about what is legitimate, as in right and just, in a given situation. I understand legitimation as a discursive competing process of rivaling actors over the dominant interpretation of a given codified or non-codified norm (Jose 2017). Consequently, I understand legitimation practices[26] as competent performances of key political figures, which are aimed at making acts of state violence appear as legitimate, i.e. legal and just, to a respective audience.

Analogous to the research on security practices, like deterrence, I understand legitimation as a practice which involves several actions. For example, the practice of deterrence consists of a number of routinized actions, among others showing military force and strong rhetoric (Adler/Pouliot 2011: 19–28). Likewise, I understand the practice of legitimation as a container for legitimacy-seeking actions (meaningful behavior) which are competently performed in a routinized way, recognizable to an audience which shares background knowledge. Each legitimacy-seeking action could be seen as one practice alone, one could argue. Similarly, norm transformation could be seen as a practice. As argued above, practice research depends on the level of aggregation. Deviating from the research on diplomacy, I will not dive into actions on the detailed level of scripts and manuals for how to be a diplomat in person, which accounts for everyday life practices. Instead, on a broader level I collect patterns of action and routines which add up to a state-actor guiding legitimation manual aimed at norm transformation.

Legitimacy, Legitimate Actions, Legitimation

Aiming to reconstruct legitimation practices, I hereinafter conceptualize the term legitimation and explain the terms justification and legality as used in this study. According to Suchman "[l]egitimacy is a generalized perception or assumption that the actions of an entity are desirable, proper, or appropriate within some socially constructed system of norms, values, beliefs, and definitions" (Suchman 1995: 574). As "a generalized perception or assumption" legitimacy is an observation made, and opinion formed that is shared by a larger crowd. This is usually a group of people who attribute legitimacy to someone or something, a defined, declared, or distinct audience. Legitimacy concerns the "actions of an entity" referring to a legitimacy-seeking individual or collective actor. The attributes "desirable, proper, appropriate" hint to a shared understanding and knowledge base

[26] I use the expression practices of legitimation as a synonym.

of the audience on what is behavior that meets the demand based on a "socially constructed system of norms, values, beliefs and definitions," which means that a shared understanding of appropriateness is inscribed in non-codified or codified norms (Suchman 1995: 574).

Building on this definition, I understand legitimacy as the congruence of actual political use of force with the shared understanding of the normatively allowed use of force (legitimate use of force) (Suchman 1995: 573). Consequently, I consider the political activity of legitimation as all efforts of government actors to persuade a defined audience that a political action or position is just and legal—thus legitimate. These attempts to establish the perception of congruence are visible in actions in and on the material world and in spoken words. Were we to imagine legitimation as a movie, for the first analytical step, we would watch and analyze the film in mute only observing the actions. In the second analytical step, we would then read the script without watching the film. Only combined—action and spoken word—will the movie unfold its full meaning.

As efforts for gaining legitimation, I consider all doings and sayings specifically aimed to generate acceptance for or prevent resistance against violence conduct among a designated audience. In terms of content, legitimation is made up of two kinds of doings and sayings: legalization and justification. Legalization I understand as the attempt to change existing legal provisions or engage in law-making procedures to make the political conduct legal. Justification encompasses all acting and arguing for compliance or norm conform behavior or arguing for the rightfulness of norm-breaking behavior using references to the law or norms and legal as well as persuasive language. Furthermore, justification includes all arguments and reasons brought forward in favor of norm-conform or reasoning for norm-deviant behavior using non-legal references.

Sources for Legitimation

Legitimation has various sources—social, historical, and political—yet, legal references play a special role, as these are already accepted and institutionally produced standards of right and wrong (Förster/Lemke 2016). Legitimation may refer to codified and non-codified norms on the national and international level. National law has already gone through a legitimate process and international law has also gone through a formal treaty-making process which grants legitimation. As a product of legitimate procedures, legal references thus already have gained legitimacy.

Legalization as activities aimed at changing existing legal provisions or engaging in law-making procedures can be acted out on the international and national level. Internationally, legalization can be accomplished through a formalized diplomatic process which involves engaging in bilateral or multilateral treaty-making processes. On the national level, law-making follows regulated legislative procedures. In the U.S., Congress must vote on new legal provisions or changes in existing provisions. Another option for U.S. presidents would be to change law or make law by presidential decree. A third option to influence legal interpretation in the United Sates and thereby not necessarily change written law but change its application is to set precedent in a legal case before a court, up to the Supreme Court.[27]

Whereas on the national level, the full range of formal and informal norm interpretation is used, on the international level, changing a norm's interpretation is more common than initiating a formal legal process, as those usually take a lot of time, organizational effort, and complicated diplomacy. In security politics, however, time is of the essence. This is visible the *Declaration of National Emergency* (Bush, Declaration of 2001-09-14) and the following events but also in executive orders which are used as a faster legalization tool than initiating congressional procedures.[28] Hence, international norms (codified or non-codified) are often re-interpreted and thus informally changed in meaning and use (Shannon 2000).

Justification, here understood as all non-legal arguments, usually refers to shared values and history. Such values are often deeply rooted in a society's identity-creating catalogue of attributes. For example, Esch describes how the Bush administration used certain narratives, which she calls myths, to gain support for policies in the war on terror (Esch 2010). Similarly, the justification of the *unlawful enemy combatant* relies on political arguments referring to tradition, the national founding ethos (referring to the Founding Fathers intentions drafting the U.S. constitution), and the shared crisis experience of the 9/11 terrorist attacks (Hühnert 2016).

Legitimation—Seeking and Granting Legitimacy

Norm research often focuses on the norm—how it emerges, changes, and eventually possibly dies; however, I want to focus on the actors involved in forwarding the norm-changing processes. Norm entrepreneurs are usually considered midwives in norm emergence. A closer look reveals that norm entrepreneurs have an agenda-setting role, by guiding attention and even creating issues for norm emergence. Security relevant events may create windows of opportunity to challenge a norm's meaning and initiate a transformation process. How norm entrepreneurs

[27] For an introduction to the political system of the United States see: Oldopp 2013.

[28] See the Appendix provided in the Electronic Supplementary Material.

set the frame for a new norm in an existing or newly created issue area is vital to the success of the norm. Norms always exist in competition to other or pre-existing norms, ideas, interests, and perceptions (Finnemore/Sikkink 1998: 897). Issue-framing efforts must acknowledge and refer to such competing or pre-existing normative frameworks (Nadelmann 1990). Thus, in the entrepreneurship phase of a norm transformation, presenting plausible alternative explanations, interpretations, and credible perceptions are part of the framing process. Establishing a new norm or fixing a transformed meaning cannot be accomplished by one actor alone. Rather, norms need acceptance, and normative meaning must be shared. This is where strategies for legitimation come in. Norm entrepreneurs need persuasion strategies in the norm emergence stage as well as in the norm transformation process (Payne 2001). Once a norm is set, norm entrepreneurs encourage other norm takers to follow the norm and promote imitation and adoption of the proposed norm interpretation. In the case of norm transformation studied here, imitation by other states is not the envisaged goal of U.S. norm transformation actions, but rather state actors' legitimation activities seek foreign states' and national votership's approval, recognition, and support.

As Thomas defines, legitimation is "the process by which actors come to believe in the normative legitimacy of an object" (Thomas 2014: 742). Whereas this definition rather focuses on legitimacy-granting activities, I am foremost interested in legitimacy-seeking activities. Legitimation understood as political positioning and efforts to persuade a defined audience is thus a public and observable activity. Consequently, legitimation efforts can only by analyzed where they occur visible, perceptible, and experienceable to the public. Thomas further explains that "[l]egitimation may occur as the result of a conscious effort to influence beliefs about what is normatively justified, or as the product of the unconscious replication of pervasive legitimacy narratives. Whereas each form of legitimacy represents property, legitimation represents action. It may either be narrowly strategic or part of a process of public discourse leading to more broadly legitimate outcomes" (Thomas 2014: 742). Thus, political actors must gain legitimacy, as legitimacy is not god-given or can be achieved by oneself but is granted by a defined audience. Legitimacy is thus reflexive: political actors are dependent on their people on the national level or on other states on the international level. Legitimation is also not arbitrary, but a deliberate, intentional effort to persuade others. As I understand this struggle for legitimation as a discursive action, I also assume that state agents actively pursue discourse strategies which include agenda-setting activities. In many cases, legitimation happens as a response to public outrage, like when press releases made torture cases in Abu Ghraib public. Here, political agenda setting is limited, but political actors still have the possibility to opt for a specific position on a certain issue. However, in other cases, political agenda setting includes the option to choose which topics are publicly treated and which issues remain secret. In any case, government actors decide which topics are dealt with and which position is presented to the audience.

Hurd further argues that legitimation is not only nationally relevant to persuade and secure voters, but also legitimation is a necessary activity on the international level to frame security political actions, gain supporters, and avoid conflict (Hurd 1999; Hurd 2007a). In the specific area of norm interpretation, state actors must give plausible reasons for actions taken (Sandholtz 2008: 107). Whereas legitimacy is the political currency on the national level, the international level lacks principles that ensure legitimate institutions and behavior in comparison. Nevertheless or because of this formal lack in legitimacy-producing institutions, on the international level legitimation remains a relevant activity. States thus need to persuade other actors (state leaders or peoples) by bringing forward convincing arguments to change normative beliefs (Sandholtz 2008: 107).

If legitimation is understood as a public act, the question arises as to why one should look at clandestine or secret government activities, as those should by definition and for practical research reasons be excluded from the study. Nevertheless, secrecy is part of the legitimacy-seeking activities in security politics, which I analyze. Secrecy is not only a free ticket on legitimation but also a killer argument in legitimation rhetoric. In terms of a free ticket, secrecy serves as the best excuse for political decision-makers not to legitimize security political actions at all: as no action is publicly known, nothing must be justified or legalized. Should a questionable action become public anyway, secrecy functions as a killer argument because the security political need for secrecy frees government actors of any further demand to justify or legalize the activities in question. As such, secrecy is a privilege of legitimate government actors, who are entrusted to decide security relevant matters in the interest of the people. With this privilege comes the trust in the promise of elected officials to act within the limits of the law. Thus, secrecy or clandestine activities signify the absence of legitimation.

Including the absence of legitimation and deliberate non-legitimation in the conceptualization of legitimation activities means for the analysis that I include all observable legitimation efforts which mention secrecy, signal the absence of legitimation, and present as efforts to evade the pressure to legitimize security political actions. The absence of legitimation is considered as part of the political strategy to legitimize political actions, and thus as a distinct activity in the set of actions adding up to legitimation practices. Moreover, in norm transformation processes I assume that secrecy hints to deliberate norm-deviating actions.

Secrecy used in a norm transformation process can be an attempt to cover up norm offenses and to ex-post legalize norm deviant actions.

Government officials function as legitimacy-seeking actors, which must appeal to a legitimacy-granting audience. Legitimacy-seeking actors include all natural persons elected to public office or officially appointed to public service as well as all judicial individuals including state institutions (commissions, government institutions, authorities, and courts). Although reciprocity is a key assumption on how legitimacy is sought and granted, I do not analyze legitimation on both sides of the process. Thus, not subject to this study is how successful government legitimation activities are, how well legitimation efforts are received, or whether and how legitimacy is granted. Rather, I analyze in detail the government's efforts to legitimize security political actions and identify legitimation activities and patterns. I thus focus on U.S. government legitimacy-seeking efforts and entrepreneurship in a norm transformation process.

The relevant audiences in the case examined here are located on two levels. On the inner state level, the relevant audience contains the U.S. people, citizens, and voters. On the interstate, international level, the relevant audience consists of the international state community and people, citizens and votership, and especially states allied to the United States. Legitimacy must be granted by the respective audiences. An audience can grant legitimacy by actively approving (informally visible in polls, or through formal channels such as elections) or by tacitly agreeing (not openly protesting or sanctioning).

Analyzing and Reconstructing Practices of Legitimation

In the following, I want to shed some light on how I recognize practices of legitimation in doings and sayings. Reconstructing practices means to observe political actions closely and to look for repetitions, patterns, and schemes. In terms of this research design, this means to observe violent actions in the considered case and to describe the political process that goes along with this use of force and application of violence to reconcile the use of force and the normative understanding. So, I look for all actions that make the use of force and application of violence seem legitimate, as in legal and just.

A legitimation practice consists of a set of distinguished actions and sequences of actions that fulfill but are not limited to the following criteria:

- Legitimation is a set of meaningful, purposeful, deliberate, and intentional actions.
- Legitimation actions are perceived as state actions by a defined audience. State action here is understood as opposed to private actions. State actions may be

performed by a single person in a public role who serves in an office. While acting individually (as in one physical person), the state official acts as a representative of an institution (here the presidency) as opposed to a private person. Although individuals in office can take personal notes on leadership style, the office comes with certain restrictions, rules, duties and demands for actions.

- These performed actions consist of observable doings with detectable consequences in and on the material world and traceable verbal expressions which convey persuasive arguments with reference to the material or idealist world.
- These actions are performed in a political and social frame of reference which builds on cultural (historical, political, and social) background knowledge. This knowledge is shared, more or less[29], by a defined community which functions as the legitimacy-granting audience. Legitimacy-seeking actors use shared background knowledge to persuade the audience, and the audience uses background knowledge to decide upon the legitimacy request.
- Legitimation is a political practice which is routinized as an inner state political process as well as an inter-state process. As such legitimation shows in reenactable patterns of action and rhetoric and constitutes a learnable and teachable performance, which can be done right or wrong.

Following these conceptual guidelines, in the subsequent analysis political actions are observed on two levels: the performative and the rhetorical level. On the performative level, I observe political actions concealing or explaining political actions and communicating with the public. On the rhetorical level, I analyze presidential speeches concerning detention and detainee treatment.

4.3 Analytical Approach: Reconstructing Legitimation Practices

This section unfolds the use of methods in the single analytical steps. The research aim in the case study is to reconstruct legitimation practices in a norm transformation process. Norm transformation is a gradual process of changing the meaning and use up to the establishing of a new norm. While existing

[29] The shared knowledge base is greater among the people of one nation, like within the United States, whereas this shared knowledge base is comparably smaller among the international community.

norms stay in effect, additional conditions and alterations in meaning eventually produce new regulations adding to a continuously existing set of norms. Norm-transforming activities are observable where norm conflicts occur. Norm conflicts occur where the interpretation in meaning and/or use of a given norm differs from the generally agreed upon meaning and/or use of the norm (violence perceived as legitimate, i.e. right and just). Norm transformation traces in (but is not limited to) formal, highly institutionalized legalization processes. Whereas national legalization processes are structured in constitutional and legislative procedures, international legalization efforts are less institutionalized. Official treaty negotiation between states leads to written international law, yet the norm transformation in the war on terror does not present as an official renegotiation of war law in an international summit. On the national level, legal alterations for security politics suggest that normative understanding has also altered the understanding of international norms, even in lack of a formal legalization process. As norm transformation can be observed and studied on the national level, deductions can be drawn from justifications concerning international norm transformation efforts.

Drawing on the conceptual work of the previous section, legitimation practices encompass an active performance in and on the material world and a rhetorical, argumentative performance traceable in political speeches. For practical research reasons I analyze these two performances in two separate steps: (1) political actions in and on the material world, seeking legitimacy for the use of force and application of violence; and (2) the political rhetoric in speeches seeking legitimacy for the use of force and application of violence. While legitimation activities are traced in both steps, for conceptual reasons each step shifts the focus on specific aspects of legitimation as in legalization and justification. Step one is more suited to track legalization activities, as these are formalized in institutionalized processes visible in institutional output and events, whereas the rhetorical analysis in step two is more suited to track justification which more obviously occurs in spoken words.

The research process is organized in fieldwork, deskwork, and textwork (see: Schwartz-Shea/Yanow 2012: 7) as summarized in the following (see Table 4.1).

Table 4.1 Working Steps in the Research Process

	Fieldwork	Deskwork	Textwork
General meaning of the working step	Archival work includes all necessary steps to search for evidence and collect relevant material for the case studies.	The interpretation and sense-making of the material include reading, categorizing, coding, and evaluating the material matching analytical criteria.	The last step in the research process includes composing the research report as a written text (independent research report, book chapter).
Step 1: Reconstructing legitimation practices in political doing in and on the material world over time	Broad research of relevant material for the case that documents legitimation activities of the administrations	Evaluating data tracing norm transformation, searching for violent activities and legitimation activities of government actors and norm conflicts, detecting practices in repeated patterns	Writing the case study, Chap. 5, which displays the legitimation activities over time, analytically structured into phases and summarizing a list of practices
Step 2: Reconstructing legitimation practices in rhetorical political doing in selected speeches	Searching for the relevant speeches of the presidents, which are of significance to reveal the legitimation of violence and norm interpretation to form a document corpus for in-depth analysis.	Evaluating selected speeches searching for rhetorical legitimation arguments of the presidents and repeated pattern adding up to legitimation practices in rhetoric.	Adding to the case study report (Chap. 5) on rhetorical legitimation activities, to account for repeated argumentative patterns and adding to the list of legitimation practices.

In the first step, I search for legitimation practices in a detailed case reconstruction of the violent acts and norm transformation process over time. Process reconstruction here means an in-depth chronological accounting of events and actions concerning the use of force and application of violence for indefinite detention and the norm-interpretation and legalization efforts made by the presidents. In this dense description, I trace events and situations hinting to norm transforming activities in which legitimation is triggered and thus practices of legitimation can be aggregated. In the second step, I search for repeated patterns of rhetoric legitimizing (legalizing and justifying) the use of force and application of violence adding up to legitimation practices in presidential speeches. I assume that rhetoric shows repeated patterns of argument that reify and strengthen the practices identified in the first step aiming at a norm transformation and finally coining a new understanding of the violence-regulating norm.

Concluding the analysis, I combine the analytical results from both steps. The resulting list conceptualizes legitimation practices in terms of denotation (definition), connotation (intension), and the examples of the practice (extension).[30] I expect to find repeated patterns of legitimacy-seeking activities building up to practices which include but may not be limited to the following: secrecy, denial, scandal/crisis management, re-interpretation of the violence-regulating norms, introduction of quasi legal constructs, belittling, marginalization, barbarization of the enemy, and formal legalization efforts.

4.3.1 Analytical Step 1: Reconstructing Legitimation Practices in Norm Transformation Processes Over Time

In the first analytical step, I reconstruct government activities in the norm transformation process and search for patterns which add up to legitimation practices in and on the material world over time. In the following, I explain the research steps I took concerning the *fieldwork* and *deskwork. Textwork* representing the research report is fully provided in Chap. 5.[31]

Fieldwork: Data Generation and Evidence Gathering

As explained, fieldwork[32] in the context of this study means the collection and processing of data suitable for reconstructing legitimation practices over time.

[30] For further guidance on concept specification see: Wonka 2007, Goertz 2006.

[31] Textwork as defined above refers to the process of writing the research report. Chap. 5 represents the research report, all structural decisions are reasoned in the report.

[32] Unlike the common approach of interpretive designs, fieldwork does not refer to field research in terms of data-generating procedures like participative observation or interview guided research. Fieldwork here mainly refers to the archival component of collecting text material for analytical purposes. Unlike interpretive approaches, which are interested in reconstructing the insights of key actors in a certain process and therefore conduct interviews, I do not seek to analyze the opinions or perceptions of single participants or specific groups. In this research approach, reconstructing practices relies on finding repeated patterns in actions, which can be traced and 'read' in government documents.

Fieldwork entails two steps: a detailed search of electronic archives and the collection of the data and securing of the findings in a structured way. My field consists of electronic archives providing written and transcribed documentation of government activities. As evidence I consider every public account for provable activity acted out by public officials. The aim of this step is to collect as much evidence as necessary to reach saturation to reconstruct the activities of the administrations concerning indefinite detention in Guantanamo. To this end, I focus on the process of violence escalation and concomitant norm transformation closely tracing government activities which foster a normative understanding of violence-enabling norms and actions.

To ensure transparency in the evidence-gathering and interpretation process, presenting and analyzing evidence needs a systematic approach. Fieldwork and deskwork partially overlap, as the material found in the comprehensive search is saved and organized. The following tables are designed to enhance transparency and to structure and guide the case study presentation. Collecting data, I pursue an iterative approach by tracing violent activities, activities of norm interpretation, and activities of violence justification and legalization. As evidence I include information based on the following proceedings. First, I search for evidence of violent actions. Here, I mainly rely on the detailed accounts of human rights organizations and investigative journalism. Archival research further includes reviewing audio-visible and text material documenting the use of force and application of violence as well as the political activities to justify and legalize the application of violence. Sources are news coverage, reports by non-governmental organizations, and the documentation provided by the government. *Torturing Democracy* (National Security Archive 2008), *Amnesty International* (2013), and the *New York Times* (Scheinkman et al. 2018; 2024) provide detailed timelines and accounts of prisoners incarcerated in Guantanamo. To further secure a broad data base, I added information to the timeline provided by *The Hill* (Hattem 2016), *The Telegraph* (Spillius/Willis 2012), and *Al Jazeera* (2022) (see Table 4.2). Since I analyze a norm transformation process, which is mainly visible in domestic legalization processes, government documents are a main source. In this search, I include government accounts as well as news coverage between September 2001 and 2017.

To organize the collected data, I use a table for evidence collection (Table 4.2) and lists of presidential documents (Table 4.3) (Eisenhardt/Graebner 2007: 29).

The tables and lists contain all documents accounting for the government activities as displayed in Table 4.2:[33]

Table 4.2 Evidence Table on Data Collection—Timeline 2001–2017

Date	Act of violence, justification, or legalization	Source

This table thus contains all information concerning Guantanamo, the detainees, and treatment in captivity. The evidence is structured chronologically, building an aggregated timeline. Also, this timeline contains information on legal activities of the government or government institutions (for example presidential decrees, USSC rulings, and congressional activities), thus displaying activities related to norm interpretation and finally norm transformation.

On a critical note, I need to address that the evidence collected in Table 4.2 is the product of journalists or human rights organizations who apply a specific focus which is not necessarily conveyed to the reader nor do these articles share the purpose of this research project. Reading the referenced timelines, the selection of information seems random and criteria for selection of information remain unstated. Taken all together, evaluating the referenced timelines as a first step is still helpful to the aims of this analysis. Partially, the referenced timelines state the same events which show a certain degree of importance to the subject of detention at GTMO. Taken together, the facts display a rather detailed account of the events surrounding indefinite detention at Guantanamo and especially document the process of legal dispute. Due to public legal criticism and the formal change in detention law through state institutions, norm transformation is well documented in i.e. presidential records, Supreme Court rulings, and congressional legislation. The referenced timelines not only account for events but also for the multitude of actors involved in the norm transformation process.

Following up on the information of the referenced timelines, I researched government and especially presidential documents accounting for the norm transformation process, which are listed in Table 4.3.[34]

[33] See Appendix provided in the Electronic Supplementary Material for a detailed account on data collection and evaluation.

[34] For a full list of documents see the Appendix provided in the Electronic Supplementary Material.

Table 4.3 Presidential Documents

Year/Date	Document Short Title	Full Document Title

On Secrecy and Clandestine Activities in the Analysis

Secrecy plays a great role in the security policies of the analyzed case and thus the absence of information or the deliberate withholding of information from the public needs addressing. Although hard to research, secrecy and clandestine actions have an impact on this study. Without clear evidence mere speculation remains. Limiting the analysis to evidence only, I exclude all activities of hearsay (possibly known unknowns) and activities consequently and successfully hidden from public account (unknown unknowns) (Rumsfeld 2002).[35] This applies mostly to acts of violence that stay in the dark and are thus part of the security political strategy but are not yet subject to legitimation efforts. However, the unknown unknowns do not influence the outcome of this study, as the focus is not on displaying a full picture on applied violence—which is where most secrecy appears—but on public legitimation for those violent actions which are known and actively or possibly questioned by the public. These legitimation actions are publicly observable. So, clandestine justification would be beside the point, as a respective audience cannot be persuaded by arguments which were never presented to them.

Nonetheless, this focus on accessible evidence also excludes classified documents that knowingly exist but have not yet been released to the public (known unknowns). This form of secrecy includes redactions and classified documents which may contain evidence of violent acts or justifications for secret acts. Non-accessibility to this information does influence the study of legitimation for indefinite detention. In the case of detention law, redactions in court rulings prohibit the public from understanding the use and application of detention law. This means that a certain blind spot remains in the legitimation strategy. Although, clearly, I cannot study all aspects of indefinite detention for the obvious lack of security clearance, I still find discussing secrecy in this study necessary. Keeping information from the public and acting in clandestine does come to the fore in specific actions and rhetoric. Thus, I consider clandestine activities and secrecy, including the act of classifying security political documents, as a specific set of actions adding to legitimation as a practice.

[35] This refers to Rumsfeld's classification at a press conference on February 12, 2002, of known knowns (things we know that we can know), unknown knows (things we could know but do not know), known unknowns (things we know that we cannot know), and unknown unknowns (things we do not know and cannot know of) (Rumsfeld 2002).

Deskwork: Data Evaluation and Interpretation

After data collection the next step is to search for patterns in legalization actions. Whereas the evidence tables (Table 4.2 and 4.3) structure the documents, construct tables (Tables 4.4 and 4.5) aim to structure the evidence in terms of the research interest. Here, I continue to use the tables from the fieldwork. More importantly, the tables take account of the government positioning towards the violent acts and the framing of the conducted violence as legitimate (just and legal). Regarding the research interest, how legitimation activities occur, in which context, by whom, and when is of key to identifying patterned actions that add up to legitimation practices. Guiding questions in this data evaluation are: what is the event, who is acting, where are they acting (time, space, position, and social context), and before and towards which audience.

In the first step, I added the columns, 'Summary: Activity and Meaning,' and 'Category: Normtransformation; Legal Activity; Detainee Treatment' as shown in Table 4.4. In these columns, I categorize the evidence in terms of norm-transforming activities. Based on the norm transformation activities, I identify phases in the process of norm development over time, applying conceptual and theoretical assumptions on norm transformation (as explained in Chap. 3). Phases were separated when legalization-related activities occurred. Here, deskwork and fieldwork overlap. Evaluating the timelines for the case study on indefinite detention, I continuously found new evidence and documents which I collected and listed in the evidence collection and listed documents.

Table 4.4 Construct Table on Timelines 2001–2017 With Added Analytical Columns

Date/ Phase	Act of Violence, Justification, or Legalization	Summary: Activity and Meaning	Category: Normtransformation; Legal Activity; Detainee Treatment	Source

In the table including presidential documents I added a column for 'Short Content Summary on Normtranformation Activities of the Administrations' structured to include phases and short summaries in content (Table 4.5).

Table 4.5 Construct Table for the Presidential Documents

Phase/ Year /Date	Document Short Title	Full Document Title	Short Content Summary on Normtranformation Activities of the Administration

Both tables result in an overall timeline structured into phases of legitimation activities which is further explained in the research report. In this timeline, I display two factors of norm transformation—the actual conduct of violence (in line with or in breach of the conventional violence-containing norm) and the political legitimation for the norm transformation actions. Summarizing fieldwork and deskwork, the tables build the ground for writing the research report. For one, the tables contain all information on Guantanamo detainees and detainee treatment in chronological order and are structured into phases of norm transformation. For another, the tables offer an overview of the legalization documents conveying the formal legalization, thus formation of a new detention law.

4.3.2 Analytical Step 2: Reconstructing Legitimation Practices in Rhetoric

In this second analytical step, I reconstruct legitimation activities from presidential rhetoric. The data collection and corpus building in the fieldwork add to the results of the first analytical step. Material in the first analytical step includes sources from a multitude of actors, including non-governmental actors, to come to a saturated picture of the violent acts and norm transformation over time. The sources in the in-depth analysis of step two are purely limited to the presidents' speeches as main legitimacy-seeking actors. However, the multitude of documents[36] listed in the evidence of the case reconstruction over time factors into the contextual sense-making process in analyzing the presidential speeches. In the deskwork, I search for argumentative patterns in the presidents' speeches to add to the set of actions that constitute legitimation practice. In the following, I describe the research proceedings in more detail.

[36] These include executive orders, Supreme Court rulings, Congress legislature, media coverage, documented activity of high-ranking government actors, like the secretary of defense or the attorney general, and declassified information from presidential memoranda.

Fieldwork: Selecting Documents for Rhetorical Analysis
For the reconstruction of argumentative legitimation practices in presidential speeches, speech records will be collected to form a document corpus for the in-depth qualitative content analysis. For an in-depth analysis of rhetorical legitimation activities, I analyze the transcripts of selected speeches that document legalization and justification of violence. To this end, I used the full collection of presidential speeches of Bush and Obama as a starting point for document selection.[37] Then, I added all presidential speeches to a MAXQDA[38] file. That accounts for 16 pdf files for each presidency (32 in total) with 1000 pages of text material on average per file. To single out relevant speeches, I searched the texts using case specific keywords for indefinite detention: Guantanamo, detainee, Geneva, *habeas*, combatant, military tribunal, and military commission.[39] After the first analytical step described in the previous section, I used those keywords that are suitable to signal that indefinite detention is the subject in the speech.[40] As I search for legitimation of indefinite detention, I look for expressions which refer to the detention, detainee treatment, or legal proceedings (sentencing or release). Using these keywords in full text searches, I auto-coded the findings in the presidential speeches in MAXQDA. However, not every finding matched the topic (see Table 4.6). So, I had to clear the findings of false matches:

[37] For a full collection of presidential speeches see: *Public Papers of the Presidents of the United Sates* (U.S. Government Information 2024). For a detailed account of government documents analyzed in this study see the Appendix provided in the Electronic Supplementary Material.

[38] For the qualitative content analysis, I worked with MAXQDA 2022 and 2024.

[39] The list of keywords is the result of a trial-and-error process. Some keywords proved to be chosen to broad, like war on terror, which was found too often in a context not relevant to the research subject. Other keywords, which might be expectable like *unlawful enemy combatant*, proved to be non-productive, as they could not be found at all or in relevant numbers. Overall, a combination of several topic-specific keywords proved most successful.

[40] Although distantly related to indefinite detention, I excluded all those text passages dealing with the war on terror in Iraq or terrorist groups other than Al Qaida. Also, I excluded text passages dealing with torture, detainee abuse, or other forms of maltreatment not related to detention at GTMO.

Table 4.6 Coding List for Text Selection Auto-Codes[41]

Keywords For Auto- coding	Match	Non-match
Guantanamo	When the passage refers to Guantanamo Bay Detention Camp	When referring to the island, foreign policy issues with Cuba not related to the detention camp, or Coast Guard matters
detainee	When referring to individuals held in Guantanamo Bay Detention Camp	When referring to individuals not held in Guantanamo Bay Detention Camp
Geneva	When referring to the *Geneva Convention of 1949*	When referring to conventions not related to detention, the town, or peace processes negotiated in the town of Geneva
habeas	When referring to *habeas* rulings or legal proceedings of Guantanamo detainees.	When referring to *habeas* issues not related to Guantanamo detainees
combatant	When referring to Guantanamo detainees	When referring to detainees not related to Guantanamo, military ranks, or conflicts not related to the war on terror and Guantanamo
military tribunal	When referring to legal proceedings related to Guantanamo detainees	When referring to military tribunals not related to the war on terror or Guantanamo detainees
military commission	When referring to legal proceedings related to Guantanamo detainees	When referring to military commissions not related to the war on terror or Guantanamo detainees

Having cleared the auto-coding findings, I marked all speech titles where findings occurred and proceeded with the deskwork.

[41] For a detailed account of the coding scheme on auto-coding see the Appendix provided in the Electronic Supplementary Material.

Deskwork: Repeated Patterns in Speech

The deskwork in this second analytical step is an in-depth qualitative content analysis of the presidential speeches selected in the fieldwork. After auto-coding the full text material, I digitally printed all speeches with findings in separate pdf documents (one speech per pdf file) and added all singled-out speeches to the analysis file in MAXQDA. For the case of indefinite detention this produced for Bush 108 speeches and for Obama 74 speeches. With these selected speeches, I continued the coding work.[42]

Considering the pragmatist, interpretive approach of this analysis, the coding scheme stems from theoretical considerations and is also further developed during the analytical process. In the first step, I started to code each speech by topic. So, I read the documents cursorily and coded them thematically using an open coding technique (a new code is used for each new topic). This resulted in the following list of 13 codes by subject for indefinite detention: Guantanamo Bay detainees, treatment of prisoners/torture, Military Commissions Act/ military tribunals, Geneva Conventions, rule of law, constitutional presidential authority, CIA program, intelligence, homeland security, surveillance law, war on terror, Usama bin Laden, and allies.[43]

Then, I further analyzed the coded segments searching for legitimation activities. Here, I used the following list of initial codes for the case: secrecy, denial, contextual framing, barbarization of the enemy, emphasizing security (stirring fears), marginalizing/banalizing, declaring an exception, referring to quasi law, legalization qua declaration, legal reasoning/(re-)interpreting existing norms, and appealing to national values (see Table 4.7) which were subsequently altered into final activity codes.[44]

---

[42] A code is the search term or the title that is assigned to a search result which is coded into a coded segment; coded segments can consist of words, sentences, or entire paragraphs.

[43] For a detailed coding scheme of the subject codes see the Appendix provided in the Electronic Supplementary Material.

[44] For a final list of activity codings and detailed coding scheme see the Appendix provided in the Electronic Supplementary Material.

Table 4.7 Initial Coding Guidelines for Rhetorical Legitimacy-Seeking Activities

Code	Meaning/Characteristic
Secrecy	The mentioning that the public would not understand these actions and should therefore not know about it, arguing that something cannot be disclosed, referring to classification and security reasons that an action and evidence thereof has to stay secret
Denial	Negating that something happened, claiming that innocence, blaming others
Contextual framing	Reference to historical events; political meaning; social meaning
Barbarization of the enemy	Characterizing the enemy as barbaric, i.e. inhuman, brutal, uncivilized and illegally acting; denying the enemy basic rights
Emphasizing security (stirring fears)	Stressing importance of (national) security; safety measures, (self-)defense, and necessity to use force
Marginalization / banalization	belittling of atrocities; denying victim rights
Declaring an exception	references to newness (of technology, situation, actors); arguing for exceptions; proclamation of a state of emergency
Referring to quasi-law	Inventing expressions that sound like law but are not part of the agreed upon body of norms or official law
Legalization qua declaration	Claiming to act within the law without further explanation
Legal reasoning, (re-)interpreting existing norms	Arguing how the norm applies to a given situation with reference to domestic, foreign, and international law; referencing favorable precedent; setting precedent for legal changes
Appealing to national values	Mentioning national values, beliefs, and shared history

The next interpretive step aims to find patterns and routines in the whole list of coded segments. In each category, I look for similarities and repetitions which add up to repeated patterns from which I can retrieve patterns of actions and routinized argumentative and acted out sequences.

Concluding from the two analytical steps, I provide a comprehensive list of meaningful actions, adding up to the practice of legitimation. The list accumulates all meaningful actions to add to a conceptual understanding of legitimation practiced in norm transformation efforts by Bush and Obama during the war on terror. Legitimation practices here combine activities in and on the material world as well as argumentative reasonings in presidential speeches. The actions are performed by competent political actors, in meaningful settings, observable for a politically relevant audience which shares a common knowledge base with the performers. The actions show patterns that are repeated over time in action and within single speeches or in several speeches. I connect these rhetorical patterns to the findings of the first analytical step, adding to the full conceptualization of legitimation practices (naming actions, listing patterns of activities and meanings in context, and offering examples for the actions), as I will present in the following research report.

Indefinite Detention in Guantanamo Bay Detention Camp

5

In this case study, I examine government activities which aim at seeking legitimacy for changes in the detention norms' meaning and use. As discussed in Chap. 2, I define indefinite detention[1] as the incarceration of men by U.S. security personnel at the designated area of the military base Guantanamo Bay Detention Camp for an unspecified amount of time, without charges, and with unclear purpose. Acknowledging the complexity of norm transformation, as developed in Chap. 3, this process involves all branches of government, yet, as presented in Chap. 4, here the analytical focus lies on the executive, i.e. the Presidents Bush and Obama. How both presidents practically worked towards seeking legitimacy for the norm transformation of detention law is subject to this analysis.

In the first section of this chapter, I trace legitimacy-seeking activities in the norm transformation process in the case of indefinite detention in GTMO. Following the transformative stages, I evaluate recurrences and changes in legitimacy-seeking actions from the planning and the installment of the camp through the legal disputes and legislative adaptations, up to the institutionalization of indefinite detention. Based on this reconstruction of legalization and justification activities over time, I evaluate legitimation actions, patterns, and routines for each president in the following Chap. 6. Then, I compare the results and discuss similarities and differences in legitimation activities. Concluding the analysis, I

[1] The terms 'detention' and 'detainee' are deliberately used by the Bush administration in order to avoid the term 'prisoner' which is regulated in the *Geneva Conventions of 1949*. In this text, I use the U.S. terminology for analytical reasons; however, this does not constitute an acknowledgment or endorsement of U.S. detention policies in the war on terror.

Supplementary Information The online version contains supplementary material available at https://doi.org/10.1007/978-3-658-49121-5_5.

D. Hühnert-Hugendubel, *Between Rules of War and Rule of Law*,
https://doi.org/10.1007/978-3-658-49121-5_5

propose a conceptual approach to legitimation practices based on the findings in the case of indefinite detention.

In this analytical step, I reconstruct the legitimation activities of Bush and Obama in the transformation from violence-containing to violence-enabling detention norms regarding activities of the government which contributed to the legalization of indefinite detention in Guantanamo Bay Detention Camp over time. Tracing legitimation activities in norm transformation basically means to account for a process of gradual change in norm use from one wording and shared meaning in use to another wording and shared meaning in use of a norm. This development, I traced in a multistage research process, as presented in Chap. 4 on fieldwork and deskwork. This chapter presents the detailed research report, the textwork, as a rich description of the political and legal developments concerning indefinite detention in Guantanamo. Combining a detailed case reconstruction and rhetorical analysis, the report features the phases of norm transformation between September 2001 and January 2018.[2]

Following Eisenhardt's proposition of a detailed case description, I display legitimacy-seeking activities based on the timelines. The analytical timeframe is set beginning with 9/11, as it marks the beginning of the war on terror. It finishes with the end of Obama's second term in office.[3] The description follows the chronology of the events based on the evaluation of seven timelines (see Table 4.2). Norm transformation is a complex process including all branches of government (presidential decrees, Supreme Court rulings, and congressional legislation). Acknowledging the multitude of actors involved, the analysis nevertheless focuses on legitimation activities of the presidents. Activities of cabinet members or government institutions are considered in terms of background knowledge and to help contextualize presidential activities.

Analyzing the full corpus of the presidential speeches, the report summarizes the result from three coding steps: (1) I auto-coded the material for detention-related keywords to select subject-related texts. (2) In these selected speeches, I

[2] The legal process includes a variety of persons. On the government side, next to the White House, the following institutions are involved: most prominently, the FBI, the CIA, and the DoD are involved as well as legal advisors to the government and the Attorney of State. On the detainees' side legal teams of defense attorneys are involved.

[3] Certainly, events that led to the attacks of September 11 will be excluded as well as events prolonging indefinite detention under Trump and Biden, as they are also not essential to answering the research question. Although indefinite detention did not start with 9/11, the attacks of 9/11 and the political actions taken in immediate response are important steps in preparing detention at Guantanamo. Also, this preparatory stage serves many arguments in justifying detention and detainee treatment which is why it is important to include this period and the documentation of political decisions in the analytical corpus.

coded subjects that were dealt with and (3) rhetorical activities in these subject-coded sections. This coding approach allows me to make statements on the following aspects. The auto-coding step limits the number of overall documents to subject relevant ones. Thus, the body of analyzed texts thematically deals with detention and detainee treatment. For this selected material, the second coding step provides results on the subjects the presidents addressed. The third coding step reveals results on how the presidents talk about these subjects, which rhetorical activities they use to position themselves on specific detention and detainee treatment related subjects by evaluating rhetorical legalization and justification actions and arguments.

Presenting the analysis over time, I show what the subjects of legitimation activities are in each phase and describe how Bush and Obama act out their legitimation strategies in the material world and in rhetoric: how they set the stage by framing subjects, which background knowledge they activate by referring to shared knowledge bases, how they react to specific questions, and what they chose to leave out.[4] Reviewing the legitimation activities chronologically provides the advantage of making developments in the legitimation strategy visible. Rhetorical adaptations in the subject definition, framing, or also in reactions (to a changed interest in the media) become visible over time. This approach allows for tracing changes in the legitimation strategies and factors in changes in the security environment and legal situation.

5.1 Phase 1: Preparations and Beginning of Norm Transformation

In Phase 1, the war on terror begins and far-reaching decisions are taken by the president and Congress which will serve the president as legal and argumentative basis to defend the detention-related policies as legal and just. On September 11, 2001, ca. 3000 people are killed in the terrorist attacks in the United States. Two planes crash into the World Trade Center, New York, one into the Pentagon in Washington, D.C., and the fourth plane crashes in Pennsylvania. More die or are injured in the attempt to save people. The attacks cause a massive shock for the American people, including its political leadership, which shows in reactions of mourning and direct response.

---

[4] All facts and documents referred to in this chapter are provided in the Appendix (see Electronic Supplementary Material).

In mourning, President Bush issues a *Proclamation Honoring the Victims of the Incidents on September 11, 2001* (Proclamation 7461). It contains the order for half-flagging and state mourning honoring the victims of September 11, 2001. On September 13, 2001, Bush issued the *Proclamation National Day of Prayer and Remembrance for the Victims of the Terrorist Attacks on September 11, 2001* (Proclamation 7462). It contains the order of a national day for prayer and remembrance in mourning of the victims of September 11, 2001.

In response to the events of 9/11, on September 14, 2001, Congress passes *The Joint Resolution to authorize the use of United States Armed Forces against those Responsible for the Recent Attacks Launched Against the United States* (AUMF), a resolution authorizing the president to the use of force. On September 18, 2001, Bush signs the AUMF into law. This resolution frames the terrorist attacks of September 11, 2001, as an act of violence which provokes the right to self-defense and authorizes the president to use military force. Thus, Congress vests the president with wartime privileges, allowing him to make far-reaching decisions without further consulting with the parliament.[5]

A further step towards the expansion of executive rights is taken when Bush issues the *Declaration of National Emergency by Reason of Certain Terrorist Attacks* (Proclamation 7463). This official declaration of a state of emergency due to the attacks of September 11, 2001, further extends the executive's rights. Bush also issues *Executive Order 13223, Ordering the Ready Reserve of the Armed Forces To Active Duty and Delegating Certain Authorities to the Secretary of Defense and the Secretary of Transportation.* This order for the ready reserve to come to active duty also provides additional authority to the DoD and Department of Transportation based on the proclaimed emergency due to the September 11, 2001, attacks.

Behind the scenes, preparations for detention begin, as the president and his team of legal advisors start a debate on where to hold prisoners made in the war in Afghanistan. The debate also includes the question how to use interrogation methods to obtain information to prevent future attacks on U.S. mainland and citizens abroad (Greenberg/Dratel 2005). During September, also a secret group called 'the War Council' forms (National Security Archive 2008). This group includes David Addington, Alberto Gonzales, Tim Flanigan, William Haynes, and John Yoo. These lawyers will advise Bush in legal terms on detainee treatment and the legal handling of indefinite detainment in Guantanamo (Greenberg/

[5] The AUMF is the president's reference for the use of executive power in detention-related actions and legal decision-making bypassing Congress and has since been subject to inner American legal debate on constitutional rights of the president in war and peace times.

Dratel 2005).[6] The Bush administration quickly finds a location to hold the captives made in Afghanistan (and later other areas) for detention and interrogation purposes.

Initiating the war on terror in Afghanistan, the legal foundations for norm transformation in detention law are laid. On October 7, 2001, Bush gives an *Address to the Nation Announcing Strikes against Al Qaida Training Camps and Taliban Military Installations in Afghanistan.* This marks the beginning of Operation Enduring Freedom, the war in Afghanistan against the Taliban and Al Qaida. Shortly after, on November 13, 2001, Bush signs the *Military Order* on *Detention, Treatment, and Trial of Certain Non-Citizens in the War Against Terrorism.* This order allows for indefinite detention without charges and without prisoners' rights to challenge their detention. The order further defines terms of detention and terms of military commissions and authorizes the Secretary of Defense to conduct trials and legal processing of detainees. However, detainees are denied any legal challenge of their detention or the military commissions verdicts in U.S. courts.

Along with the military defense strategy, preparatory steps for capturing and detaining declared terrorists are taken by the Bush administration in the media. Already on September 16, 2001, Dick Cheney, Vice President, had given an interview to NBC's Meet the Press stating that intelligence operations in the dark will be necessary. In his statements he characterizes the enemy as terrorist network (namely Al Qaida and Usama bin Laden) and announces violence against the enemy including secret operations. After the beginning of the war in Afghanistan, on November 14, 2001, Dick Cheney speaks before the Chamber of Commerce (*Remarks by the Vice President to the U.S. Chamber of Commerce*). In his speech, he states that terrorists, should they be captured alive, should be brought before military tribunals. He further argues that terrorists are not lawful combatants and will not be treated as prisoners of war by the United States. Finally, on December 27, 2001, in a press conference at the Pentagon, Secretary of Defense, Donald

[6] In "The Torture papers. The Road to Abu Ghraib" Greenberg and Dratel (2005) collect numerous documents, among them memoranda and presidential orders, giving a detailed insight into the debate among members of the Bush administration, members of government institutions, and legal counsels. All documents deal with specifics of detainee treatment concerning interrogation methods and modalities of captivity. This includes a debate on the installation of Guantanamo in a territory that was argued to be outside the scope of national and international law (see documents in Greenerg and Dratel (2005) created between 2001–2002). The collection of documents also contains the two memoranda, which later became known as the "Torture Memos," written by Bybee and Yoo.

Rumsfeld, admits to journalists that preparations are made for holding detainees from Afghanistan in Guantanamo Bay, Cuba.

Meanwhile, on November 16, 2001, Bush signs Executive Order 13235 on *National Emergency Construction Authority*. This order contains the authorization of the DoD to use emergency regulations based on the emergency declared after the terrorist attacks of September 11, 2001. On December 12, 2001, Bush signs Executive Order 13239 on the *Designation of Afghanistan and the Airspace Above as a Combat Zone*. While official steps are taken towards conflict determination in preparation of combat and detainee treatment behind the scenes, preparations for detention are discussed in detail. On December 28, 2001, John Yoo argues to Jim Haynes in a memorandum from the U.S. Department of Justice to the Pentagon arguing against *habeas rights* (Greenberg/Dratel 2005: 29–37). On January 9, 2002, John Yoo sends a memorandum to Jim Haynes arguing that the *Geneva Conventions* do not apply to Taliban and Al Qaida fighters and that the president has the power to suspend the law as he sees fit (Greenberg/Dratel 2005: 38–79).

Analyzing speeches in Phase 1, the documents cover the period after 9/11 up to the transfer of detainees to Guantanamo. Thus, in this first phase right after the terrorist attacks, the war on terror is beginning in Afghanistan and the hunt for Usama bin Laden starts, but Guantanamo is only in preparation. The focus on the subjects set by Bush is on the conventional war on terror. The two other dominant topics, which appear rather in Question-and-Answer sessions are military tribunals and Usama bin Laden. A lot of questions are directed at the current situation concerning the hunt for bin Laden and on the use of military tribunals. As the *Military Order* provides the possibility for military tribunals many questions address how the president intends to use these courts, even though no use case has been presented up to this point. So, the treatment and legal processing of potential detainees is subject to debate and subject to presidential legitimacy-seeking rhetoric early on. This is further represented in the legitimacy-seeking activities in this phase: the dominant activity over all topics is 'claiming pursuit to justice' followed by 'emphasizing security' and then 'enemy characterization,' and 'appealing to national values.'

Separated by topic, in the subject 'war on terror,' Fig. 5.1 shows that 'claiming pursuit to justice,' 'emphasizing security,' and 'appealing to national values' as well as 'characterizing the enemy' are the dominant activities. Thus, these are the legitimacy-seeking actions that Bush himself undertakes (see Fig. 5.1).

Codesystem	Guantanamo Bay detainees	treatment of prisoners/ torture	Military Commissions Act/ military tribunals	Geneva Convention	rule of law	constitutional presidential authority	war on terror	Usama bin Laden	allies	CIA program	intelligence	homeland security	SUMME
admitting defeat													
admonishing													
announcing/commenting new detention law			1										1
appealing to national values			1				9						10
applying new detention law													
applying the law												2	2
calling on Congress/working w Congress													
characterizing the enemy			2				6		1				9
claiming presidential power			4										4
claiming pursuit to justice			4				17	4	1			3	29
commenting USSC/court decisions													
committing to international law													
criricizing democrats													
criticizing Congress													
criticizing past actions													
declaring a presidential order			1										1
denying/defending/offering alternative explanation			1										1
emphasizing accountability													
emphasizing legality			1				1						2
emphasizing rule of law			1										1
emphasizing security			8				13					4	25
emphasizing transparency													
explaining prosecution of detainee maltreatment													
explaining security politics													
explaning cooperation							1		1				2
explaning/defending detainee treatment													
expressing gratitude							1		2				3
(re-)interpreting the law			1				1						2
keeping secrets			1				3						4
listing acomplishments													
proposing legislation													
referring to quasi-law													
reporting on war progress							2	1					3
revoking national memory							1						1
stressing newness of the war													
SUMME			26				55	5	5			9	100

Fig. 5.1 Code Relations—Activities and Subject—Phase 1

Looking at the activities in the single topics in this phase, the subject 'war on terror' dominates with the activities: 'claiming pursuit to justice,' 'emphasizing security,' 'appealing to national values,' and 'characterizing the enemy' (see Fig. 5.1). These are the legitimizing activities Bush uses when he sets the stage for justifying the use of force. Noteworthy is that the 'pursuit to justice' comes before 'emphasizing security.' 'Claiming pursuit to justice' is not only the declared objective of the military mission but also the aim for U.S. and cooperative efforts in fighting terrorism. According to Bush, the war on terror is the "calling of the 21st century" and restoring justice the main aim in the war on terror (Bush, Remarks at 2006–10–02: 1746). However, although Bush makes references to the judicial system and emphasizes the superiority of the American (legal) system, 'claiming pursuit to justice' remains a rather open category. This rhetorical activity is mainly applied in relation to military operations but not necessarily to law enforcement. How exactly justice will be achieved is not further described beyond the claim: "They think they can run, and we'll tire. They think they can hide, and we will tire. But they have sorely misunderstood America. They don't understand our will and our determination. This great land is united to bring freedom to the world. We will bring them to justice, and we will prevail." (Bush, Remarks at 2001–12–04: 1473).

Evaluating rhetorical activities across all subject-coded segments, 'emphasizing security' is used most often in Bush's legitimacy-seeking effort, both in self-set topics and in reaction to questions. He mainly uses this activity in reference to terror prevention and the preservation of national security. Regarding captives, Bush emphasizes that capturing terrorists ensures security. "My job is to protect the United States people from further attack. And that's exactly what I'm going to do and, at the same time, bring Al Qaida to justice." (Bush, Remarks Prior 2001–12–05: 1488).

Noticeable in this regard is that Bush lists the captivation of terrorists in large numbers by U.S. and coalition forces as a main accomplishment in the early stage of the war on terror. While emphasizing the importance of allied efforts, Bush also stresses the need for information-sharing.

> And it's not just America. There are a lot of other countries who have participated with us, and that's heartening. We've got great intelligence-sharing now, around the world. I've been able to say to a lot of leaders, face to face, 'You tell us when they're coming, and if we find out something about you, we'll let you know, too.' And that's important. It's important to know as much information as possible about the enemy. It's important to try to figure out where they hide and their intentions. It helps to have a vast coalition willing to share that kind of information. (Bush, Remarks at 2001–11–29: 1461)

'Appealing to national values' appears as an activity code in connection to valuing freedom and liberty, emphasizing America and the shared mourning of terrorism victims, as well as honoring the constitution. "[...] I want the people of the world to understand that our great Nation will never forgo the values that have made us unique; that we believe in democracy and rule of law and the Constitution." (Bush, Remarks Prior 2001–12–05: 1487).

The activity 'characterizing the enemy' mainly occurs in the topics 'war on terror,' 'Usama bin Laden,' and 'military tribunals.' The statements enforce that the United States are fighting a war, which was declared by the enemy, who is characterized as "the most evil kinds of people" (Bush, Remarks Following 2001–11–19: 1425). Also, enemy characterization extends to everyone helping, harboring, and collaborating with terrorists. "And as we speak, we're enforcing the doctrine that makes it plain that not only do we seek the terrorists, but we also hold governments that harbor them and feed them and house them and hide them accountable for their behavior, as well." (Bush, Remarks at 2001–11–29: 1461).

In Q/A sessions Bush has to position himself towards questions concerning the search for bin Laden and the use of military tribunals.

> Every morning I wake up and read the threat assessments. The evil ones still intend to harm America. And if it's in our national security interests, to bring people to justice, I will use a military tribunal. And I may give you one example of why I would use one. We haven't used one yet; it's simply an option. If we capture an Al Qaida representative—if we capture a murderer, and in order to convict that murderer it would require us giving means of how we knew he was guilty that would jeopardize the security of the United States, he'll be tried in a military tribunal. (Bush, Remarks Prior 2001–12–05: 1487)

Especially concerning bin Laden, the dominant activities are 'claiming pursuit to justice' and 'characterizing the enemy.' As head of Al Qaida and held responsible for 9/11, bin Laden functions as the personification for the hunted terrorist and is the most concrete enemy figure in this first stage of the war on terror. Bush emphasizes that he is searched for and "he will be brought to justice" (Bush, Remarks Welcoming 2001–12–28: 1548). This search is also subject to secrecy, as Bush denies concrete information and offers general assessments and progress reports.

> Listen, if our military knew where Mr. bin Laden was, he would be brought to justice. We're hunting him down. He runs, and he hides. But as we've said repeatedly, the

> noose is beginning to narrow; the net is getting tighter. But this is a difficult assignment. Things happened very quickly in Afghanistan recently, as—went to show that our strategy was a well-thought-out strategy. But the objective is yet to be achieved, and we're not leaving until we do achieve the objective. (Bush, Remarks Following 2001–11–19: 1424)

Overall, the war on terror and bin Laden function as background information and framing, drawing a picture for the specific interpretation of the law for captives in the war on terror. Although this is not a trending topic in Bush's war on terror rhetoric, the decision not to apply the *Geneva Conventions* to captives from Afghanistan comes up in Q/A sessions. Legal questions often concern military tribunals established in the *Military Order*. When asked about military tribunals, why he chose not to apply the *Geneva Conventions* or the national court system, Bush dominantly 'emphasizes security' before 'claiming pursuit to justice' and 'presidential authority.'

> We're fighting a war, Terry, against the most evil kinds of people. And I need to have that extraordinary option at my fingertips. I ought to be able to have that option available should we ever bring one of these Al Qaida members in alive. It's our national interests; it's our national security interests we have a military tribunal available. It is in the interests of the safety of potential jurors that we have a military tribunal. (Bush, Remarks Following 2001–11–19: 1425).

This quote underlines the preparatory stage in the war on terror and that Bush sees justice as a matter at his discretion. As commander in chief, he emphasizes security and interprets his role in preserving national security and closely connects the option of military tribunals to national security. However, the quote also indicates the possibility of terrorist suspects being killed in combat, as captivity is stated to be a hypothetical. Claiming presidential power, he emphasizes that decisions on how to prosecute terrorist captives are up to the president claiming justice as a matter for the commander in chief. This decision is frequently questioned, and Bush repeatedly affirms his decision with reference to security and secrecy. As such, military tribunals are presented as extraordinary institutions, which according to Bush are a necessary means to preserve national security and the security of the judicial and military personnel. Even though Bush emphasizes that military tribunals are only a hypothetical option, he repeatedly states two clarifications. First, he makes clear that no American citizen will be tried before a military tribunal, these are only for non-American citizens subject to the *Military Order*. Second, referring to U.S. courts, he emphasizes the superiority of the

U.S. legal system and legal prosecution in terms of fairness compared to terrorist methods.

Explaining the need for military tribunals, Bush uses secrecy as a main argument:

> In other words, this is an ongoing conflict. There are still real threats. And I, in order to get a conviction of a murderer, will not jeopardize the people of the United States. I will not show our secrets. I will not tip our hand. I will not let the world at large, particularly our enemy, understand how we put a case together if it's going to jeopardize and compromise national security secrets of the United States of America. (Bush, Remarks Prior 2001–12–05: 1487)

Again, Bush 'emphasizes security' and prioritizes national security over public transparency of judicial procedures. Prosecuting detainees is thus tightly connected to national security, as an open trial is seen as a strategic disadvantage. Furthermore, prosecuting detainees here does not only serve the pursuit of criminal offenses but also is claimed to have an effect on future national security, as Bush states: "In a court of law, there would be all kinds of questions that might compromise our ability to gather incredibly important intelligence to prevent the next attack from happening to America." (Bush, Remarks at 2001–21–04: 1479). Thus, posecuting detainees in civil courts is ruled out by Bush for intelligence reasons and to grant national security. This explanation underlines the intention to treat detainees who are accused of terrorist activities not in the legal framework of criminality but in the context of (inter)national security.

Concluding, this phase is coined by three sets of activities preparing for indefinite detention, concerning the organization and realization of detainment and for the legal argument. The first set of activities encompasses the direct reaction to 9/11, by declaring the national emergency and preparing to meet the attacks with means of war. In this respect, event-framing of 9/11 and terrorist threats in a setting of war is a main issue in political rhetoric. The second set of activities includes the beginning of the conventional war in Afghanistan in reaction to the terrorist attacks and to prevent further attacks, as argued. In preparation and implementation, authorization of government institutions is a main subject in legal efforts and accompanying rhetoric. In this regard, first legalization steps are taken to empower the president for decision-making on detention and distance U.S. violent acts from existing normative standards and establishing exceptions and preparing for the introduction of new detention regulations. The third set of activities includes the planning for a military detention facility in Guantanamo Bay as a prison for interrogation and information gaining and punishment. In this regard, claims for the pursuit of justice, emphasizing security needs, and enemy characterization are key activities in legitimacy-seeking efforts.

5.2 Phase 2: Beginning of Indefinite Detainment

Phase 2 between January 2002 and May 2004 marks the beginning of indefinite detention in Guantanamo and the beginning of the norm-transformation process. As prepared in Phase 1, the Bush administration denies detainee's *Geneva Rights* and POW status as well as constitutional rights. With the label *unlawful enemy combatant*, the Bush administration introduces quasi-legal terms and offers new interpretations concerning detainees' status, treatment, and legal processing rights (Hühnert 2016).

The beginning of 2002 marks the beginning of detainment and denial of rights. On January 11, 2002, the first 20 captives are brought to Guantanamo, Camp X-Ray.[7] The number of detainees grows to 156 by the end of January 2002. During January and February 2002, legal arguing continues behind the scenes of the White House and the Departments of Defense and Justice. This is documented in several memoranda, in which the legal status of the detainees is discussed. On January 11, 2002, William Taft argues in a memorandum to John Yoo, criticizing Yoo's argument regarding the status of detainees (National Security Archive 2008). On January 22, 2002, Jay Bybee argues in a memorandum to Jim Haynes in favor of denying POW-status to non-state actors (Greenberg/Dratel 2005: 81–117). On January 25, 2002, Alberto Gonzales argues in a memorandum to President Bush for denying the detainees *Geneva Rights* (Greenberg/Dratel 2005: 118–121). Opposed to these arguments, on January 26, 2002, Colin Powell argues in a memorandum to Alberto Gonzales in favor of applying the *Geneva Conventions* fearing negative consequences for U.S. troops and diplomatic complications (Greenberg/Dratel 2005: 122–125).

Based on these consulting legal debates, Bush takes the first steps to set the legal status of Guantanamo detainees. On January 18, 2002, Bush decides to deny Guantanamo detainees POW status. This decision is reflected in a memorandum, dating January 19, 2002, from Rumsfeld to the Joint Chiefs of Staff, ordering to deny Al Qaida and Taliban POW status (Greenberg/Dratel 2005: 80). Formally, this decision is expressed in a presidential memorandum of February

[7] Experience reports by former inmates or defense attorneys provide ample information about the camp, the conditions of captivity, and interrogation methods as well as other forms of maltreatment (Constitution Project Task Force Report 2013; Wilson 2003; Maran 2006: 154; McNeal 2009; Smith 2005, 2007).

7, 2002, from President Bush to Vice President, Secretary of State, and Secretary of Defense, concerning the status of Al Qaida and Taliban fighters, at Guantanamo and abroad and declaring *Common Article 3* of the *Geneva Conventions* not applying to them (National Security Archive 2008). Furthermore, legal counsels discuss court rulings and proceedings for the detainees, as documented in a letter to President Bush from February 1, 2002, in which John Ashcroft discusses courts entertaining detainee cases (Greenberg/Dratel 2005: 126–128). These actions mark not only the beginning of indefinite detention as a violence practice but also express the legal position of the Bush administration, denying international protective rights and the application of U.S. law, yet discussing alternating legal solutions.

These legal proceedings are accompanied by supporting statements of members of the Bush administration. On January 22, 2002, Donald Rumsfeld defends the detention policy at Guantanamo at a press conference answering critical questions about the treatment of prisoners after conditions of the temporary camp had become public. Rumsfeld calls the prisoners a danger to U.S. security and military personnel and claims that the detainees are treated humanely despite the non-application of *Geneva Rights*. The non-application of the *Geneva Convention* he defends by arguing that neither Taliban nor Al Qaida fighters meet the necessary criteria. In a press statement in late January 2002, Dick Cheney and Donald Rumsfeld characterize Guantanamo detainees as extremely dangerous.

By setting up the camp and denying rights, the norm-transformation process begins with an act of norm contestation and continues with the establishment of a quasi-legal category of the *unlawful enemy combatant* (Bush decision of 18 January 2002; memorandum of 7 February 2002).[8] What started as an executive project—the denial of *Geneva Rights* and constitutional rights—is taken to the judiciary, as U.S. Courts start dealing with *habeas* petitions. On February 21, 2002, a challenge of detention is dismissed by a federal judge. The legal debate and court rulings on prisoner petitions continue, as the Bush administration guided by legal counseling seeks to dominate the interpretation of detention law. The Bush administration's position is shown in exchanged memoranda. In a memorandum titled *Re: Possible Habeas Jurisdictions over Aliens Held in Guantanamo Bay, Cuba*, Patrick F. Philbin and John Yoo write to William J. Haynes

[8] Although during 2001 and 2002 various synonyms of the term *unlawful enemy combatant* are used throughout correspondence, I here use the full term as it was later adopted in the *Detainee Treatment Act* (2005) and defined in the *Military Commissions Act of 2006*. On a detailed analysis of the conceptual development and legitimation of the term *unlawful enemy combatant* see: Hühnert 2016.

(General Counsel, Department of Defense), preparing an argument for the incarceration of captives from Afghanistan. The authors state that detainees held in GTMO would have no constitutional rights to *writ habeas corpus*, since Guantanamo remains outside the legal jurisdiction of U.S. courts (Greenberg/Dratel 2005: 29–37).

From 2002 to 2004, indefinite detention increases with the rising number of detainees brought to GTMO and new regulations are step by step introduced for detainment, treatment, and trial.[9] On April 25, 2002, Camp Delta is complete, a permanent building for the detainees, on April 28, the detainees are transferred there from Camp X-Ray, taking a step towards the normalization of indefinite detention without trial in GTMO.[10] Following the declared promise, that no U.S. citizen will be held at GTMO, Yaser Hamdi is transferred to U.S. mainland on April 5, 2002, after discovering he was born in the U.S. The number of prisoners rises to 680 in May 2003, before in mid-May repatriation starts. By mid-2003, the number of detainees in Guantanamo reaches its peak with about 684 prisoners. Up to this point, the Bush administration had only transferred 42 prisoners to their home countries or other places.

After detention is established, the discursive focus turns to detainee treatment. The rest of 2002, interrogation and interrogation methods[11] are discussed, designed, and implemented at Guantanamo. On March 14, 2003, Yoo issues a legal assessment of interrogation methods in a memorandum to Haynes. On April 16, 2003, as documented in a memorandum, Rumsfeld allows interrogation methods including sleep deprivation and isolation to be applied at Guantanamo. Meanwhile, the interrogation program is further implemented and the war on terror extends to the second battlefield with the War in Iraq starting on March 19, 2003, and ending per proclamation by May 1, 2003.

---

[9] According to reports of defense attorneys, government agencies systematically complicated the prisoners' access to legal counsel (Smith 2007). Numerous defense attorneys report that GTMO security personal prevented attorney client meetings and government officials actively sowed mistrust (Denbeaux/Boyd-Nastad 2007; Smith 2005; Smith 2007).

[10] Having started bringing captives mainly from Afghanistan to Guantanamo in 2002, the Bush administration enlarged the camp in the following years. Camp X-Ray was the first, followed by more permanent, solidly build Camps Iguana, Delta, and Echo (Kurnaz 2007).

[11] See Timelines in the Appendix (provided in the Electronic Supplementary Material) where events are listed between August 1, 2002, and December 2, 2002. These items of evidence are excluded from this report, as they are proof of the development of the interrogation program and the use of torture but do not explicitly contain information on indefinite detention.

Throughout 2003, public criticism builds up concerning detainee treatment in captivity and the Bush administration faces legal challenges before the Supreme Court. On May 27, 2003, the president of the *International Committee of the Red Cross* demands improved legal proceedings for the detainees in a meeting with members of the U.S. administration. On October 9, 2003, the *Red Cross* issues a warning concerning the deteriorating health conditions of the Guantanamo detainees. However, the Bush administration continues to establish quasi-legal regulations for the detention and prosecution of the detainees. On March 21, 2002, the Bush administration announces new regulations for military tribunals. On July 3, 2003, Bush designates six detainees to military tribunals, two of them are later released to the UK without charges or trial. In this stage, the U.S. judiciary confirms the Bush administration's legal position on detainee status and rights. On March 11, 2003, the Federal Appeals Court rules that GTMO detainees have no rights in U.S. courts. However, on November 10, 2003, the Supreme Court agrees to hearings on detainee rights to access civil courts to challenge their detention, questioning the legality of the new detention policy of the Bush administration.

Nevertheless throughout 2004, the Bush administration proceeds with military trials and continues to enlarge the prison by opening Camp 5 (in May 2004). On February 23, 2004, the Bush administration starts pressing first charges against detainees: Ali Hamza al-Bahlul and Ibrahim al-Qosi are charged with conspiracy to commit war crimes. Meanwhile the public criticism continues. On January 21, 2004, five military lawyers working on GTMO cases state that some of the military commission rules are unconstitutional. On January 30, 2004, the ICRC criticizes that detainees are placed outside the legal system, without clear perspective on trial, duration of captivity, or legal options. In late April 2004, the Bush administration faces the torture scandal of Abu Ghraib (April 28, 2004). On April 30, 2004, Bush distances the U.S. activities from abusive detainee treatment, denying that U.S. forces commit torture. While indirectly connected to the debate on detainee treatment in GTMO, the upcoming debate on torture also extends to the detainee treatment and the necessity and legality of indefinite detention in Guantanamo.

Whereas Phase 1 was a preparatory stage, Phase 2 marks the beginning of indefinite detention without charge or trial, as well as the denial of *Geneva Convention* status and rights to the detainees and the introduction of new legal ideas for detention and trial. The speeches in this phase cover many upcoming security political issues, as the trending topics show. Evaluated by topic as displayed in Fig. 5.2, above all in Bush's speeches the 'war on terror' remains the most prominent issue before 'Guantanamo detainees' and 'homeland security.' Thus, the topics display the ongoing war on terror which intensifies in Afghanistan and then spills to Iraq in 2003. In this regard, cooperation in the war on terror becomes an important issue. Concerning U.S. national security, the conception of homeland security and the establishment of the joint department come up. Underlining the security stress of the situation and the need for justification and explanation, the leading activities are 'emphasizing security,' 'appealing to national values,' and 'explaining security politics' as well as 'reporting on war progress.'

However, as transfers to Guantanamo increase, more questions are directed at the president concerning detainee treatment and prosecution. In press conferences journalists keep bringing up questions concerning detainee prosecution and trials. However, not only journalists ask about the detainees, but also the detention of foreign nationals keeps coming up in press conferences with state leaders. Also, of great concern for journalists is the progress in the search for bin Laden. However, Bush remains secretive about the whereabouts of bin Laden, referring to the safety of military personnel. Also, questions about military trials are answered reluctantly. Concerning detainee treatment, the torture scandal[12] in Abu Ghraib falls in this period and extends to general concerns for detainee treatment. On torture, Bush is very clear in repeatedly giving the same answer: this was a mistake, it is not what the Unites States stand for, the United States do not torture, this will be prosecuted, and the United States abide by the rules forbidding torture. Whereas homeland security remains an often-mentioned topic, allies, and military tribunals are mentioned less (see Fig. 5.2).

[12] I include statements on torture in the examination of political rhetoric when statements refer to an overall assessment of detainee treatment or specific concerns for GTMO detainees and their treatment.

Codesystem	Guantanamo Bay detainees	treatment of prisoners/ torture	Military Commissions Act/ military tribunals	Geneva Convention	rule of law	constitutional presidential authority	war on terror	Usama bin Laden	allies	CIA program	intelligence	homeland security	SUMME
admitting defeat													
admonishing													
announcing/commenting new detention law													
appealing to national values	3	1					60		1			1	66
applying new detention law													
applying the law	1		1				7						9
calling on Congress/working w Congress							6					6	12
characterizing the enemy	4						37				1	1	43
claiming presidential power							5					1	6
claiming pursuit to justice	5						15					1	21
commenting USSC/court decisions													
committing to international law		2		1									3
criricizing democrats													
criticizing Congress												1	1
criticizing past actions													
declaring a presidential order													
denying/defending/offering alternative explanation		3					2						5
emphasizing accountability													
emphasizing legality	1	4					1						6
emphasizing rule of law							2						2
emphasizing security	8	1		1			68		2			13	93
emphasizing transparency													
explaining prosecution of detainee maltreatment	1	6											7
explaining security politics	3	2					59		3			12	79
explaning cooperation	5	1	1				25		5		1		38
explaning/defending detainee treatment	14	1	2	2			3					1	23
expressing gratitude	1						15		1				17
(re-)interpreting the law													
keeping secrets							5						5
listing acomplishments	1						7		2				10
proposing legislation												3	3
referring to quasi-law	1												1
reporting on war progress	5			2			41		1				49
revoking national memory	2	1					29		1		1	1	35
stressing newness of the war							7				2		9
SUMME	55	22	4	6			394		16		5	41	543

Fig. 5.2 Code Relations—Activities and Subject—Phase 2

Evaluating rhetorical activities by topics, dominant activities in the subject 'war on terror' are 'emphasizing security,' 'appealing to national values,' 'explaining security politics,' 'reporting on war progress,' 'characterizing the enemy,' 'explaining cooperation,' and 'revoking national memory.' This list shows that legal topics play a subordinate role in public speech. These activities are used to deliver a framing for the war, portraying the role of the military in Afghanistan as liberators of the Afghan people from a brutal regime that murdered civilians, oppressed women, and supported Al Qaida.

Next to the 'war on terror,' the subject 'GTMO detainees' dominates speeches with the leading activities 'explaining/defending detainee treatment,' 'emphasizing security,' and 'characterizing the enemy.' Although legal questions come up, judicial issues are mentioned rather marginally. In 'explaining/defending detainee treatment' Bush emphasizes that the detainees are treated well and in full compliance with international law. This statement is further supported by emphasizing security, when Bush prioritizes national security: "And so our country is mindful of the need to respect people's rights. But I want to assure you, we will do, within our power, within the Constitution of the United States, what it takes to defend the American people. My most important job is to protect innocent Americans, and this is exactly what I'm going to do." (Bush, The President's 2002–02–13: 226). While 'emphasizing security,' Bush also refers to means within the legal framework of the constitution. However, he also signals, that "the need to respect people's rights" comes after fulfilling security duties for the American people.

Concerning legal treatment, Bush makes sure that detainees are not considered POW but illegal combatants, overall painting strong verbal images. 'Characterizing the enemy,' Bush repeatedly calls the enemy "killers" (Bush, The President's 2002–01–28: 126), often in connection with explaining the treatment the detainees are receiving from U.S. security personnel and the terms of their captivity (in Question-and-Answer sessions). However, Bush also repeatedly states that he and his departments and legal advisors agree that international law, namely the *Geneva Conventions*, does not apply to the GTMO detainees.

> A couple of things we agree on: One, they will not be treated as prisoners of war; they're illegal combatants. Secondly, they will be treated humanely. And then, I'll figure out—I'll listen to all the legalisms and announce my decision when I make it. But we're in total agreement on how to—on whether or not—on how these prisoners, or detainees, excuse me, ought to be treated. And they'll be treated well. (Bush, The President's 2002–01–28: 123).

As this accidental mix up of the terms prisoner and detainee indicates, in this phase the status definition is not fully decided. Bush further argues that GTMO detainees do not qualify as POW but are considered illegal combatants. He also underlines that it is up to his decision how the detainees will be ranked in status and how they will be treated, emphasizing his power as commander in chief and president. In this phase, the Bush administration prepares for and finally introduces the term *unlawful enemy combatant*, a term that closely resembles international legal phrasing but is not part of official international treaties.[13] Emphasizing that the United States act in compliance with international and *Geneva* provisions, Bush stresses that GTMO detainees receive medical care and ensures they are treated well.

Yet, Bush stresses the U.S. commitment to the *Geneva Conventions* and the importance of the treaty. Concerning the GTMO detainees, Bush assures that detainees are treated "in the spirit of the Geneva Conventions" (Bush, The President's 2002–01–28: 125). Regarding the criticism theat the *Geneva Conventions* are outdated, Bush clearly denies: "No, the Geneva Conventions are not outdated, and it's a very important principle. First of all, Terry, we are adhering to the spirit of the Geneva Convention. When you say you're holding the prisoners in the manner you are—we're giving them medical care; they're being well treated." (Bush, The President's 2002–01–28: 125).

While promissing commitment to the *Geneva Conventions*, not applying them to GTMO detainees is repeatedly explained referring to the newness of the war, placing the enemy outside the sovereign state system.

> And so I am looking at the legalities involved with the Geneva Convention. In either case, however I make my decision, these detainees will be well treated. We are not going to call them prisoners of war, in either case, and the reason why is, Al Qaida is not a known military. These are killers. These are terrorists. They know no countries. And the only thing they know about countries is when they find a country that's been weak, and they want to occupy it like a parasite. [...] And so the prisoners, detainees, will be well treated. They just won't be afforded prisoner-of-war status. I'll decide beyond that whether or not they can be noncombatants under the Geneva Convention, or not. I'll make that legal decision soon. But this administration has made the decision they'll be well treated. Long before they arrived at Guantanamo Bay did we make that decision. (Bush, The President's 2002–01–28: 126)

In fulfilling his reporting duties to Congress on war progress in Afghanistan and regarding the detainees at Guantanamo, Bush officially declares international legal consistency: "We currently hold approximately 550 enemy combatants at Guantanamo. All are being treated humanely and, to the extent appropriate and

[13] On the development and meaning of the term *unlawful enemy combatant* see: Hühnert 2016, Greenberg/Dratel 2005.

consistent with military necessity, in a manner consistent with the principles of the Geneva Conventions of 1949." (Bush, Letter to 2002–09–20: 1628). And similarly: "We currently hold more than 600 enemy combatants at Guantanamo Bay. All are being treated humanely and, to the extent appropriate and consistent with military necessity, in a manner consistent with the principles of the Geneva Conventions of 1949." (Bush Letter to 2003–03–21: 285).

Concerning the torture scandal, many questions come up regarding the treatment and status of the detainees. Talking about prisoner abuse, Bush 'emphasizes legality' and underlines the commitment of the United States to the *Geneva Conventions*.

> In recent days, America and the world have learned of shocking conduct in Iraqi prisons by a small number of American service men and women. These individuals had been given the responsibility of overseeing Iraqis in American custody and doing so in a decent and humane manner consistent with U.S. law and the Geneva Conventions. Instead we have seen shameful images of prisoners being subjected to abuse and humiliation. Such practices do not reflect our values. They are a stain on our country's honor and reputation. (Bush, The President's 2004–05–08: 830).

Bush clearly distances the U.S. official detainee treatment from the abusive treatment with reference to U.S. values.

Concerning legal treatment and military tribunals, Bush repeats the same rhetoric from 2001 in March 2002 (see Bush, Exchange With 2002–03–20: 458). He also continues to refer to secrecy and security as the main reasons to install military tribunals. However, in this phase, Bush only mentions military tribunals twice, and only when asked.

> Well, we're still in the process of getting as much information from the detainees as possible. Remember, these are—the ones in Guantanamo Bay are killers. They don't share the same values we share. They would like nothing more than to come after Americans or our friends and allies. And so, therefore, it's in our national interest to make sure we know enough about them before we decide what to do with them. So there's a process—ongoing process to get as much information as we can from the prisoners, the detainees. Some talk; some don't talk. (Bush, Exchange With 2002–03–20: 458)

Again, Bush emphasizes that military tribunals will be used for security reasons: "I told you, if any evidence that is required to convict them jeopardizes the national security interests of the country, we'll use the tribunal." (Bush, Exchange With 2002–03–20: 458). This continues the argument from the first phase, that military tribunals will be necessary, as certain information will have to be kept secret to keep military and judicial personnel safe.

Evaluating rhetorical activities, the dominant actions across all topics in this phase are 'emphasizing security,' 'explaining security politics,' 'appealing to national values,' 'reporting war progress,' and 'characterizing the enemy.' These activities are strongly connected with framing the 'war on terror' as background for detainee treatment and prosecution. Whereas this issue framing continues from Phase 1, a slight shift is noticeable in 'characterizing the enemy.' Shortly after 9/11, Usama bin Laden represented the dominant enemy figure, however in Phase 2, 'enemy characterization' shifts to Al Qaida and Taliban as main targets in the war on terror. Still, the activity of 'characterizing the enemy' stays tightly connected to the 'war on terror' as to the topic of 'GTMO detainees.' Another shift in activities sticks out: 'claiming pursuit to justice' is no longer focused on bin Laden and connected to military tribunals, which decline in importance. In Phase 2, 'claiming pursuit to justice' is mainly used while talking about the 'war on terror' and about 'GTMO detainees.'

5.3 Phase 3: Legal and Political Dispute

Starting with the transfer of the first detainees to Guantanamo, Phase 2 includes the events up to the Supreme Court ruling on *Rasul v. Bush* where the third phase begins. Phase 3 marks a period from mid-2004 through September 2006 in which the judiciary and the executive fight over the determination of detainee rights. In 2004, Bush campaigns for a second term in office, eventually leading to his re-election in November 2004. The beginning of this phase is marked by a turn towards *habeas corpus rights*, courts' declaring the illegality of indefinite detention, and driving the Bush administration towards implementing status reviews of the detainees. The Supreme Court takes a vote in favor of detainee rights concerning *due process* and *habeas corpus*. On June 28, 2004, the Supreme Court rules on *Rasul v. Bush*. According to this ruling, the GTMO detainees have the right to challenge their detention in a legal process. Furthermore, the court declares that U.S. citizens have *due process* rights. On November 8, 2004, a U.S. District Court rules that the military commissions are unlawful in the current form.

The Supreme Court ruling on *Rasul v. Bush* marks the beginning of the legal and political dispute on detainee rights in the United States. In *Rasul*, the Supreme Court rules that GTMO detainees have the legal right to *writ habeas corpus* and

U.S. citizens have *due process* rights. This ruling poses a strong contradiction to the legal interpretation of detainee rights applied to Guantanamo up to this point which had mainly relied on the *Military Order* of November 13, 2001. The order mentions military tribunals as an option to try GTMO detainees. Furthermore, Bush had heavily relied on the war powers granted to him by the AUMF and the power vested in him to decide on detainee status and treatment. With *Rasul v. Bush*, the legalization by declaration policy applied by the Bush administration so far is restrained by the court and the Bush administration is forced to start *Combatant Status Review Tribunals* (CSRTs) to determine the detainees' legal status.

These court decisions drive the Bush administration towards a legalization process of indefinite detention. In response to the rulings, the Bush administration initiates an assessment process. On July 7, 2004, the Pentagon starts the *Combatant Status Review Tribunals* (CSRTs) to determine the detainees' status, with *Review Tribunals* starting on August 13, 2004, and *Administrative Review Boards* for annual reviews and assessment of the prisoner's captivity being implemented on September 14, 2004. By March 29, 2005, the *CSRTs* are complete: 558 detainees were assessed, 38 no longer qualify as enemy combatants and are cleared for release.

Meanwhile, public criticism concerning detainment and detainee treatment continues to build up pressure on the Bush administration with prominent support. A lawsuit from the *Associated Press* against the Department of Defense which began with charges being pressed on April 19, 2005, leads to the forced release of 2000 pages of redacted Guantanamo detainee testimony on May 20, 2005. On May 25, 2005, *Amnesty International* demands the closure of Guantanamo Bay Detention Camp, followed by former U.S. Presidents Cater and Clinton, UN experts, and other human rights organizations.

Between 2004 and 2005, the legal dispute centers around military commissions. The Bush administration continues towards the legalization of military commissions and takes legislative steps towards the creation of a new detention law. In mid-2005, the formation of a new detention law is initiated. On July 15, 2005, the U.S. Court of Appeals for the District of Columbia Circuit Court overrules the halt on military commissions by Judge Robertson. Military commissions are free to continue. In the *Detainee Treatment Act* (DTA 2005), which is signed into law by President Bush on September 30, 2005, the new detention law is officially formalized. On November 10, 2005, Senate approves to withhold *habeas corpus rights* from GTMO detainees. On December 30, 2005, the *Detainee Treatment Act* becomes law: it bans cruel, inhuman, or degrading treatment of prisoners but sets restrictions on detainee rights to challenge detention. This is a major step towards a new detention law which formalizes the quasi-legal terms and provisions that had been challenged by the Supreme Court rulings. The Bush administration thus responds to the demands of the rulings in favor of detainee rights by formal legislation which limits detainee rights. This legal dispute ends in the *Detainee Treatment Act of 2005*, which constitutes the first formal congressional approach to a new detention law. The DTA 2005 formally withholds *habeas rights* from detainees held at GTMO. However, the legal dispute goes into another round, as the Supreme Court starts hearings on *Hamdan v. Rumsfeld* concerning the legality of the detention based on *Geneva Conventions* and *U.S. Military Code of Uniform Justice*, on March 28, 2006.

Throughout 2006, criticism of detention policies continues while the Bush administration releases more prisoners. On February 15, 2006, the UN issues a report recommending the closure of Guantanamo. On February 23, 2006, a *Freedom of Information Act* ruling orders the Pentagon to release the identities of prisoners to the *Associated Press.* On February 27, five UN experts issue a report on Guantanamo, arguing that international law is applicable and questioning the U.S. interpretation of the *Torture Convention.* On April 20, 2006, the Department of Defense releases 558 prisoners from Guantanamo. In May, repatriations continue while some detainees attempt to commit suicide and riots break out. The Pentagon admits that 75 detainees are on hunger strike. On June 10, 2006, the Department of Defense reports three suicides as a result of a protest of the continued imprisonment: Mani Shaman Turki al-Habardi al-Utaybi (Saudi Arabia), Yasser Talal al-Zahrani (Saudi Arabia), and Ali Abdullah Ahmed (Yemen).[14]

Phase 3 ends with the USSC ruling on *Hamdan v. Rumsfeld* on June 29, 2006, concerning the use and conduct of military tribunals. The court rules that GTMO detainees have the right to pursue cases of *habeas corpus* in U.S. civilian courts. The court also rules that the military tribunals initiated by the Bush administration violate international law and U.S. constitutional law. Again, a Supreme Court ruling challenges Bush in his legal position on detainee rights. On July 12, 2006, Bush thus repeals his directive of February 2002 (see Phase 1) and accepts the court's judgement that the *Geneva Conventions* apply to the detainees in Guantanamo. What seems like a return to violence-containing norm and law is but a

[14] On files and detention history of single detainees see: Guantanamo Docket of the New York Times (Scheinkman et al. 2018).

temporary acknowledgement of yet another legal challenge to be worked out in legislation. This shows for one in the fact that detention in GTMO is continued and more prisoners arrive. However, more detainees arrive in September. Especially so-called 'high-value detainees,' accused of plotting the 9/11 attacks, are transferred to GTMO. On September 6, 2006, 14 so-called 'high-value detainees' are relocated from a CIA black-site to Guantanamo. On September 26, 2006, the *Red Cross* visits these new prisoners, signaling continued interest in U.S. detention policies and detainee treatment in GTMO. For another, in reaction to this ruling, Bush starts working with Congress on legislation that clarifies the application of *Common Article 3* to detention in GTMO, a legal debate and legislative process, which continues in Phase 4.

The events also characterize the president's rhetoric. In this phase, trending topics remain the 'war on terror' followed by 'GTMO detainees' and 'military tribunals' before 'detainee treatment/torture,' 'CIA program,' 'Usama bin Laden,' and 'allies' (Fig. 5.3). Less mentioned are 'Geneva Conventions,' 'surveillance law,' 'intelligence,' 'presidential authority,' and 'homeland security.' Especially the rhetoric in 2004 is largely dominated by the upcoming elections. In this campaigning time, very little speeches contain keywords for the search of detention topics. In 2006 the judicial dispute continues with the Supreme Court ruling on military commissions. This also shows in the speeches, as Bush reacts to the rulings and is questioned on the consequences of the rulings for detention policies. Dominant rhetorical activities are 'emphasizing security,' 'explaining/defending detainee treatment,' 'explaining security politics,' and 'characterizing the enemy' as Fig. 5.3 shows.

Codesystem	Guantanamo Bay detainees	treatment of prisoners/ torture	Military Commissions Act/ military tribunals	Geneva Convention	rule of law	constitutional presidential authority	war on terror	Usama bin Laden	allies	CIA program	intelligence	homeland security	SUMME
admitting defeat													
admonishing													
announcing/commenting new detention law	3		9	2			1			4			19
appealing to national values	3		1				32	1		4			41
applying new detention law			2							2			4
applying the law							7						7
calling on Congress/working w Congress	4		24	2			9			6	4	1	50
characterizing the enemy	15		4	2			45	2	1		1	1	71
claiming presidential power	2			1			5	1			1		10
claiming pursuit to justice	15		13				14	2		2		1	47
commenting USSC/court decisions	13		12	3			1	1		2	3		35
committing to international law	3		10	11						1			25
criricizing democrats			1				6	1		1	1		10
criticizing Congress													
criticizing past actions													
declaring a presidential order													
denying/defending/offering alternative explanation	4	4	5	4			4	1					22
emphasizing accountability													
emphasizing legality	8		13	7			3	1		5			37
emphasizing rule of law	4						2	1		2			9
emphasizing security	25		20	1			76	6		21	4	5	158
emphasizing transparency	6						1						7
explaining prosecution of detainee maltreatment	4		2	1			1						8
explaining security politics	11	1	2				62	2	3	2	4	2	89
explaning cooperation	6						27	1	4				38
explaning/defending detainee treatment	45	4	14	6			8	1	1	24	3		106
expressing gratitude	3		3				4		1				11
(re-)interpreting the law	2		3	5									10
keeping secrets	2						2			1	2		7
listing acomplishments	1						11	1					13
proposing legislation	1		14	2			2			3	2		24
referring to quasi-law	2			1					1				4
reporting on war progress	3						25	2					30
revoking national memory	3		2				39	1		1	1		47
stressing newness of the war	1			1			9				1		12
SUMME	189	9	154	49			396	25	11	81	27	10	951

Fig. 5.3 Code Relations—Activities and Subject—Phase 3

Concerning the 'war on terror,' dominant activities are 'emphasizing security,' 'explaining security politics,' and 'characterizing the enemy.' After that, 'revoking national memory,' 'explaining cooperation,' 'appealing to national values,' and 'reporting on war progress' are used. Especially when 'emphasizing security,' the focus shifts with a changing security environment and the progressing war on terror from Afghanistan to Iraq. While in earlier phases retribution for 9/11 and finding bin Laden are main purposes in war on terror related rhetorical activities, in Phase 3 greater security goals are mentioned, like taking an active role in the peace process in the Middle East and making the war on terror a joint project in terms of a U.S. led security architectures for the Middle East and Iraq.

Another line of argument is dominant in this period, as the following quote shows. Rather on the defensive, Bush argues for his strategy regarding critical debates with European coalition partners who face public criticism, especially concerning the war in Iraq.

> But I don't buy into the theory that taking actions to defend yourself causes extremists to murder people. I think that's part of their ideology. I think it's part of their methodologies. As a matter of fact, this notion about kind of tolerating the world as it is and hope for the best didn't work. It led to an attack on our country where 3,000 people died. Now, look, I fully understand, in Europe that was a traumatic—a dramatic moment, but it was a passing moment. For us, it was a change of philosophy and a change of attitude, and that's been part of the issue with Europe. And I will continue to reach out to explain that our national consciousness was affected deeply by that attack. (Bush, Interview With 2005–05–05: 746)

With the war on terror progressing to Iraq, Bush faces growing criticism from European civil societies and governments. On the one hand, Bush argues for support. On the other hand, he affirms his strategy in Iraq by referring to Al Qaida spreading throughout the countries of the Middle East, defending the war on Iraq as liberating the Iraqi people and saving the world from a tyrant who wanted to use weapons of mass destruction. When asked about protests, Bush acknowledges criticism and refers to freedom of speech. At the same time, he states, that this kind of freedom was not afforded to the Iraqi people. Furthermore, Bush stresses that he will not wait for another attack to happen and accuses Democrats of sitting around and waiting for the best. Moreover, as stated in the quote above, Bush explains that 9/11 was a traumatic moment in Europe but caused a lasting change in the United States. He repeatedly states that 9/11 was a lasting, security and threat perception changing event for the United States. This statement signifies a change in the justification over time. The rhetoric stays focused on

9/11 but changes: while in the beginning retribution was in the center of arguing for detention, the prevention of future attacks and safekeeping of Americans comes to the fore with growing distance from the event. Also, increasing in the justification argument is the difference in ideology. 'Emphasizing security' and 'characterizing the enemy,' Bush progressively speaks of a fight between civilization and barbaric enemies. He also claims that the entire western civilization is at stake in this conflict.

> We're engaged in a global struggle, and the entire civilized world has a stake in its outcome. [...] I've spoken with leaders of foreign governments and worked with them to address their concerns about Guantanamo and our detention policies. I'll continue to work with the international community to construct a common foundation to defend our nations and protect our freedoms. Free nations have faced new enemies and adjusted to new threats before, and we have prevailed. Like the struggles of the last century, today's war on terror is, above all, a struggle for freedom and liberty. The adversaries are different, but the stakes in this war are the same. We're fighting for our way of life and our ability to live in freedom. (Bush, Remarks on 2006–09–06: 1619)

Concerning Guantanamo detainees, the dominating activities are 'explaining/defending detainee treatment,' 'emphasizing security,' 'claiming pursuit to justice,' 'characterizing the enemy,' and 'commenting USSC decisions.' In this phase, 'explaining/defending detainee treatment' plays a significant role, especially since Bush's policy on detainee treatment is declared illegal by the Supreme Court decision and the detention strategy questioned by the highest U.S. court. Thus, Bush defends his decisions and continues to emphasize security concerns. "I think we probably had about 800 or so people detained there, and remember, Klaus, I made a decision as to what to do with people swept off of a battlefield who didn't wear uniforms. I mean, this is a different kind of war. I made the decision they would be treated humanely, just like the Geneva Accords insist, and they have been." (Bush, Interview With 2005–06–330: 1175). He repeats his decision and the reasons for the deviance from the *Geneva Convention* and repeats his arguments: for the detainee status, for the treatment, and because of the new kind of war.

Concerning detainee treatment, Bush uses the activities 'claiming pursuit to justice,' 'characterizing the enemy,' and 'commenting USSC decisions' to defend his policies and to stress that detainee treatment is humane:

> [...] the pictures people saw about the prison—prison abuse is different from the detainees in Guantanamo. We're working our way forward so that they—and our courts, by the way, are adjudicating this. It is a clear, transparent review of the decision I made by the courts, so everybody can see it. And they're being argued in the

> courts as we speak. People are being treated humanely. They were illegal noncombatants, however, and I made the decision they did not pertain to the Geneva Convention. They were not—these were terrorists. (Bush, Interview With 2005–05–05: 749)

Concerning the USSC decision, Bush emphasizes his willingness to work with Congress to fulfill the court's demands and uses 'characterizing the enemy' to emphasize his argument.

> And we'll work with the United States Congress. They [the courts] have said, work with the Congress. I have been waiting for this decision in order to figure out how to go forward. I want to move forward. First of all, I stand by the decision I made in removing these people from the battlefield. See, here's the problem: These are the types of combatants we have never faced before. They don't wear uniforms, and they don't represent a nation-state. They're bound by an ideology. They've sworn allegiance to individuals but not to a nation. The Geneva Conventions were set up to deal with armies of nation-states. You've got standard rules of war. (Bush, The President's 2006–07–07: 1339)

Although abiding by the court's demands, Bush still emphasizes his decisions as right with reference to the newness of the war. He further underlines his argument with 'characterizing the enemy' as not abiding by the rules of war and not being part of the sovereign state system but a member of a terrorist network, and as extremely dangerous. Thus, Bush affirms the meaning of international law for state actors while stressing the need for special rules applying to terrorists.

A specific topic also related to the 'CIA program' remains the accusations of torture and detainee treatment bordering on torture. In this regard, Bush remains clear in his continued denial of wrongdoing.

> These times of increasing terror challenge the world. Terror organizations challenge our comfort and our principles. The United States will continue to take seriously the need to question terrorists who have information that can save lives. But we will not compromise the rule of law or the values and principles that make us strong. Torture is wrong no matter where it occurs, and the United States will continue to lead the fight to eliminate it everywhere. (Bush, Statement on 2004–06–26: 1142)

While denying torture and affirming the U.S. compliance with the torture norm, Bush continues to 'emphasize security' and the importance of detainee questioning for the national security.

One of the main legal challenges after the Supreme Court decisions on detainee treatment in this period for the Bush administration is to come to a legal solution with Congress which allows for the CIA program to continue. This program is important to Bush, as he stresses that the continuance of the program is vital to gaining information from detainees in order to prevent and detect plans for future attacks. Furthermore, Bush affirms the importance of the CIA program in the pursuit of justice.

> The CIA program has detained only a limited number of terrorists at any given time, and once we've determined that the terrorists held by the CIA have little or no additional intelligence value, many of them have been returned to their home countries for prosecution or detention by their governments. Others have been accused of terrible crimes against the American people, and we have a duty to bring those responsible for these crimes to justice. So we intend to prosecute these men, as appropriate, for their crimes. (Bush, Remarks on 2006–09–06: 1617)

When mentioning the 'CIA program,' 'explaining/defending detainee treatment' is used as well as 'emphasizing security.'

> This program has been subject to multiple legal reviews by the Department of Justice and CIA lawyers; they've determined it complied with our laws. This program has received strict oversight by the CIA's Inspector General. A small number of key leaders from both political parties on Capitol Hill were briefed about this program. All those involved in the questioning of the terrorists are carefully chosen, and they're screened from a pool of experienced CIA officers. Those selected to conduct the most sensitive questioning had to complete more than 250 additional hours of specialized training before they are allowed to have contact with a captured terrorist. (Bush, Remarks on 2006–09–06: 1616–1617)

The following quote shows that Bush is not only on the defense but also wants to keep the detention program running by arguing for the legality and necessity of the program.

> I want to be absolutely clear with our people and the world: The United States does not torture. It's against our laws, and it's against our values. I have not authorized it, and I will not authorize it. Last year, my administration worked with Senator John McCain, and I signed into law the Detainee Treatment Act, which established the legal standard for treatment of detainees wherever they are held. I support this act. And as we implement this law, our Government will continue to use every lawful method to obtain intelligence that can protect innocent people and stop another attack like the one we experienced on September the 11th, 2001. (Bush, Remarks on 2006–09–06: 1617)

So, he clearly distances the detention program from torture, as he has always stated on the matter. Bush strictly denies that torture was part of any official U.S.

security strategy, and he emphasizes the institutional embedding of the detention program, as he argues.

Noteworthy is that when detainee treatment is mentioned, finding a legal solution mainly prioritizes assuring impunity for the security personnel.

> As we work with Congress to pass a good bill, we will also consult with congressional leaders on how to ensure that the CIA program goes forward in a way that follows the law, that meets the national security needs of our country, and protects the brave men and women we ask to obtain information that will save innocent lives. For the sake of our security, Congress needs to act and update our laws to meet the threats of this new era. And I know they will. (Bush, Remarks on 2006–09–06: 1619)

In this quote, Bush repeats his security political mindset concerning national security. This emphasis on national security he connects with background knowledge like national values and the fight for shared values, and ideas. These are core national values which have a historical meaning and tradition in the United States. These values function as identity building blocks for the U.S. citizens and are thus relatable to for the listeners. Bush thus refers to shared values, beliefs, tradition, and national history to appeal to the (voting) audience.

In this third phase, the speeches cover the entire legislative process of the *Military Commissions Act 2006*, beginning with the presentation of the draft to Congress and ending with Bush signing the act into law. Concerning 'military tribunals,' the following activities dominate the speech: 'calling Congress to action,' 'emphasizing security,' 'proposing legislation,' 'explaining/defending detainee treatment,' 'emphasizing legality,' 'claiming pursuit to justice,' 'commenting USSC decisions,' 'committing to international law,' and 'announcing/commenting new detention law.'

In his official statement on passing the draft to Congress by 'explaining/defending detainee treatment,' Bush emphasizes that he follows the Supreme Court ruling and intends to work with Congress. Further, he emphasizes his role in the process and the importance of this new legislation not only historically but also for national security. Although military tribunals are no new measure in U.S. criminal prosecution in war times, Bush accentuates that this is the first time in history that Congress is deciding on a legal framework for military tribunals. Bush also emphasizes having found regulations for *unlawful enemy combatants*. 'Commenting USSC decisions,' he claims to improve regulations by avoiding *Common Article 3* which he criticizes as not sufficiently clear in wording and meaning. Continuing the legalization path for detention taken with the *Detainee Treatment Act (2005)*, the draft *MCA (2006)* further legalizes the status of *unlawful enemy combatants*.

> I transmit for the consideration of the Congress draft legislation entitled the 'Military Commissions Act of 2006.' This draft legislation responds to the Supreme Court of the United States decision in Hamdan v. Rumsfeld, 126 S. Ct. 2749 (2006), by establishing for the first time in our Nation's history a comprehensive statutory structure for military commissions that would allow for the fair and effective prosecution of captured members of al Qaeda and other unlawful enemy combatants. The Act also addresses the Supreme Court's holding that Common Article 3 of the Geneva Conventions applies to the conflict with al Qaeda by providing definitions rooted in United States law for the standards of conduct prescribed by Common Article 3. (Bush, Message to 2006–09–06: 1620)

What shows in rhetoric despite criticism of the USSC is that the president follows his constitutional and legally prescribed role concerning the branches of government and he abides by the ruling of the Supreme Court. However, he also makes clear throughout the entire process of adapting detention law that he does not agree with the court decisions. Bush openly criticizes the Supreme Court not only for the decisions but also, more fundamentally, for making politics and prescribing legislation instead of only reading the law. However, although Bush abides by the Court mandates, he also makes use of his maneuvering room, fixing his interpretation, and making rules which appeal to the envisaged detainee treatment strategy. Bush proposes legislation to Congress that meets his strategic demand, thereby not restoring detention law in the policies but rather transforming the law to legalize detention policies.

In arguing for the *Military Commissions Act 2006* as proposed to Congress, Bush clearly voices his concern that U.S. security personnel could be prosecuted for war crime offenses:

> In its ruling on military commissions, the Court determined that a provision of the Geneva Conventions known as Common Article Three applies to our war with Al Qaida. This article includes provisions that prohibit 'outrages upon personal dignity' and 'humiliating and degrading treatment.' The problem is that these and other provisions of Common Article Three are vague and undefined, and each could be interpreted in different ways by American or foreign judges. And some believe our military and intelligence personnel involved in capturing and questioning terrorists could now be at risk of prosecution under the War Crimes Act, simply for doing their jobs in a thorough and professional way. (Bush, Remarks on 2006–09–06: 1619)

His concern is, however, not with the treatment of the detainees but rather with the legal terms, which could pose a litigation risk for U.S. forces. This line of argument shows that Bush prioritizes securing the rights of the security personnel over defining humane regulations for detainee treatment. Bush fosters formally legalizing detainee treatment and questioning methods, aiming to make prosecution of security forces less likely. This proposed legislation thus strengthens the safety and security of U.S. forces but not the rights of detainees. These legal efforts of the Bush administration mark a fundamental difference to the original intentions of the *Geneva Conventions (1949) Common Article 3*, which grants protection to captives of unclear status from arbitrary use of state power.

Bush criticizes the USSC and the unspecific reading of *Common Article 3*. Bush further claims that the programm which is so vital for national security was put to a halt by the USSC (Bush, The President's 2005–06–20: 1023). He criticizes the court for not protecting the good but serving the evil. Here, the president again uses the dichotomy between good and bad to create an image of the judiciary in terms of the USSC jeopardizing the nation's safety and standing in the way of preserving national security.

> Now, the Court said that you've got to live under Article 3 of the Geneva Convention, and the standards are so vague that our professionals won't be able to carry forward the program, because they don't want to be tried as war criminals. They don't want to break the law. These are decent, honorable citizens who are on the frontline of protecting the American people, and they expect our Government to give them clarity about what is right and what is wrong in the law. And that's what we have asked to do. (Bush, The President's 2006–09–15: 1650)

As much as Bush emphasizes the importance of the law and the constitution, he also emphasizes that this law is exclusive—it only protects Americans—and that the law should not be in the way of security.

As the following quote shows, Bush asks Congress to pass the *Military Commissions Act 2006*, repeating the intention to pass law that achieves legal security for the U.S. security personnel, and not to enhance legal rights of prisoners or ameliorate the conditions of their captivity.

> So today I'm asking Congress to pass legislation that will clarify the rules for our personnel fighting the war on terror. First, I'm asking Congress to list the specific, recognizable offenses that would be considered crimes under the War Crimes Act so our personnel can know clearly what is prohibited in the handling of terrorist enemies. Second, I'm asking that Congress make explicit that by following the standards of the Detainee Treatment Act, our personnel are fulfilling America's obligations under Common Article Three of the Geneva Conventions. Third, I'm asking that Congress make it clear that captured terrorists cannot use the Geneva Conventions as a basis to sue our personnel in courts—in U.S. courts. The men and women who protect us should not have to fear lawsuits filed by terrorists because they're doing their jobs. (Bush, The President's 2006–09–06: 1619)

The aim of the legislation, as Bush emphasizes, is also to specify wrongful detainee treatment in order to create legal certainty for U.S. security personnel. Furthermore, he also clarifies that detainees should be prevented from using the *Geneva Conventions* to gain legal advantage over U.S. security personnel. Finally, Bush comments on the passing of the *Military Commissions Act 2006*, by applauding Congress for having continued the detention program.

> Today the House passed legislation that would allow this vital program to continue and help keep our country safe. The 'Military Commissions Act of 2006' addresses the Supreme Court's ruling regarding the application of Common Article 3 of the Geneva Conventions and clarifies the standards for U.S. personnel who detain and question unlawful enemy combatants. The act also creates a comprehensive statutory structure for military commissions so that we can prosecute suspected terrorists. (Bush, Statement on 2006–09–27: 1708)

Here Bush emphasizes that the passed legislation is in line with the USSC demand and creates more clarity concerning the use and interpretation of international law, for U.S. security personnel in detention facilities concerning treatment and questioning of detainees. Formally, the *MCA 2006* legalizes the status introduced in the *Detainee Treatment Act*, the *unlawful enemy combatant*. Furthermore, the *MCA 2006* includes procedural guidelines for the conduct of military commissions (military tribunals). Having stalled on prosecuting detainees in Guantanamo, with reference to the upcoming court decisions and pending legislation, Bush now emphasizes that detainee trails can be pursued.

5.4 Phase 4: Formal Legalization of New Detention Law

In Phase 4 from October 2006 to mid-2008, the new detention law is formally legalized when the *Military Commissions Act 2006* is signed into law and Bush issues the 2007 Executive Order 13440 on secret detention. As the legal debate continues during this phase, Bush keeps criticizing that *Common Article 3* is too unspecific and needs to be clarified in the interest of security against the prosecution of military and security personnel.

In 2006, reacting to the USSC rulings in favor of detainee rights, the Bush administration motions for legislation towards a new detention law concerning detainee status, treatment, and regulations for prosecution. On October 17, 2006, the *Military Commissions Act 2006* is signed into law by President Bush adding to the *Detainee Treatment Act 2005* a significant part of the new detention law. The

MCA 2006 denies GTMO detainees the right to *writ habeas corpus* and allows for the continuation of the detention program. This legislation is approved by the U.S. Court of Appeals ruling (February 20, 2007) which states that U.S. federal courts have no jurisdiction on *habeas* cases of GTMO detainees based on the *MCA (2006)*. The prison is even enlarged, as Camp 6 opens in December 2006.

Throughout 2007, indefinite detention continues despite releases or clearance of detainees, secret detention is legalized, and military commissions continue. On March 18, 2007, two UK citizens, Ahmed Rahidi and Ahmed Belbacha, are authorized for release. Yet, they remain in indefinite detention because the UK refuses to receive them. Also, military commissions continue at Guantanamo. On March 26, 2007, David Hicks[15], an Australian citizen, pleads guilty. He is convicted to serve nine months of prison in Australia by a military commission on March 30, 2007. During this year, the prison receives new detainees. On March 26, 2007, Abdul Malik Abdul-Jabbar arrives in GTMO in a direct transfer to the camp. On April 27, 2007, the Pentagon states that Iraqi Abd al-Hadi al-Iraqi was transferred from CIA captivity to GTMO.

Throughout 2007 and 2008, the new detention law is expanded and actively applied. On July 20, 2007, President Bush issues an Executive Order on the *Interpretation of the Geneva Conventions Common Article 3 as applied to a Program of Detention and Interrogation Operated by the Central Intelligence Agency* (Executive Order 13440) specifying regulations for CIA detention and interrogation, reaffirming compliance with international law, and stressing interrogation as means to receive terrorism preventing information. Military commissions continue, which shows that the new detention law is actively applied.[16] On August 9, 2007, the Pentagon declares that 14 detainees, who had been in captivity since September 2006, are 'enemy combatants.' On May 13, 2008, the U.S. administration requests the death penalty for five Guantanamo detainees in a military commission, including prisoners Khalid Sheikh Mohamed, Wali bin Attash, Ramzi bin al-Shibh, Ali Abd al-Aziz Ali, and Mustafa al Hawsawi who are accused of having been involved in the 9/11 attacks. In June 2008, they are sued at Guantanamo.

---

[15] The conviction of David Hicks is reversed by the U.S. Military Appeals Court on February 18, 2015.

[16] For examples of motions on behalf of the Bush administration to convict detainees in military commissions see the Appendix provided in the Electronic Supplementary Material.

The situation in the prison remains tense, as several deaths and more information on detainee maltreatment are reported. On May 30, 2007, the GTMO administration declares the death of a detainee from Saudi Arabia, Abdul Rahman Ma'ath Thafir al-Amri, due to suicide. In December 2007, an Afghan prisoner dies of cancer in captivity. On December 6, 2007, the Director of the CIA admits that videos of interrogations including those showing waterboarding and other enhanced interrogation methods from 2002 were destroyed by the CIA in 2005. On February 5, 2008, the CIA Director confirms waterboarding on three secret captives between 2002 and 2003. Yet, transfers to the camp continue. On March 14, 2008, the Pentagon declares that Muhammad Rahim al Afghani is brought to GTMO as a 'high value detainee.' Also in 2008, Bush returns without approval the *Intelligence Authorization Act for Fiscal Year 2008*. The bill would have established more oversight to CIA operations and applied *U.S. Army Field Manual* standards to the CIA program, effectively preventing interrogation methods like waterboarding and other means of so-called enhanced interrogation methods.

In Phase 4, the dominant topics in speeches are 'war on terror' and 'GTMO detainees,' before 'CIA program' and 'intelligence,' followed by 'homeland security,' 'Military Commissions Act/ military tribunals,' 'treatment of prisoners/ torture,' 'surveillance law,' and 'allies' (see Fig. 5.4). Across all topics mentioned, 'emphasizing security' is still the dominant activity, followed by 'explaining security politics' and 'explaining detainee treatment.' Starting with the signing of the *Military Commissions Act 2006*, this phase continues the discussion from Phase 3 on the legislative process with Congress. Overall, Bush's rhetoric shows a shift towards legal topics, less regarding the GTMO detainees but more focusing on the competence afforded to the security forces.

Codesystem	Guantanamo Bay detainees	treatment of prisoners/ torture	Military Commissions Act/ military tribunals	Geneva Convention	rule of law	constitutional presidential authority	war on terror	Usama bin Laden	allies	CIA program	intelligence	homeland security	SUMME
admitting defeat													
admonishing													
announcing/commenting new detention law		1	9										10
appealing to national values			6	1			16			1			24
applying new detention law			1	2						2			5
applying the law							4						4
calling on Congress/working w Congress		1	1	1			2			1			6
characterizing the enemy	1			1			16	3		3			24
claiming presidential power				1						3			4
claiming pursuit to justice			5				2		1				8
commenting USSC/court decisions	1		1										2
committing to international law			1	1						1			3
criricizing democrats	1						8			2		1	12
criticizing Congress				1			1			12	3		17
criticizing past actions													
declaring a presidential order													
denying/defending/offering alternative explanation	3						1						4
emphasizing accountability													
emphasizing legality	1	3	2	3						4			13
emphasizing rule of law	1										1		2
emphasizing security	2	1	9	2			52	2	1	13	2	1	85
emphasizing transparency													
explaining prosecution of detainee maltreatment													
explaining security politics							28		1	4	2	1	36
explaning cooperation							4						4
explaning/defending detainee treatment	7	4	5	2			5	1		11	2		37
expressing gratitude			1				2			1		1	5
(re-)interpreting the law													
keeping secrets		4		2						7			13
listing acomplishments							2						2
proposing legislation							2						2
referring to quasi-law													
reporting on war progress							9						9
revoking national memory			6				16			1		1	24
stressing newness of the war							9						9
SUMME	17	14	47	17			179	6	3	66	10	5	364

Fig. 5.4 Code Relations—Activities and Subject—Phase 4

Concerning the evaluation by topics, in the 'war on terror' the dominating activities are 'emphasizing security,' 'explaining security politics,' 'revoking national memory,' 'appealing to national values,' and 'characterizing the enemy.' While 'emphasizing security' and 'explaining security politics' have been dominant activities throughout all phases of norm transformation, 'revoking national memory' has been used less dominantly. In this phase, however, 'revoking national memory' is used especially during the mid-term election campaign for Congress in October through November 2006. 'Revoking national memories' is used to remind the voters of the terrorist attacks and the security issues connected with the newness of the war.

The activity 'emphasizing security' is mainly used in this phase in campaign talk for the mid-term elections, in connection with the activities 'criticizing Democrats' and 'explaining security politics' in the war on terror. Bush keeps arguing for an offensive strategy abroad to keep the homeland safe. He uses reminders of the progress made in the war. 'Emphasizing security,' Bush names the protection of the nation as a top priority of political issues in the election.

> And so I vowed—and the reason I know this is because, you see, we've got to be right 100 percent of the time to protect you. And the enemy has got to be right one time. (Bush, Remarks at 2006–10–04: 1769)

By presenting these odds, the president defends his security strategy and stirs up fear of future attacks while emphasizing his role in safekeeping the nation. Bush again frames the 'war on terror' as the calling of the 21st century, a battle between civilization and barbarity, moderate forces and extremists, tyrants and freedom loving democratic states.

This rhetoric also shows in 'characterizing the enemy.' While Bush defends an offensive strategy, he also emphasizes the defensive necessity of the use of force abroad. In this regard, the president repeatedly defends his strategy to go after the harboring nations in counterterrorism, like Afghanistan, calling the Taliban barbaric. This dichotomy between civilization and barbarity is used in the activities 'defending security politics,' 'characterizing the enemy,' and 'defending detainee treatment.'

> Now, the lesson I have learned from September the 11th was two—one—many, but two of the most notable ones were, if you find somebody harboring a terrorist, they're equally as guilty as the terrorists and must be held to account. And that's why we removed the Taliban from Afghanistan and freed 25 million people from the clutches of a barbaric regime. (Bush, Remarks at 2006–10–02: 1746)

Concerning the characterization of the enemy, Bush mainly argues that Al Qaida spilled from Afghanistan to Iraq where they keep planning terrorist attacks, Usama bin Laden is mentioned a legitimation figure in the war in Iraq.

As 'claiming pursuit to justice' was dominantly used in earlier phases, the activity is still used but decreasingly. Yet, especially during the election campaign this activity comes to the fore.

> You can't negotiate with these people. Therapy is not going to work. [Laughter] The best way to deal with this enemy is to bring them to justice before they hurt the American people again. (Bush, Remarks at 2006–10–02: 1746)

Bush here repeats his offensive war strategy, based on using military force based on intelligence insights. The expression to bring the enemy to justice before Americans could be harmed underlines the preemptive/preventive turn of Bush's security strategy. This can also be read as a hint towards the change in his detention strategy. With building up of criticism and the growing tensions in Guantanamo, Bush starts exploring drones as a means to eliminate terrorists on the ground instead of capturing them.

With the mid-term elections coming up on November 7, 2006, speeches are directed at supporting candidates and 'criticizing Democrats' increases as an activity in this phase. Main issue of this criticism is the Democrats' voting on the prolonging of the *PATRIOT Act* and on the legislation concerning the terrorist surveillance and the CIA program to detain and question terrorists. In campaign speeches Bush follows the same line of argument: he emphasizes his own contribution to national security and that of his party and the candidate he supports, then starts criticizing Democrats for neglecting national security over other political issues by referring to certain votes in Congress. Bush emphasizes that Democrats follow a wait-and-see strategy which he criticizes as passive and not leading to success in defending the United States against terrorism, as sums up in the following quote:

> It's important for people in this district and around the country to understand there is a different mindset. You cannot wait to respond to an attack. You got to act before the attack. (Bush, Remarks at 2006–11–05: 2029)

Mainly, he repeatedly emphasizes the importance of national security, while accusing Democrats of having no plan for national security.

However, Bush hardly mentions the topic of GTMO detainees during the campaign, except when listing accomplishments in the war on terror. When the topic comes up in Q/A, the president repeats his intention to close GTMO and to go forward with detainee transfers while complying with the *Torture Convention.* In this regard, he points to repatriation problems, as many countries are reluctant to take in former detainees and transferring detainees to the United States is no option. When confronted with the accusation that after a year of time, Bush had not fulfilled his claim to close Guantanamo, Bush reacts defensive and offers an alternative explanation: "And you say nothing has taken place. I strongly disagree with that. First of all, we are working with other nations to send folks back. Again, it's a fairly steep order. A lot of people don't want killers in their midst, and a lot of these people are killers. Secondly, of course, we want to make sure that when we do send them back, they're treated as humanely as possible." (Bush, The President's 2007–08–09: 1059). Again, Bush uses a mix of accusing the enemy, characterized as bad people, and killers, and of commitment to legal proceedings. Concerning the possibility of trials, Bush states:

> The other issue was whether or not we can get people to be tried. One of the things I'm anxious about, want to see happen, is that there to be trials. Courts have been involved with deciding how to do this, and Defense is trying to work out mechanisms to get the trials up and running. And the sooner we can get that up and running, the better it is, as far as I'm concerned. I don't want to make any predictions about whether Guantanamo will be available or not. I'm just telling you it's a very complicated subject. (Bush, The President's 2007–08–09: 1059)

In this statement, Bush refrains from decisive language, but rather vaguely blames legal and security institutions for complicating the matter.

After the 'war on terror,' the 'CIA program' is the trending topic in this phase which mainly deals with detainee treatment. Concerning the 'CIA program,' the dominant activities are 'emphasizing security,' 'explaining detainee treatment,' 'criticizing Congress,' and 'keeping secrets.' On the question of the detainee treatment bordering on torture (as revealed by a *Red Cross* report) Bush only denies by stating "I haven't seen it. We don't torture." (Bush, The President's 2007–08–09: 1059). What is presented as an incident in this quote is part of a repeated effort of denial of torture and defense of detainee treatment. Concerning GTMO detainees, next to detainee treatment in captivity, detainee prosecution remains a pressing topic. Concerning trials for remaining prisoners Bush refers to legal issues: "Well, some of the detainees are going to need to be tried in our court system. The crimes were such that we believe they ought to be brought to justice in a U.S. court system, which is—it's having a little trouble getting started because we've had a few court challenges for our court system. The whole purpose of the exercise was to send people home and try those who remain."

(Bush, Interview With 2008–01–04: 15). Again, Bush criticizes the court system for not delivering justice. He further says on the prosecution of GTMO detainees:

> And so what people got to understand is, we'll make decisions based upon law. We're a nation of law. Take Guantanamo, look, I'd like it to be empty. On the other hand, there's some people there that need to be tried. And there will be a trial, and they'll have their day in court, unlike what they did to other people. No, there's great concern about—and I can understand this—that these people be given rights, but they're not willing to grant the same rights to others. They'll murder, but you got to understand, they're getting rights. And I'm comfortable with the decisions we've made, and I'm comfortable with recognizing this is still a dangerous world. (Bush, Interview With 2008–02–14: 196)

Bush strongly emphasizes the meaning of the law and its application. He also refers to doubts as to give detainees rights and repeats his interpretation of the law as exclusive to Americans. The president expresses his agreement with not granting detainees rights due to a lack of reciprocity. This statement alludes to one of Bush's core arguments that although the so-called killers did not afford the same respectful, fair treatment to their victims, the U.S. treatment is still fair granting undeserving people privileges. Bush thus claims to take the moral high road. Despite all criticism, Bush continues to defend his decisions as right referring to national security.

A specific topic in this phase is the use of military commissions, as on October 17, 2006, Bush signs the *Military Commissions Act 2006* into law. After the *2005 Detainee Treatment Act* this is the document which contains the new detention law. As this is the main legislative act in the norm transformation, Bush's accompanying speech is significant in content and analyzed in more detail in the following.

On signing the *Military Commissions Act 2006* Bush emphasizes in his speech the meaning of this act as "one of the most important pieces of legislation in the war on terror" (Bush, Remarks on 2006–10–17: 1857). He further stresses the success of the CIA program in countering and preventing terrorism in the past and for the future. Furthermore, the president mentions that the bill makes trials possible. This announcement is noteworthy because Bush had to postpone prosecution of detainees due to the court rulings demanding additional legislation through Congress (Bush, Remarks on 2006–10–17: 1857). Following his war on terror rhetoric, Bush 'emphasizes security,' 'claims pursuit to justice,' and 'revokes national memories':

> The bill I sign today helps secure this country, and it sends a clear message: This Nation is patient and decent and fair, and we will never back down from the threats to our freedom. One of the terrorists believed to have planned the 9/11 attacks said he hoped the attacks would be the beginning of the end of America. He didn't get his wish. We are as determined today as we were on the morning of September the 12th, 2001. We'll meet our obligation to protect our people, and no matter how long it takes, justice will be done. (Bush, Remarks on 2006–10–17: 1858)

Bush again emphasizes his role in proposing this legislation to Congress, using 'explaining security politics' and 'defending detainee treatment':

> When I proposed this legislation, I explained that I would have one test for the bill Congress produced: Will it allow the CIA program to continue? This bill meets that test. It allows for the clarity our intelligence professionals need to continue questioning terrorists and saving lives. This bill provides legal protections that ensure our military and intelligence personnel will not have to fear lawsuits filed by terrorists simply for doing their jobs. (Bush, Remarks on 2006–10–17: 1858)

The president continues to argue in favor of the CIA program, which stands at the core of his detention policy. The phrasing in this speech resembles the rhetoric Bush used throughout Phase 3, campaign talk, and publicly accompanying the legislation process leading to the passing of the *MCA 2006*. He repeats his exclusive idea of the law, which is supposed to protect U.S. security personnel from prosecution for detainee maltreatment. Bush further states that the specifications in the law are beneficial to U.S. security personnel in treating detainees by 'defending detainee treatment' and 'appealing to national values':

> This bill spells out specific, recognizable offenses that would be considered crimes in the handling of detainees so that our men and women who question captured terrorists can perform their duties to the fullest extent of the law. And this bill complies with both the spirit and the letter of our international obligations. As I've said before, the United States does not torture. It's against our laws, and it's against our values. (Bush, Remarks on 2006–10–17: 1858)

Bush also defends the detainee treatment by praising the CIA program for having delivered key information in the prevention of terrorist attacks. By reporting that terrorists had planned attacks using biological and chemical weapons, which are highly dangerous and belong into the category of weapons of mass destruction, he further stirs fears. Bush thus links to arguments which were used to justify the war in Iraq and refers to a threat scenario that has been drawn up since 9/11. He mentions several examples where the CIA program has successfully prevented already planned attacks from happening, thus underlining not only the meaning but also the success of the program. In this regard, Bush repeats his criticism of the USSC and the Democrats in the legal debate and in the mid-term election for causing the CIA program to pause. Next to the importance of the program for national security, Bush stresses that the *MCA* paves the way to terrorist prosecution. He thus invalidates major points of criticism he had to face in the legal dispute throughout Phases 3 and 4. 'Revoking national memory,' Bush is connecting the *MCA* to his post-9/11 proposition of military commissions, which he sees in line with historically used military tribunals. Again, Bush implicitly criticizes the USSC for questioning his decision's legality, while stressing his own role in the legislative process and 'claiming pursuit to justice':

> The bill I'm about to sign also provides a way to deliver justice to the terrorists we have captured. In the months after 9/ 11, I authorized a system of military commissions to try foreign terrorists accused of war crimes. These commissions were similar to those used for trying enemy combatants in the Revolutionary War and the Civil War and World War II. Yet the legality of the system I established was challenged in the court, and the Supreme Court ruled that the military commissions needed to be explicitly authorized by the United States Congress. (Bush, Remarks on 2006–10–17: 1859)

'Claiming pursuit to justice' Bush offers solace and retribution to the families of the victims of terrorist attacks. Emphasizing justice for American losses, Bush also 'revokes national memories' and 'appeals to national values.' By telling from personal experience and by telling anecdotes brought to his attention he makes the stories emotionally appealing:

> Last month, on the fifth anniversary of 9/11, I stood with Americans who lost family members in New York and Washington and Pennsylvania. I listened to their stories of loved ones they still miss. I told them America would never forget their loss. Today I can tell them something else: With the bill I'm about to sign, the men our intelligence officials believe orchestrated the murder of nearly 3,000 innocent people will face justice. (Bush, Remarks on 2006–10–17: 1857)

Concerning military commissions, Bush emphasizes not only that these courts meet security needs but also stresses the legality of the tribunals based on a joint effort of the legislative and the executive. He further highlights the qualities of the prosecution in military commissions:

> These military commissions will provide a fair trial, in which the accused are presumed innocent, have access to an attorney, and can hear all the evidence against them.

> These military commissions are lawful, they are fair, and they are necessary. (Bush, Remarks on 2006–10–17: 1859)

Bush circles back to the attacks attributed to Al Qaida (9/11, the attack on the USS Cole, and the attacks on the American Embassies in Kenia and Tanzania), which have been mentioned frequently in war on terror rhetoric (Bush, Remarks on 2006–10–17: 1859). He also repeats his 'claim to pursuit of justice' like in the beginning of the war on terror:

> When I sign this bill into law, we will use these commissions to bring justice to the men believed to have planned the attacks of September the 11th, 2001. [...] With our actions, we will send a clear message to those who kill Americans: We will find you, and we will bring you to justice. (Bush, Remarks on 2006–10–17: 1859)

Acknowledging the political and legal debate on the bill and expressing gratitude for the support in Congress, Bush places the *MCA 2006* in a wider historical context, 'revoking national memory' and 'appealing to national values':

> Over the past few months, the debate over this bill has been heated, and the questions raised can seem complex. Yet, with the distance of history, the questions will be narrowed and few: Did this generation of Americans take the threat seriously, and did we do what it takes to defeat that threat? Every Member of Congress who voted for this bill has helped our Nation rise to the task that history has given us. Some voted to support this bill even when the majority of their party voted the other way. I thank the legislators who brought this bill to my desk for their conviction, for their vision, and for their resolve. (Bush, Remarks on 2006–10–17: 1859)

As this quote shows, Bush claims the *MCA 2006* to be the necessary legislation for the defense of the country. He further underlines this in the closing remarks referring to 9/11, mourning the victims, once again 'revoking national memories,' 'appealing to national values,' and 'characterizing the enemy':

> There is nothing we can do to bring back the men and women lost on September the 11th, 2001. Yet we'll always honor their memory, and we will never forget the way they were taken from us. This Nation will call evil by its name. We will answer brutal murder with patient justice. Those who kill the innocent will be held to account. With this bill, America reaffirms our determination to win the war on terror. [...] And now, in memory of the victims of September the 11th, it is my honor to sign the Military Commissions Act of 2006 into law. (Bush, Remarks on 2006–10–17: 1859)

Concluding, this phase contains the main formal legalization steps for a new detention law. Although Bush justifies the detention program with national security and enemy characterization as evil and presents legal solutions, the legal dispute continues as the following phase shows.

5.5 Phase 5: Towards Institutional Ending of Detainment

Phase 5 from June 12, 2008, to June 2009, marks the turn towards ending indefinite detention. Whereas Bush had already signaled to empty the camp in Phase 4, the presidential campaign of Barack Obama prioritizes closing GTMO as one of the leading topics. As this phase covers the presidential turnover from Bush to Obama in January 2009, the first section here covers the events and rhetoric of Bush's last months in office up until the end of his presidency. The second section of this phase covers Obama's first months in office up to June 2009.

Section 1: June 12, 2008—January 19, 2009
In this phase from June 12, 2008, to January 19, 2009, the legal dispute over detainee rights continues. In 2008, several courts rule in favor of detainee rights. On June 12, 2008, the Supreme Court rules on *Boumediene v. Bush*, in favor of *habeas* rights of GTMO detainees before U.S. courts. This decision declares the *Military Commissions Act of 2006* illegal and again demands legislative action from Congress. Indefinite detention is resolved in some cases through further legal proceedings and releases. As military commissions continue in July and August of 2008, Yemini prisoner Salim Hamdan is found guilty of supporting terrorism and sentenced to five years in captivity. On October 7, 2008, due to a Washington D.C. Court decision, 17 Chinese Muslim detainees are ordered to be released who had been held without charges. In November 2008, Salim Ahmed Hamdan, the driver of Usama bin Laden, is released after being convicted for supporting terrorism. On November 20, 2008, due to a U.S. District Court order, five detainees out of six which were granted *habeas* rights based on *Boumediene v. Bush* are released. In December 2008, five detainees connected to 9/11 plead guilty. On December 5, 2008, the Supreme Court accepts a hearing on the case of Ali al-Marri.[17] On December 11, 2008, the Armed Services Committee issues

[17] Although Ali Al-Marri is held on U.S. mainland and is thus not a GTMO detainee, the case is mentioned here to show that the Supreme Court is dealing with different challenges to the detention law.

a report on the mistreatment on detainees. In January 2009, Susan Crawford, member of the Bush administration, admits in a public statement that Mohammed al-Qahtani was tortured while in U.S. custody. This statement stands in stark contrast to President Bush's rhetoric, who denies torture allegations brought forward against the United States and affirms U.S. commitment to the *Torture Convention.*

In Bush's last months in office, topics in the remaining documents which check detention-related keywords are the 'war on terror' and 'GTMO detainees.' Dominant activities overall remain 'emphasizing security,' 'denying/defending/offering alternative explanations,' and 'commenting on USSC decisions' (see Fig. 5.5).

Concerning the 'war on terror,' Bush continues his rhetorical activities. In this topic dominant activities are 'emphasizing security,' 'explaining cooperation,' 'explaining security politics,' 'reporting on war progress,' and 'characterizing the enemy.' In this topic campaign-related speech is also dominant, in support of presidential candidate Senator McCain.

Regarding GTMO detainees, the president faces another challenge in terms of legislative efforts towards a new detention law. On June 12, 2008, the Supreme Court rules on *Boumediene v. Bush*, overruling the *Military Commissions Act of 2006* and grating GTMO detainee *habeas* rights before U.S. civil courts. Concerning the topic of 'GTMO detainees' the dominant activities are 'commenting USSC decisions' and 'denying/defending/offering alternative explanations.' 'Emphasizing security' is used less as a rhetorical activity. When asked about the USSC ruling, Bush replies that he will accept the court's decision. However, he sides with the overruled judges. So, he criticizes the ruling and emphasizes that the overruled judges were more concerned with national security. Again, Bush shows his respect for the institution but argues against the court decision. He underlines this notion in his description of the court:

"First of all, it's the Supreme Court decision. We'll abide by the Court's decision. That doesn't mean I have to agree with it. It's a deeply divided Court, and I strongly agree with those who dissented that. And their dissent was based upon their serious concerns about U.S. national security." (Bush, The President's 2008–06–12: 797).

Bush repeats his criticism of the Supreme Court in the presidential run up for Senator McCain in 2008. The president not only questions certain rulings, but he argues with the judges interpretation of their own role. His main point is that the Supreme Court judges do not interpret the constitution but engage in the politics of legislation.

> We received a fresh reminder of the importance of the courts last week. A bare majority of five Supreme Court Justices overturned a bipartisan law that the United States

Codesystem	Guantanamo Bay detainees	treatment of prisoners/ torture	Military Commissions Act/ military tribunals	Geneva Convention	rule of law	constitutional presidential authority	war on terror	Usama bin Laden	allies	CIA program	intelligence	homeland security	SUMME
admitting defeat													
admonishing													
announcing/commenting new detention law													
appealing to national values							1						1
applying new detention law													
applying the law							2						2
calling on Congress/working w Congress	1												1
characterizing the enemy	1						4						5
claiming presidential power													
claiming pursuit to justice													
commenting USSC/court decisions	5												5
committing to international law													
criricizing democrats							1						1
criticizing Congress													
criticizing past actions													
declaring a presidential order													
denying/defending/offering alternative explanation	5												5
emphasizing accountability													
emphasizing legality													
emphasizing rule of law													
emphasizing security	2						10						12
emphasizing transparency													
explaining prosecution of detainee maltreatment													
explaining security politics	1						5						6
explaning cooperation							6						6
explaning/defending detainee treatment	1						3						4
expressing gratitude													
(re-)interpreting the law													
keeping secrets													
listing acomplishments							1						1
proposing legislation													
referring to quasi-law													
reporting on war progress							4						4
revoking national memory							1						1
stressing newness of the war													
SUMME	16						38						54

Fig. 5.5 Code Relations—Activities and Subject—Phase 5—Bush

> Congress passed, and I signed, to deliver justice to detainees at Guantanamo Bay. With this decision, hardened terrorists—hardened foreign terrorists now enjoy certain legal rights previously reserved for American citizens. This is precisely the kind of judicial activism that frustrates the American people. And the best way to change it is to put Republicans in charge in the Senate and John McCain in the White House. (Bush, Remarks at 2008–06–18: 848)

Again, Bush repeats that he will work with Congress to prosecute GTMO detainees, while claiming that the court complicated the judicial processes (Bush, The President's 2008–07–15: 1021). Also, the exclusive character of Bush's understanding of the law shows. According to Bush, American law is for the American people and is not supposed to extend to terrorists who are the declared enemy. Bush further argues that the USSC overruled previous Supreme Court decisions and especially Congress decisions, implying that the Supreme Court is acting against the people. Bush claims that *Boumediene v. Bush* overrules a Congress decision and thus the majority vote of the people's representatives. "We saw the power of judges in Boumediene v. Bush. There, a 5—4 majority rejected the carefully crafted procedures Congress established for detainees held at Guantanamo Bay in response to a prior Supreme Court decision. And for the first time, the Court awarded foreign terrorists held overseas legal rights previously reserved for American citizens." (Bush, Remarks to 2008–10–06: 1273).

Confronted with President-elect Barack Obama's criticism of Guantanamo damaging U.S. moral standing in the world, Bush denies the accusation and presents his own point of view:

> I strongly disagree with the assessment that our moral standing has been damaged. It may be damaged amongst some of the elite, but people still understand America stands for freedom, that America is a country that provides such great hope. [...] Now, I understand that Gitmo has created controversies. But when it came time for those countries that were criticizing America to take some of those detainees, they weren't willing to help out. And so, you know, I just disagree with the assessment [...]. (Bush, The President's 2009–01–12: 1559)

In his final press conference, the departing president takes stock, defending his policies and his detention program:

> And in terms of the decisions that I had made to protect the homeland, I wouldn't worry about popularity. What I would worry about is the Constitution of the United States and putting plans in place that makes it easier to find out what the enemy is thinking, because all these debates will matter not if there's another attack on the homeland. The question won't be, you know, were you critical of this plan or not. The question is going to be, why didn't you do something? Do you remember what it

> was like right after September the 11th around here? In press conferences and opinion pieces and in stories—that sometimes were news stories and sometimes opinion pieces—people were saying, 'How come they didn't see it? How come they didn't connect the dots?' Do you remember what the environment was like in Washington? I do. When people were hauled up in front of Congress, and Members of Congress were asking questions about, 'How come you didn't know this, that, or the other?' And then we start putting policy in place—legal policy in place—to connect the dots, and all of a sudden people were saying, 'How come you're connecting the dots?' [...] But I'm more concerned about the country and our—how people view the United States. They view us as strong, compassionate people who care deeply about the universality of freedom. (Bush, The President's 2009–01–12: 1559–1560)

Bush claims to sacrifice his own popularity for the gain in security. Again, Bush 'appeals to national values' like freedom and liberty and emphasizes his commitment to the constitution. 'Emphasizing national security,' he strongly defends his decisions. Also, Bush 'revokes national memory' by referring to the political situation right after 9/11. His statement underlines the need to close the information gap by engaging in an information-gathering detention program. The president here also repeats that the project of his two terms in office was to solve the problem of a failing intelligence apparatus and to establish a functioning information-gaining program to solve the security breach by gaining information to learn to know the enemy and find out his plans to prevent further attack. In his closing remarks, President Bush repeats his threat perception and remains focused on terrorism and attack prevention handing over to Obama: "The most urgent threat that he'll have to deal with, and other Presidents after him will have to deal with, is an attack on our homeland. You know, I wish I could report that's not the case, but there's still an enemy out there that would like to inflict damage on America, Americans. And that will be the major threat." (Bush, The President's 2009–01–12: 1554). The Supreme Court ruling seems like a reversal of the norm transformation and certainly counts as a setback in the Bush administration's executive efforts to regulate detainee rights. Considering the overall development throughout all stages, the ruling and thus demand for an adaptation of the *Military Commissions Act 2006* should be considered a feedback loop in the transformation of detention norms but does not constitute a complete reversal of the norm transformation process.

Section 2: January 20, 2009—June 11, 2009

When President Obama takes office on January 20, 2009, 245 detainees remain in Guantanamo. Up to this point, the Bush administration had released or transferred

533 prisoners (NYT Guantanamo Docket 2020[18], Amnesty 2013).[19] During the presidential run up in 2008, closing the camp had been a major campaign issue. After winning the 2008 presidential elections, Obama highly prioritizes the closure of Guantanamo.

On January 20, 2009, on his first day in office, shortly after his inauguration, Obama signs three executive orders to facilitate the closure of the camp within one year. The first, *Executive Order 13491 Ensuring Lawful Interrogation* (Obama 2009: EO 13491), revokes President Bush's 2007 *Executive Order 13440*[20], reinstituting the application of the *Geneva Conventions*, namely *Common Article 3*, as minimum standard in interrogations and detention. Obama thereby reestablishes U.S. commitment to *Common Article 3* and all national and international regulations concerning torture.[21] The EO further limits interrogation methods to *Army Field Manual 2–22.3*. Obama also orders the closure of CIA detention facilities and grants access to detention facilities and detainee information to the *Red Cross*. To determine further proceedings for the remaining prisoners, Obama establishes the *Special Interagency Task Forces* tasked with the evaluation of interrogation methods and possible transfer of detainees without violating international law. The second, *Executive Order 13492 Review and Disposition of Individuals Detained at the Guantánamo Bay Naval Base and Closure of Detention Facilities* (Obama 2009: EO13492), orders the review of detainees and closure of the Camp. Those detainees who had not been determined or treated as enemy combatants by the DoD become subject to review. The EO demands the closure

[18] The information cited here can be found on the website's subsection "Overview" available online: https://www.nytimes.com/ interactive/projects/guantanamo (access date: 23 September 2020).

[19] See website's subsection "Overview" available online: https://www.nytimes.com/interactive/projects/guantanamo (accessed 24 September 2020).

[20] Executive Order 13440 "Interpretation of the Geneva Conventions Common Article 3 as Applied to a Program of Detention and Interrogation Operated by the Central Intelligence Agency" determines "that members of al Qaeda, the Taliban, and associated forces are unlawful enemy combatants who are not entitled to the protections that the Third Geneva Convention provides to prisoners of war" (Bush 2007, Executive Order 13440: 40707). He further refers to the *2005 Detainee Treatment Act* and stresses the president's authority to "interpret the meaning and application of the Geneva Conventions" (Bush 2007, Executive Order 13440: 40707).

[21] According to Obama's Executive Order the U.S. detention policy shall comply with: "Federal torture statute, 18 U.S.C. 2340–2340 A, section 1003 of the Detainee Treatment Act of 2005, 42 U.S.C. 2000dd, the Convention Against Torture, Common Article 3, and other laws regulating the treatment and interrogation of individuals detained in any armed conflict" (Obama 2009: EO 13491: 4894).

of the Camp within one year and commands the release or transfer to the home country or third countries, or other U.S. detention facilities suiting the security needs for the remaining prisoners. Those detained are subject to immediate status review. The EO also puts a halt to military commissions. The third, *Executive Order 13493 Review of Detention Policy Options* (Obama 2009: EO 13493), further specifies the establishment of the *Special Interagency Task Force.*[22]

Throughout 2009, international criticism continues while the number of detainees in Guantanamo is reduced further, and Obama adheres to his plan. On February 23, 2009, Binyam Mohamed is transferred to the UK. On March 15, 2009, the ICRC issues a report on mistreatment of prisoners. On April 16, 2009, secret memoranda of the Department of Defense are released which cover the secret interrogation program of the CIA between 2002–2005. On May 5, 2009, Lakhdar Boumediene is transferred to France. On May 15, 2009, Obama announces to continue military tribunals in a changed form. On May 21, 2009, in a speech on national security Obama repeats his plans to close the detention facility. However, he does not succeed in changing detention law to end indefinite detention. On June 1, 2009, Mohammad Ahmed Abdullah Saleh a Hanashi dies at GTMO. On June 9, 2009, Ahmad Ghailani is tried on U.S. mainland in a federal trial. On June 11, 2009, Mohammed el Gharani is released, he had been 14 years old at the time of his capture.

Coming into office, Obama emphasizes his envisaged turn in security politics mainly concerning detention policies and the war on terror. Thus, in this first phase of Obama's presidency, the dominant topics are 'GTMO detainees' before 'war on terror,' 'detainee treatment/torture' and followed by 'rule of law,' 'presidential authority,' 'allies,' and 'military commission/military tribunals.' Dominant activities across all topics are 'emphasizing security,' 'explaining/ defending detainee treatment,' 'appealing to national values,' 'emphasizing rule of law,' and 'criticizing past actions' (see Fig. 5.6). Although the emphasis on security remains high, compared to Bush, Obama shows a turn in rhetoric. Setting the tone for a change in foreign and security politics, Obama uses 'emphasizing the rule of law' as a prerequisite for peace and security and thereby emphasizes truthfulness to core American values to restore Americas role and prestige in the world. This change in tone shows especially in Obama's interpretation of the constitutional presidential authority. Here the dominant activities are 'keeping secrets,' 'emphasizing security,' and 'transparency.' Moreover, his change in rhetoric shows concerning treatment/torture. Here the activities 'explaining/

[22] In the following also called: Guantanamo Review Task Force.

Codesystem	Guantanamo Bay detainees	treatment of prisoners/ torture	Military Commissions Act/ military tribunals	Geneva Convention	rule of law	constitutional presidential authority	war on terror	Usama bin Laden	allies	CIA program	intelligence	homeland security	SUMME
admitting defeat													
admonishing													
announcing/commenting new detention law	8		2				2						12
appealing to national values	8	6	1		3	2	12						32
applying new detention law	2		1										3
applying the law													
calling on Congress/working w Congress	3												3
characterizing the enemy							1						1
claiming presidential power	2	6				1	1						10
claiming pursuit to justice	6		3			1	1						11
commenting USSC/court decisions	3	1				1							5
committing to international law	1												1
criricizing democrats													
criticizing Congress							1						1
criticizing past actions	6	11	1		2								20
declaring a presidential order	4						1						5
denying/defending/offering alternative explanation		2	1										3
emphasizing accountability		1			1	2	1						5
emphasizing legality	1						1						2
emphasizing rule of law	11	3	1		1		3						19
emphasizing security	20	16			1	6	15	1					59
emphasizing transparency	2	2				4							8
explaining prosecution of detainee maltreatment		4			1								5
explaining security politics	2	3	1				10		4				20
explaning cooperation	12	1					2		6				21
explaning/defending detainee treatment	34	15	3				1	1					54
expressing gratitude	4								3				7
(re-)interpreting the law			1										1
keeping secrets	1	7				7							15
listing acomplishments	1						1						2
proposing legislation						2							2
referring to quasi-law													
reporting on war progress							1						1
revoking national memory	1				1		4						6
stressing newness of the war							1						1
SUMME	132	78	15		10	26	59	2	13				335

Fig. 5.6 Code Relations—Activities and Subject—Phase 5—Obama

defending detainee treatment,' 'emphasizing security,' 'criticizing past actions,' and 'keeping secrets' are dominant activity codes.

Concerning detention policies, releasing three executive orders related to detention policies on his first day in office clearly set the stage for a turn in detention policy towards closing Guantanamo definitively, for stopping the CIA program, and for fostering legal prosecution of the remaining detainees. While Obama also stresses ending indefinite detention, some of his actions continue a track started by the Bush administration, like the decrease in detainee numbers through transfers to countries of origin or third-party countries. By setting the timeframe to one year, Obama set a clear benchmark for achieving the goal to close the detention center.

Relating to the 'war on terror,' the president introduces major changes, aiming to end the wars in Iraq and Afghanistan, striving for troop withdrawal and towards a strategic shift from offensive war fighting to civil-military engagement. Dominant activities are 'emphasizing security,' 'appealing to national values,' 'revoking national memory,' and 'emphasizing rule of law.' Obama sets a different tone concerning the 'war on terror' by changing the strategic focus. Stressing the importance of diplomacy, Obama does also 'emphasize national security,' but he 'emphasizes national values' and the rule of law to achieve security. In this regard, he calls for a "new era of American leadership" (Obama, Remarks at 2009–01–22: 9). In his *Remarks at the State Department* he emphasizes "enduring values" as way towards national security:

> The world needs to understand that America will be unyielding in its defense of its security and relentless in its pursuit of those who would carry out terrorism or threaten the United States. And that's why, in this twilight struggle, we need a durable framework. The orders that I signed today should send an unmistakable signal that our actions in defense of liberty will be just as our cause, and that we the people will uphold our fundamental values as vigilantly as we protect our security. Once again, America's moral example must be the bedrock and the beacon of our global leadership. (Obama, Remarks at 2009–01–22: 9)

When security was emphasized by Bush, it was always separated from rule of law by a but. To the contrary, Obama connects security "and" values and rules of law. As he repeatedly states, the war on terror is a complex problem, which cannot be solved by the United States alone but must be solved with partners in a global effort. Nonetheless, he still sees the United States in a leading role, yet, in a leading role of a cooperative effort. Obama mainly focuses on diplomacy and shifts towards a military-civilian engagement for the military role. He speaks of collective security, regional partnerships, a military civilian program for

Afghanistan, and the long-term goal being retrieving troops. To Obama "security in the 21st century is shared", nevertheless, he emphasizes the U.S. commitment to lead (Obama, Remarks at 2009–01–22: 11). In April 2009, he lists his accomplishments in the strategic shift:

> I also campaigned on the promise that I would change the direction of our Nation's foreign policy, and we've begun to do that as well. We've begun to end the war in Iraq, and we forged with our NATO allies a new strategy to target Al Qaida in Afghanistan and Pakistan. We have rejected the false choice between our security and our ideals by closing the detention center at Guantanamo Bay and banning torture without exception. And we've renewed our diplomatic efforts to deal with challenges ranging from the global economic crisis to the spread of nuclear weapons. (Obama, The President's 2009–04–29: 584)

In Obama's rhetoric, Usama bin Laden is not the figure of national security to mobilize for a war on terror. In pursuing terrorism, Obama rather 'emphasizes national values' as a guarantee for national security. Obama critically reflects the decisions made with reference to the newness of the war on terror: "After 9/11, we knew that we had entered a new era; that enemies who did not abide by any law of war would present new challenges to our application of the law; that our Government would need new tools to protect the American people, and that these tools would have to allow us to prevent attacks instead of simply prosecuting those who tried to carry them out." (Obama, Remarks at 2009–05–21: 691). Although Obama agrees with the assessment that the war on terror poses a new, unprecedented conflict scenario that demands new strategies, he does not agree with the actions taken in response but criticizes past decisions:

> Unfortunately, faced with an uncertain threat, our Government made a series of hasty decisions. I believe that many of these decisions were motivated by a sincere desire to protect the American people. But I also believe that all too often, our Government made decisions based on fear rather than foresight; that all too often, our Government trimmed facts and evidence to fit ideological predispositions. Instead of strategically applying our power and our principles, too often we set those principles aside as luxuries that we could no longer afford. And during this season of fear, too many of us—Democrats and Republicans, politicians, journalists, and citizens—fell silent. In other words, we went off course. And this is not my assessment alone. It was an assessment that was shared by the American people, who nominated candidates for President from both major parties who, despite our many differences, called for a new approach, one that rejected torture and one that recognized the imperative of closing the prison at Guantanamo Bay. (Obama, Remarks at 2009–05–21: 691)

One of his main points of criticism is that national values and the adherence to the rule of law were sacrificed for national security. Although he criticizes past decisions, he also agrees with some of the assessments.

> Now let me be clear: We are indeed at war with Al Qaida and its affiliates. We do need to update our institutions to deal with this threat. But we must do so with an abiding confidence in the rule of law and due process, in checks and balances and accountability. For reasons that I will explain, the decisions that were made over the last 8 years established an ad hoc legal approach for fighting terrorism that was neither effective nor sustainable, a framework that failed to rely on our legal traditions and timetested institutions and that failed to use our values as a compass. And that's why I took several steps upon taking office to better protect the American people. (Obama, Remarks at 2009–05–21: 691)

Obama admits that strategic shifts are necessary to defeat Al Qaida. However, he proposes a different approach compared to Bush. Obama 'emphasizes the rule of law' and the constitutional principles. Obama 'criticizes the past decisions' which were not in accordance with the U.S. legal principles and system. Therefore, he proposes several measures, which he lists as his accomplishments:

> First, I banned the use of so-called enhanced interrogation techniques by the United States of America. Now, I know some have argued that brutal methods like waterboarding were necessary to keep us safe. I could not disagree more. As Commander in Chief, I see the intelligence; I bear the responsibility for keeping this country safe. And I categorically reject the assertion that these are the most effective means of interrogation. What's more, they undermine the rule of law. They alienate us in the world. They serve as a recruitment tool for terrorists and increase the will of our enemies to fight us, while decreasing the will of others to work with America. They risk the lives of our troops by making it less likely that others will surrender to them in battle and more likely that Americans will be mistreated if they are captured. In short, they did not advance our war and counterterrorism efforts; they undermined them. And that is why I ended them once and for all. (Obama, Remarks at 2009–05–21: 691–692)

By introducing these measures, Obama questions main pillars of the Bush administration's defense strategy. One main turn Obama takes concerns interrogations. Whereas Bush emphasized the need for the CIA interrogation program as a guarantee for national security, Obama strongly opposes and declares enhanced interrogation methods illegal. He also emphasizes that this form of interrogation and detainee treatment in his opinion is a threat to national security rather than a guarantee.

In this phase, Obama mentions GTMO detainees mainly with reference to the first three executive orders he signs to set his plan in motion to close the detention center and change detainee treatment. Here the dominant activities are 'explaining/defending detainee treatment,' 'emphasizing security,' 'emphasizing rule of law,' 'explaining cooperation,' 'appealing to national values,' 'criticizing past actions,' 'pursuit to justice,' and 'announcing new detention law.'

On May 15, 2009, Obama makes a statement on military commissions. The activities used in this statement are 'appealing to national values,' 'claiming pursuit to justice,' 'denying/defending/offering alternative explanations,' 'explaining security politics,' and 'interpreting the law.' In his statement, Obama reminds the audience of the historical meaning of military commissions in the United States and admits to the fitness of these tribunals "for trying enemies who violate the laws of war, provided that they are properly structured and administered" (Obama, Statement on 2009–05–15: 655). He also explains his past support for both military commissions and Article III courts in prosecuting terrorists, while criticizing past decisions: "In 2006, I voted in favor of the use of military commissions. But I objected strongly to the Military Commissions Act that was drafted by the Bush administration and passed by Congress because it failed to establish a legitimate legal framework and undermined our capability to ensure swift and certain justice against those detainees that we were holding at the time." (Obama, Statement on 2009–05–15: 655). Obama further criticizes the Bush administration for inefficiency in trying GTMO detainees. Furthermore, the president announces changes to the procedures in military commissions explaining detainee treatment and emphasizing the rule of law:

> The rule changes will ensure that: First, statements that have been obtained from detainees using cruel, inhuman, and degrading interrogation methods will no longer be admitted as evidence at trial; second, the use of hearsay will be limited, so that the burden will no longer be on the party who objects to hearsay to disprove its reliability; third, the accused will have greater latitude in selecting their counsel; fourth, basic protections will be provided for those who refuse to testify; and fifth, military commission judges may establish the jurisdiction of their own courts. These reforms will begin to restore the commissions as a legitimate forum for prosecution, while bringing them in line with the rule of law. (Obama, Statement on 2009–05–15: 655)

Concluding, Obama announces to continue working with Congress to make terrorist prosecution more effective and use federal courts. He continues to emphasize security and the rule of law (Obama, Statement on 2009–05–15: 655).

In a speech, which Obama holds a speech on May 21, 2009, he restates his will to close GTMO. He criticizes the Bush administration for failing to achieve justice with military commissions. Obama argues that in seven years only three trials were held. He also defends his repatriation plans by referring to the fact that two thirds of the prisoners had already been released by the Bush administration. While Obama stresses his determination to close GTMO, he also expresses his awareness for the problems of repatriation due to international resistance to take in former detainees and for staying in accordance with the *Torture Convention.* He also repeats that GTMO give the United States a bad reputation and criticizes past decisions:

> There is also no question that Guantanamo set back the moral authority that is America's strongest currency in the world. Instead of building a durable framework for the struggle against Al Qaida that drew upon our deeply held values and traditions, our Government was defending positions that undermined the rule of law. In fact, part of the rationale for establishing Guantanamo in the first place was the misplaced notion that a prison there would be beyond the law, a proposition that the Supreme Court soundly rejected. Meanwhile, instead of serving as a tool to counter terrorism, Guantanamo became a symbol that helped Al Qaida recruit terrorists to its cause. Indeed, the existence of Guantanamo likely created more terrorists around the world than it ever detained. (Obama, Remarks at 2009–05–21: 692)

Obama further explains his plan to close GTMO and his plan for detainee treatment—he wants to try GTMO detainees before U.S. federal courts for violations of U.S. law in an effort to reintegrate terrorist prosecution into the U.S. legal system.

> First, whenever feasible, we will try those who have violated American criminal laws in Federal courts, courts provided for by the United States Constitution. Some have derided our Federal courts as incapable of handling the trials of terrorists. They are wrong. Our courts and our juries, our citizens, are tough enough to convict terrorists. The record makes that clear. Ramzi Yousef tried to blow up the World Trade Center. He was convicted in our courts and is serving a life sentence in U.S. prisons. Zacarias Moussaoui has been identified as the 20th 9/11 hijacker. He was convicted in our courts, and he too is serving a life sentence in prison. If we can try those terrorists in our courts and hold them in our prisons, then we can do the same with detainees from Guantanamo. (Obama, Remarks at 20005–21: 693)

Obama stresses that U.S. courts are fit to prosecute terrorists and tries to restore trust in the judicial system, by citing past court decisions. Also, he proposes to prosecute and detain GTMO detainees on U.S. mainland.

Overall, Obama keeps emphasizing that national security is the priority and that Al Qaida must be fought but also stresses the importance of abiding by the rule of law. Obama 'emphasizes national security' which also entails preventing future attacks: "Let me repeat: I am not going to release individuals who endanger the American people. Al Qaida terrorists and their affiliates are at war with the United States, and those that we capture, like other prisoners of war, must be prevented from attacking us again." (Obama, Remarks at 2009–05–21: 694–695). However, having said that, he draws conclusions for the defense strategy concerning detention policies:

> Now, having said that, we must recognize that these detention policies cannot be unbounded; they can't be based simply on what I or the executive branch decide alone. And that's why my administration has begun to reshape the standards that apply to ensure that they are in line with the rule of law. We must have clear, defensible, and lawful standards for those who fall into this category. We must have fair procedures so that we don't make mistakes. We must have a thorough process of periodic review so that any prolonged detention is carefully evaluated and justified. (Obama, Remarks at 2009–05–21: 694–695)

As argued here, Obama announces to determine the rules for detention of terrorists in writing. This can be read as an effort to reverse the decision-making of the Bush administration where decisions on detainee treatment were often reserved for the president or referred to the Department of Defense.

> Even as we clean up the mess at Guantanamo, we will constantly reevaluate our approach, subject our decisions to review from other branches of Government as well as the public. We seek the strongest and most sustainable legal framework for addressing these issues in the long term, not to serve immediate politics, but to do what's right over the long term. By doing that, we can leave behind a legacy that outlasts my administration, my Presidency, that endures for the next President and the President after that, a legacy that protects the American people and enjoys a broad legitimacy at home and abroad. (Obama, Remarks at 2009–05–21: 697)

Although Obama strengthens his promise to close GTMO, he emphasizes that he does not want to decide foreign policy by presidential order, which he criticized Bush for, but wants to work with Congress. At the time, closing Guantanamo was not controversial but a bipartisan agreement, so Obama could expect support from Congress on the issue.

Yet, in this speech, Obama includes the option of indefinite detention without trial for security reasons:

> Now, finally, there remains the question of detainees at Guantanamo who cannot be prosecuted yet who pose a clear danger to the American people. And I have to be honest here: This is the toughest single issue that we will face. We're going to exhaust every avenue that we have to prosecute those at Guantanamo who pose a danger to our country. But even when this process is complete, there may be a number of people who cannot be prosecuted for past crimes, in some cases because evidence may

> be tainted, but who, nonetheless, pose a threat to the security of the United States. Examples of that threat include people who've received extensive explosives training at Al Qaida training camps, or commanded Taliban troops in battle, or expressed their allegiance to Usama bin Laden, or otherwise made it clear that they want to kill Americans. These are people who, in effect, remain at war with the United States. (Obama, Remarks at 2009–05–21: 694)

Concluding this phase regarding norm transformation, Obama not only ordered to close Guantanamo but also vowed to reestablish the rule of law in detainee treatment when he took office, emphasizing the importance of the *Geneva Conventions* in the war on terror. However, although the steps taken early in the Obama administration show commitment to the rule of law and signal turnback in the norm transformation, by the end of this phase, Obama's actions indicate that some developments towards violence-enabling norms during the Bush administration are irreversible. As the following phase shows, Obama will not only fail to close GTMO but also ends up institutionalizing a transformed detention law.

5.6 Phase 6: Institutionalization of Indefinite Detention

In Phase 6, despite ongoing efforts to close GTMO and first signs to reverse the norm transformation in detention law in Phase 5, Obama fails to realize his plans but rather progressively contributes to the de facto and de jure institutionalization of the new detention law. In July 2009, Obama's plans to close Guantanamo are first delayed and finally, in November 2009, publicly dismissed. However, detainee trials continue in the second half of 2009. Furthermore, on October 28, 2009, Obama signs the *Military Commissions Act 2009*, which amends the *MCA 2006* signed by Bush. The amendment emphasizes the U.S. commitment to the *Geneva Conventions*. One of the major changes is that the term *unlawful enemy combatant*, which had been controversial, is replaced with the term *unprivileged enemy belligerent* in opposition to *privileged belligerents* (the latter being covered by the *Geneva Conventions* according to the *MCA 2009*). With this wording the Obama administration emphasizes commitment to international law but also continues to legalize a status-definition outside the international legal provisions, issuing *unprivileged belligerents* to trial in military commissions. On November 13, 2009, Attorney General, Eric Holder, announces that five prisoners connected to 9/11 will be tried in the United States. The same prisoners had been tried by a military commission under Bush in 2008. However, Obama's plans to transfer detainees to a high security prison in Illinois on U.S. mainland, are blocked by Congress on December 15, 2009.

In 2010, Obama's deadline officially expires, and the institutionalization of indefinite detention further progresses. On January 22, 2010, the Department of Justice finds that 50 detainees remain indefinitely in custody without charges or trial, as reported by the *Guantanamo Review Committee*. On January 25, 2010, due to the deteriorating security situation, detainee transfers to Yemen are officially put on hold by the White House in compliance with the *Torture Convention*. In April 2010, the Pentagon releases new rules for military commissions, which include the right to indefinitely detain individuals despite acquittal. This decision further institutionalizes the new detention law. On December 22, 2010, Congress passes a bill limiting the president's capability to try GTMO detainees in U.S. civil courts. Obama signs it into law, thus, supporting legislation which continues and institutionalizes indefinite detention and further limits the options for detainee releases. Meanwhile indefinite detention is further reduced by legal processing of detainees and releases. In July 2010, Ibrahim al-Qosi pleads guilty and is sentenced to 14 years of prison. In October 2010, Omar Khadr pleads guilty, who had been 15 years old at his capture in Afghanistan in July 2002. He is sentenced to 40 years in prison, the verdict is shortened to eight years, one in U.S. captivity followed by a transfer to Canada in September 2012. On November 9, 2010, the Department of Justice declares that no one will be charged for destroying the video tapes on interrogation, thus limiting the prospects for prosecution of detainee maltreatment and torture during interrogations.

In 2011, legislation passed through Congress which further institutionalizes indefinite detention and prevents the closure of Guantanamo. On January 7, 2011, the *Ike Skelton National Defense Authorization Act for Fiscal Year 2011* is signed by Obama (Obama, Statement on 2011–01–07). Passages in the bill prevent closing Guantanamo and prison transfers. On March 7, 2011, Obama issues *Executive Order 13567* allowing military trials at GTMO. On April 4, 2011, Attorney General, Eric Holder, announces that the five detainees connected to 9/11 will be tried before a military commission revising the decision to try them before a U.S. court. On April 20, 2011, charges against Abd al Rahim are announced before a military commission, who is further prosecuted in September and November 2011. Shortly after, on May 31, 2011, the military commission on the five detainees connected to 9/11 begins. The Obama administration asks for the death penalty. In December 2011, Obama does not veto the *2012 National Defense Bill* which allows for the possibility of indefinite detention without charges and further expands the ban on prisoner transfers. However, Obama strongly criticizes the provisions included in the bill on detainee rights and opposes indefinite detention (Obama,

Statement on 2011–12–31: 1573–1574). On June 11, 2012, the Supreme Court denies the appeals of seven detainees on *habeas corpus*. With the decision to deny *habeas* petitions of seven GTMO detainees, the Supreme Court approves the decisions of the District and Appeals Courts and accepts the legislation of the Bush administration which legalizes indefinite detention.

Indefinite detention continues throughout Obama's first and second term in office, as closing GTMO remains an open conflict between the president and Congress. Several detainees die, some are convicted, or released. On January 6, 2011, Saeed Farhi bin Mohammed, who had been detained since 2002, is transferred to Algeria against his will because he feared persecution. His detention had been declared illegal by a U.S. court in 2009. On February 18, 2011, Sudanese Noor Uthman Muhammed is sentenced to 14 years of prison after pleading guilty before a military commission. In exchange for his plea and cooperation in other cases he was released after 34 months. Also, secrecy and detainee rights in captivity remain issues in public debate, as *WikiLeaks* releases material on the detainees on April 24, 2011 (WikiLeaks 2011). In February 2011, two detainees die, another commits suicide in May, yet another dies in September 2011.

On April 19, 2012, the DoD announces the release of two Uiguri prisoners, Ahmed Mohamed and Abdul Razek, and their transfer to El Salvador. Although they had been cleared of charges, the detainees had waited for transfer, as no country would take them in, and they could not return to China because they feared persecution. In September 2012, another prisoner dies. By December 2012, 166 detainees remain in captivity in Guantanamo. The number is further reduced by several releases. Another hunger strike starts in March 2013, and the military starts force-feeding the detainees. On July 5, 2014, Guantanamo detainee lawyers file a motion to grant inmates religious rights and attain communal prayers. On September 26, 2015, UK resident Shaker Aamer is released from Guantanamo. Yet, on February 23, 2016, the Obama administration issues a four-part plan to close Guantanamo to Congress (Obama, Remarks on 2016–02–23). In 2016, ten Yemini detainees are released to Oman, nine detainees from Yemen are released to Saudi Arabia, and 15 detainees are released to the United Arab Emirates.

In Phase 6, the topics 'war on terror' and 'GTMO detainees' are trending before 'allies' and followed by 'constitutional authority,' 'rule of law,' 'bin Laden,' 'homeland security,' '*Geneva Conventions*,' 'detainee treatment/torture,' 'surveillance,' and, finally, 'military tribunals.' Overall, the 'war on terror' remains the dominant topic, before 'GTMO detainees' and followed by 'allies,' 'homeland security' and 'rule of law.' Concerning 'GTMO detainees,' Obama's focus is clearly on closing the detention facility and thus finding solutions for

Codesystem	Guantanamo Bay detainees	treatment of prisoners/ torture	Military Commissions Act/ military tribunals	Geneva Convention	rule of law	constitutional presidential authority	war on terror	Usama bin Laden	allies	CIA program	intelligence	homeland security	SUMME
admitting defeat	1											2	3
admonishing	2												2
announcing/commenting new detention law	5	2				3	5						15
appealing to national values	39	1			6		30	1	5		1	1	84
applying new detention law	8						21						29
applying the law	2						15						17
calling on Congress/working w Congress	30										1		31
characterizing the enemy	3			1	1		14	1				2	22
claiming presidential power	16				2	5	9						32
claiming pursuit to justice	23	2	1		1			1					28
commenting USSC/court decisions													
committing to international law	1			4			1						6
criricizing democrats													
criticizing Congress	42					4	4						50
criticizing past actions	1												1
declaring a presidential order		2											2
denying/defending/offering alternative explanation	2						1						3
emphasizing accountability						2	1						3
emphasizing legality	5										1		6
emphasizing rule of law	16	1		1	2		9		1				30
emphasizing security	70		1		3	1	121	5	8			6	215
emphasizing transparency	1					2							3
explaining prosecution of detainee maltreatment			1										1
explaining security politics	18			1	2		117	3	7			11	159
explaning cooperation	9						51		17			4	81
explaning/defending detainee treatment	104		1	1			24						130
expressing gratitude	4				1		1		3				9
(re-)interpreting the law													
keeping secrets	4						12						16
listing acomplishments	1				1		6	1					9
proposing legislation													
referring to quasi-law													
reporting on war progress	7						46	1				1	55
revoking national memory	9				2		14	1				1	27
stressing newness of the war							2						2
SUMME	423	8	4	8	21	17	504	14	41		3	28	1071

Fig. 5.7 Code Relations—Activities and Subject—Phase 6

prosecution and repatriation. Other issues regarding detainee treatment are subordinate to this foreign and security political goal of closing GTMO. Dominant activities across all topics are 'emphasizing security,' 'explaining security politics,' 'explaining,' 'defending detainee treatment,' 'explaining cooperation,' and 'appealing to national values' (see Fig. 5.7).

Evaluating Phase 6 by activities, speeches on 'GTMO detainees' are dominated by 'explaining/defending detainee treatment,' 'emphasizing security,' 'criticizing Congress,' 'appealing to national values,' 'calling on Congress,' and 'claiming pursuit to justice.' Throughout his presidency Obama repeats his message that national security is his priority including fighting terrorism which he sees as a continuous threat to the United States. Despite the terrorist threat Obama emphasizes the need to uphold the commitment to the rule of law. Politically, he continues to oppose to keeping Guantanamo open, which becomes a challenge, especially after terrorist attacks like the attacks on Christmas day 2009 (see speech Obama, Remarks Following 2010–01–05). Despite political resistance building up during 2010, Obama stays the course of his argument: "There's been no bigger propaganda weapon for many of these extremists than pointing to Guantanamo and saying that we don't live up to our own ideals. And that's something that I strongly believe we have to resist, even if it has some costs to it and even if it's not always the most politically popular thing to do." (Obama, Question and 2010–02–01: 128).

According to Obama, Guantanamo is an obstacle and a potential to increase terrorist threats to America.

Closing GTMO and ending indefinite detention become increasingly difficult, for political and practical reasons. Politically, the majorities shift in Congress during Obama's first term in office, closing GTMO is no longer a bipartisan issue. Practically, the Obama administration faces repatriation issues, which make detainee transfers more difficult. The biggest obstacle becomes resistance forming in Congress to allow detainee transfers for prolonged detainment to detention facilities in the United States. On the one hand, Obama works with the existing standards of the new detention law, on the other hand, he runs into problems concerning *due process* based on the evidence gathering, captivation, and legal proceedings in the past. One of the big problems for *due process* remains the quality of the evidence:

> One of the toughest problems is what to do with people that we know are dangerous, that we know are—have engaged in terrorist activity, are proclaimed enemies of the United States, but because of the manner in which they were originally captured, the circumstances right after 9/11 in which they are interrogated, it becomes difficult to

> try them, whether in a Article III court or in a military commission. Releasing them at this stage could potentially create greater danger for the American people. And so how do we manage that? And that's what this team has been looking at. Are there ways for us to make sure these folks have lawyers, to make sure that these folks have the opportunity to challenge their detention, but at the same time, making sure that we are not simply releasing folks who could do us grievous harm and have shown a capacity and willingness to engage in brutal attacks in the past? (Obama, The President's 2010–12–22: 1947)

While Obama stresses following the rule of law, he also includes the possibility of prolonged detention for security reasons, thus contributing to the norm transformation towards violence-enabling norms and its institutionalization.

The conflict over GTMO detainees increases in 2011, as Congress starts putting budget restrictions on detainee transfers, severely limiting the president's capability to proceed with repatriation. One of the main issues is the *Executive Order 13567* of Obama which allows detainee transfers to a detention facility on U.S. mainland. Posing budget restrictions and reporting duties, Congress limits Obama's capabilities to transfer detainees to the U.S. mainland.

Congress keeps limiting Obama's powers in terms of detention policy and detainee treatment. With reference to the deteriorating economic situation, Obama criticizes Congress. He argues that GTMO is too expensive, referring to the millions in spending on detention abroad as compared to lower costs that detention in U.S. maximum security facilities would be. "Well, I think it is critical for us to understand that Guantanamo is not necessary to keep America safe. It is expensive. It is inefficient. It hurts us in terms of our international standing. It lessens cooperation with our allies on counterterrorism efforts. It is a recruitment tool for extremists. It needs to be closed." (Obama, The President's 2013–04–30: 353). Obama keeps trying to disengage national security from keeping Guantanamo running. While emphasizing security, he lists the multiple disadvantages in terms of national financial and budgetary issues, national security, and international cooperation, and reaffirms his demand to close the detention camp. Obama grows increasingly frustrated with Congress restricting the president in following up on his plan to close GTMO while the situation at the camp remains tense. When asked about force-feeding of prisoners, Obama replies:

> I don't want these individuals to die. Obviously, the Pentagon is trying to manage the situation as best as they can. But I think all of us should reflect on why exactly are we doing this? Why are we doing this? I mean, we've got a whole bunch of individuals who have been tried who are currently in maximum security prisons around the country. Nothing's happened to them. Justice has been served. It's been done in a way that's consistent with our Constitution, consistent with due process, consistent with

> rule of law, consistent with our traditions. […] So we can handle this. (Obama, The President's 2013–04–30: 354)

While showing sympathy for the traumatic experience of 9/11 and showing empathy for reactions to the terrorist attacks, Obama continues to criticize Congress for preventing detainee prosecution on U.S. mainland, stressing the severity of the problem.

> And I understand that in the immediate aftermath of 9/11, with the traumas that had taken place, why, for a lot of Americans, the notion was somehow that we had to create a special facility like Guantanamo and we couldn't handle this in a normal, conventional fashion. I understand that reaction. But we're now over a decade out. We should be wiser. We should have more experience in how we prosecute terrorists. And this is a lingering problem that is not going to get better. It's going to get worse. It's going to fester. And so I'm going to, as I said before, examine every option that we have administratively to try to deal with this issue, but ultimately, we're also going to need some help from Congress, and I'm going to ask some folks over there who care about fighting terrorism, but also care about who we are as a people to step up and help me on it. (Obama, The President's 2013–04–30: 354)

However, the conflict with Congress keeps building up, especially with budged discussions tightening in 2015. Obama continues to repeat his intention to work with Congress to shut down Guantanamo for the sake of security by emphasizing the consequences of GTMO.

> But I think we can make a very strong argument that it doesn't make sense for us to be spending an extra $100 million, $200 million, $300 million, $500 million, a billion dollars, to have a secure setting for 50, 60, 70 people. And we will wait until Congress has definitively said no to a well-thought-out plan with numbers attached to it before we say anything definitive about my executive authority here. I think it's far preferable if I can get stuff done with Congress. (Obama, The President's 2015–12–18: 1592–1593)

Also, Obama keeps emphasizing his intention to work with Congress. He stresses that he wants to propose a plan for closing GTMO to which Congress can agree, instead of bypassing Congress with executive orders. He also repeats one of his main arguments, that GTMO is a liability to national security: "We know that. We see the Internet traffic. We see how Guantanamo has been used to create this mythology that America is at war with Islam. And for us to close it is part of our counterterrorism strategy that is supported by our military, our diplomatic, and our intelligence teams." (Obama, The President's 2015–12–18:1593).

On February 23, 2016, Obama gives *Remarks on Closing the Detention Facilities at the United States Naval Base Guantanamo Bay, Cuba,* in which he reminds the audience that by the time he took office closing GTMO was a bipartisan issue even supported by President Bush. He summarizes efforts to close the camp and points to problems in cooperation with Congress. He reaffirms his appeal to Congress to close the detention center after seven years of trying.

> When I first ran for President, it was widely recognized that this facility needed to close. This was not just my opinion. This was not some radical, far-left view. There was bipartisan support to close it. My predecessor, President Bush, to his credit, said he wanted to close it. It was one of the few things that I and my Republican opponent, Senator John McCain, agreed on. And so, in one of my first acts as President, I took action to begin closing it. And because we had bipartisan support, I wanted to make sure that we did it right. I indicated that we would need to take our time to do it in a systematic way and that we had examined all the options. And unfortunately, during that period where we were putting the pieces in place to close it, what had previously been bipartisan support suddenly became a partisan issue. Suddenly, many who previously had said it should be closed backed off because they were worried about the politics. The public was scared into thinking that, well, if we close it, somehow, we'll be less safe. And since that time, Congress has repeatedly imposed restrictions aimed at preventing us from closing this facility. (Obama, Remarks on 2016–02–23: 181)

Finally, in September 2016 Obama admits that he could not close Guantanamo and thus end indefinite detention. Nevertheless, he lists his accomplishments as he succeeded in reducing prisoner count:

> With respect to Guantanamo, it is true that I have not been able to close the darn thing—[laughter]—because of the congressional restrictions that have been placed on us. What is also true is, we have greatly reduced the population. You now have significantly less than a hundred people there. There are some additional transfers that may be taking place over the next 2 months. There is a group of very dangerous people that we have strong evidence of having been guilty of committing terrorist acts against the United States. But because of the nature of the evidence—in some cases, that evidence being compromised—it's very difficult to put them before a typical Article III court. And that group has always been the biggest challenge for us. My strong belief and preference is that we would be much better off closing Gitmo, moving them to a different facility that was clearly governed by U.S. jurisdiction. We'd do it a lot cheaper and just as safely. (Obama, The President's 2016–11–14: 1516)

Up to the end of Obama's presidency, he repeats his position to close the camp.

> Congress disagrees with me, and I gather that the President-elect does as well. We will continue to explore options for doing that. But keep in mind that it's not just a

> matter of what I'm willing to do. One of the things you discover about being President is that there are all these rules and norms and laws and you've got to pay attention to them. And the people who work for you are also subject to those rules and norms. And that's a piece of advice that I gave to the incoming President. (Obama, The President's 2016–11–14: 1516)

Concerning the 'war on terror,' the dominant activities are 'emphasizing security,' 'explaining security politics,' 'explaining cooperation,' 'reporting on war progress,' 'appealing to national values,' and 'explaining/defending detainee treatment.' 'Characterizing the enemy' is an activity Obama mainly uses in the 'war on terror,' but less when talking about 'GTMO detainees.' 'Keeping secrets' mainly occurs regarding the topics 'GTMO detainees' and 'war on terror.' While closing GTMO dominates Obama's rhetoric concerning indefinite detention, legal matters are subordinate to the security function of ending detention in Guantanamo.

The investigation period finishes with the end of Obama's second term in office before the inauguration of Donald Trump. About 40 detainees remain in indefinite custody at that point of time. However, the detention center remains contested. Indefinite detention of individuals not citizen to the United States at Guantanamo remains legal on the grounds of U.S. law. Under Obama the security political discourse regarding detainee rights mainly focused on closing GTMO, ending torture and other forms of maltreatment, and strengthening the rule of law. While Obama failed to close Guantanamo due to resistance in Congress, he managed to reverse violence-enabling developments in the transformation of detainee rights. However, he was not able to reverse the entire process. Rather, the detention law put in place by Bush in part continued in use and in part amended, still including the possibility of indefinite detention without charges or trial, thus transformed.

6 Towards a Practice of Legitimation

The presidents adapt their legitimation strategies with upcoming security situations, changes in the security environment, and the progressing norm transformation process. As the evaluation of legalization actions and justificatory rhetorical activities in Chap. 5 shows, legitimacy-seeking activities vary to a certain degree in each phase. By analyzing the phases, I reconstructed how indefinite detention was planned and prepared for, how it was implemented, which legal conflicts arose, and how finally indefinite detention was formally legalized in a new detention law. Furthermore, I described how the new detention law was further institutionalized even though political activities worked towards the closure of the detention camp under late Bush and during the Obama presidency.

This reconstruction of the norm-transforming activities builds the ground for reconstructing the presidents' role in the norm transformation and for further analyzing practices—reoccurring actions, routines, and repeated patterns—of formal legalization and rhetorical justification that constitute legitimation practices. In the following, I evaluate the presidents' commonalities and differences with regard to their approaches to legalization and justification of transformed detention law. While both presidents are known for their different approaches to foreign policy, the analysis also shows that they shared common ground, especially regarding the role of the presidency. Although some formal aspects predict the role, the presidents have room to shape their individual foreign policy style and strategy in justificatory rhetoric. Furthermore, the evaluation displays which topics were relevant for the presidents—either set by them in person or confronted with by the media. In addition to subject setting and framing, which are already strong

Supplementary Information The online version contains supplementary material available at https://doi.org/10.1007/978-3-658-49121-5_6.

D. Hühnert-Hugendubel, *Between Rules of War and Rule of Law*,
https://doi.org/10.1007/978-3-658-49121-5_6

legitimation activities, I focus on rhetorical activities in the single subject codes to display how both presidents framed issues and built their legitimacy-seeking arguments.

6.1 Role Interpretation and Leadership Style

The first conceptual building block for legitimation is a powerful actor's decision on role interpretation and leadership style. This sets the tone for the strategic direction of security policies regarding the use of power, cooperation style, and mindsets in terms of core values, beliefs, and ideas and functions as basis for decision making. Based on the evaluation of the topics and rhetorical activities, differences in role interpretation and leadership style of both presidents become apparent. Bush and Obama share some similarities in role interpretation and restrictions qua office, and both use executive power to foster legalization processes. However, the presidents act differently due to varying leadership styles and political mindsets concerning values, beliefs, and ideas which influence their positions in legal matters of detention policies. These commonalities and differences are visible reviewing the presidents' security political leadership in the capacity of commander in chief, the interpretation of the executive role in legalization processes, and the positioning in the constitutional system, as I discuss in more detail in the following.

Commander in Chief Role

Concerning presidential duties as commander in chief in the war on terror, both presidents emphasize their willingness to take leadership. Both stress national security as top priority and their commitment to U.S. security personnel. In this capacity the presidents appeal to national values and use shared history to illustrate the envisaged security political goals. Both presidents show great respect for the military, in terms of care and respect for veterans, commitment to active forces, responsibility for budgetary questions, and care and empathy for military families. Mainly, the responsibility as commander in chief shows in emphasizing the responsibility to protect the nation from terrorist threats by stressing national security as top priority and emphasizing the U.S. role in the world.

Although both accentuate their duties as commander in chief, Bush and Obama differ greatly on positions regarding how to fight terrorism, and on how the United States should exercise a global leadership role. Bush emphasizes the rule of force and U.S. global leadership in his security political strategy in the war on terror. According to Bush, the fight against terrorism is the main security political challenge for him as commander in chief. Security is to be achieved with force as a necessary means to fight terrorism. Security in terms of winning the war against terror is an American responsibility and to be achieved under American leadership with the help of allies. Guantanamo is a necessary facility to hold terrorists, who were withdrawn from the battlefield. According to Bush, GTMO is thus a guarantee for security for two reasons. For one, detaining terrorists withdraws them from activity, and for another, terrorists are a valuable source for information in terrorism prevention.

Obama in contrast emphasizes the rule of law and cooperation in his approach to foreign and security politics in the war on terror. He underlines U.S. responsibility to assume a global leadership role while defining security as a shared burden. Obama stresses diplomacy as a main means to a cooperative security effort fighting terrorism and reduces active combat engagement of U.S. troops. Fundamentally disagreeing with his predecessor, Obama regards GTMO as a security liability and cause for damage to the U.S. reputation. Gaining information from GTMO detainees through interrogation is not a means to prevent terrorist attacks but is used as a tool by terrorists for mobilization against the United States. Hence, Obama proposes the return to the rule of law, to process GTMO detainees, and eventually close the facility (Obama, Remarks at 2009-05-21: 692).

Executive Role and Cooperation with Institutions in Realizing Detention Policy
Concerning the interpretation of the executive role in legalization processes, Bush and Obama show respect for the constitution and the separation of powers as constitutional principle and work with the other branches of government to achieve political goals. Although both presidents emphasize security, they take different stances on how to reach security goals within the legal framework and changing the legal framework. Nevertheless, working on detention policies within the constitutional confinement of the presidency causes conflicts with Congress and the Supreme Court for both presidents.

Bush uses the executive powers available to him as a wartime president in a state of emergency. Based on the AUMF, Bush interprets his executive powers in terms of having decision-making prerogatives concerning detainee rights and the use of force. He emphasizes his leadership in setting the tone in the war on terror and determining detention policies without consulting Congress. Bush's far-reaching empowerment on the use of force and application of violence raised dispute over the wartime privileges of the president and legal competences in detainee rights as pushing constitutional boundaries of the presidency.

More than once Bush is forced by the Supreme Court to engage in formal legalization processes with Congress on detainee rights. For example, in 2004, the Supreme Court established the right of *habeas corpus* for the Guantanamo prisoners in *Rasul v. Bush* and *Hamdi v. Rumsfeld* (Greenberg et al. 2008). Such court rulings in favor of or against the Bush administration's actions forced the administration to engage in further formal legal steps, thus, contributing to the norm transformation and its institutionalization. So, Congress had to work out legislative groundwork for detainee treatment which forwarded the norm transformation towards violence-enabling norms. The results of this process, namely the *2005 Detainee Treatment Act* and the *2006 Military Commissions Act* fulfill the court's demand but remain open to interpretation concerning both detainee treatment and detainee rights.

However, Bush continues to claim his leadership role throughout his presidency as he emphasizes that he is in control over the legislative processes, that he has a strong opinion on legal decisions, and that he does not regret or question past decisions. Moreover, Bush criticizes the Supreme Court for making law, instead of ruling on the use of the law. Despite the conflicts with the court, Bush shows respect for the constitutional system and its institutions, accepting the role of the judiciary and legislation in legal matters. For instance, when the Supreme Court ordered the Bush administration to install a legal process for the prisoners at Guantanamo to challenge their detention, Bush emphasized his role in proposing legislation and called on Congress to make the right decision (Bush, Remarks on 2006-09-06: 1617).

While Bush faces several Supreme Court rulings which question his legal choices concerning detainee treatment, Obama faces conflicts with a divided Congress and shifting majorities finally causing the closure of Guantanamo to fail. Obama's overall approach in changing detention law is more oriented towards cooperation with other branches of government, rather than executive dominance in decision-making processes. Obama emphasizes rule of law, separation of powers, and the will of the people represented in Congress to work out legal issues. Although Obama uses executive orders to express his political goals in detention policies, he emphasizes his willingness to work with Congress even on controversial questions and in complicated matters of detention policies. Furthermore, he criticizes the Bush administration for reserving so many detention-related decisions for the executive and rather emphasizes the rule of law (as opposed to the rule of the executive) and works towards a more substantial regulatory framework. Although his presidential terms are marked by open conflict with a Republican dominated Congress, he keeps emphasizing that he will refrain from using executive orders in favor of working out bipartisan compromises. However, despite

Obama's cooperative efforts, he ends up in a deadlock with Congress. Eventually, Congress prevents the president from accessing funds to transfer remaining detainees to high security detention facilities on U.S. mainland, thus effectively blocking the closure of Guantanamo and continuing indefinite detention.

Mindsets—Values, Beliefs, and Ideas

Reviewing the positions and role interpretations of Bush and Obama, the presidents differ in their political mindsets concerning ideas, beliefs, and values and thus propose different strategies to achieve goals in detention policies during the war on terror. Bush relies on war time privileges and uses executive power to realize policies favoring a rule of force with military deployment in the war on terror. Achieving justice is a military task in Bush's anti-terror strategy and detention serves security political goals. On the contrary, Obama follows a rule of law approach favoring conflict settlement and cooperative efforts over the show of force and application of violence. Achieving justice is a judicial task in Obama's approach to returning to *Geneva Rights* and legal processing of detainees to finally close Guantanamo.

As the analysis of the norm transformation process has shown, both presidents have the same constitutional prerequisites but choose to act very differently in their role as presidents regarding leadership style as commander in chief, their use of presidential power in legal processes, and their relationship in cooperation or conflict with Congress and the Supreme Court. Overall, the legal proceedings of both presidencies show that the interpretation of the role and personal leadership style influence legalization processes and normative development. Decisive factors for norm transformation are security political ambitions (nationally and regarding foreign and international political leadership); political mindsets (beliefs, values, ideas); constitutional role interpretation of executive leadership (with regard to the use of force, the rule of law, and executive rights in legislation); respect for the division of labor between the three branches of government (in terms of executive rights, cooperative efforts, and subordination in legislative and judiciary matters). These identity-revealing role interpretations and leadership style build the ground for the alignment of the presidents' legitimation strategy showing in the aspects of legitimation discussed in the following.

6.2 Legalization Activities by Actions, Patterns, and Routines

The second building block for legitimation as a strategic practice consists of legalization activities. According to the role interpretation and leadership style each president uses executive tools available to them to influence law-making and law-changing processes. Drawing from the evaluation of the norm transformation efforts over time, I review the Bush and Obama administrations' formal and rhetorical legalization activities contributing to a change in detention law. This includes a review of the presidents' use of official legalization tools available to them by the authority vested in them by the constitution, as well as the rhetorical framing they used to accompany official legalization acts. In the following, I review how each president performed legalization actions and discuss similarities and differences between Bush and Obama.

Formal Legalization Steps towards Norm Transformation
The making of a new detention law in U.S. domestic law and the introduction of new status terminology for terrorist detainees during the war on terror constitute a case of norm transformation. As argued in Chap. 3, a norm transformation occurs when an existing robust norm stays in effect, but a new rule or a changed meaning is added to the existing norm. A new norm may result from an official legal process and/or a new normative understanding may result from the repeated stating of the changed interpretation of the norm in meaning and use. Any new norm or normative understanding will have to be institutionalized to be established and strengthened in meaning and use. Summarized, these theoretical stages translate into the following legalization steps in the norm transformation process.

The first phase is a preparatory stage coined by ignorance and secrecy, as norm violations or illegal actions are planned for or happen without public knowledge or political acknowledgement. Shortly after 9/11, preparatory steps for detention and legal arguments were taken towards the norm transformation when the Bush administration plans to deny potential Taliban and Al Qaida detainees POW status and declares that the *Geneva Conventions* do not apply to terrorists. Concerning potential detainee prosecution, the first step towards a change in detention law is taken with the *Military Order of November 13, 2001* (Military Order), which grants the possibility of military tribunals to try terrorists.

The second phase constitutes the norm-entrepreneurship phase during which the original norm stays in effect while additional meaning is introduced for specific aspects of the norm's scope of application. As the first detainees arrive at GTMO, the denial of *Geneva Rights* is made official, a new status is introduced with the quasi-legal term *unlawful enemy combatant*, and military tribunals based on the *Military Order* are discussed for prosecution.

In the third phase, the legal dispute begins when the alternating legal interpretation of detainee rights by the Bush administration is called into question by the Supreme Court. While detainee count is increasing in GTMO, the political and legal debate evolves, soon involving courts and the USSC. The ruling on *Hamdan v. Rumsfeld* forces the Bush administration to work on further legislation on detention regulations with Congress. The legal debate and dispute throughout all branches of government lead to the first formal legalization of the new detention law when the *2005 Detainee Treatment Act* is passed, which formally legalizes the term *unlawful enemy combatant* as status definition and denies *habeas rights* to GTMO detainees.

In the fourth phase, after the passing of the *DTA 2005*, another phase marked by political normalization of the new provisions and legal dispute follows. Once again, the USSC decides on *habeas rights.* In 2006, USSC rulings demand further work of the Bush administration with Congress. The passing of the *Military Commissions Act 2006* further legalizes new detention law, by restating the status definition and finalizing military commissions as prosecution institutions.

In Phase 5, Bush finishes his second term and Obama takes over as president, initiating a revision of the new detention law and urging legislation to ameliorate detainee rights. Whereas Bush had already started reducing prisoner count and claims to want to close the detention center, Obama prioritizes Guantanamo on his first day in office. With Obama taking office, the president starts with three executive orders, ordering the closing of GTMO and banning cruel and inhumane treatment of detainees. With these orders Obama initiates the reversal of the norm transformation.

The sixth phase is marked by institutionalization of the transformation in detention law. During the remainder of his time in office, Obama attempts to reverse some of the new detention law. Although he does succeed in ameliorating some conditions, he also contributes to institutionalizing the new detention law, thus, contributing to the norm transformation. Obama signs an executive order issuing the transfer of GTMO detainees to a high-security prison in Illinois. Although this is an initiative to dial back Bush's detention policy, these efforts fail due to Congress denying necessary funds. Obama tries to reverse the new detention rules which he criticized as undermining the rule of law. With the passing of the *Military Commissions Act 2009*, he works with Congress to amend the *MCA 2006*. However, Obama does not succeed with his initial plan to integrate GTMO detainee prosecution in the U.S. court system. Finally, the *MCA 2009* constitutes another change in detention law, as the *unlawful enemy combatant* is replaced with the *unprivileged enemy belligerent* proposing a wording which again resembles international legal terminology but remains different from official treaty law. Overall, the *MCA 2009* continues the special legal treatment of terrorists deviating from international war law despite emphasis of compliance with *Geneva Rights*. Moreover, indefinite detention remains a reality. Hence, Obama amends but also institutionalizes transformed meaning and use of detention norms.

Executive Legalization Actions
Legalization actions lead to informal and formal changes in law and thus signify the most visible transformation in violence-regulating norms. Although legalization is a complex process reserved for the legislation, during the war on terror the executive plays a distinctive role in shaping legal processes towards norm transformation. Both presidents have used executive power to shape the legalization process of the emerging detention law. However, their legalization actions reflect their role interpretation and leadership style. Based on the constitution, the president as representative of the executive branch of government can sign or reject legislation passed by Congress. Moreover, the president has the power to use his executive authority to initiate legislative procedures. The following documents were used to shape the norm transformation: proclamation, memorandum, notice, executive order, and military order. As orders function as directives, the first three presidential documents are relevant in analyzing legalization activities, since they convey background-setting and fulfill issue-framing functions. Likewise, notices, memoranda, letters, messages, determinations, and orders serve the communication of legal matters with other branches of government or government institutions.

With regard to the norm transformation process here, proclamations fulfill mainly framing and accentuating functions. Proclamations are mainly used to inform people about holidays, commemorations or other occasions. Often proclamations are issued to bestow honors, express grief and condolences, or accentuate topics of national importance, below the legalization threshold. In this case, proclamations play a background-setting role, as they are not as legally important as executive orders. However, proclamations may be used to set the stage, for instance, when proclaiming a state of emergency or *National Day of Remembrance*. Similarly, notices are mainly used to prolong the state of emergency declared after 9/11, as both presidents used notices for the yearly renewal of the state of emergency due to the terrorist attacks of 9/11.

Among the presidential documents, memoranda play a special role in the preparation of indefinite detention during the Bush administration. Memoranda are mainly used for communication, as position papers and legal discussion within the administration. Bush also uses memoranda to pass down specific orders on detainee treatment to the DoD in his function as commander in chief, especially in the first two phases of the norm transformation process. The Bush administration kept many documents secret. Emphasizing transparency and accountability, Obama published many government documents, among those many memoranda, thus granting insights into government correspondence.

Executive orders give the president the option to issue directives managing the operations of the federal government (Federal Register 2024) which is beneficial under time pressure and provides the opportunity to bypass Congress. Executive orders play a vital role in President Bush's approach to the war on terror. Having proclaimed a state of emergency after 9/11, which is regularly renewed, and using the AUMF as authorization, he relies on executive orders to issue his decisions on detention-related rules bypassing Congress. Especially the *Military Order of November 13, 2001*, which Bush issued, is relevant to norm transformation, as it sets the legal grounds for the prosecution of detainees outside the U.S. court system. With this tool Bush uses his power as commander in chief to adapt the rules of detainee treatment and reserve himself the possibility to decide upon prosecution of captives in the war on terror. Obama, on the contrary, criticizes Bush's use of executive power bypassing Congress and diverting decisions to the president and the subordinate secretaries. Obama also uses executive orders to emphasize his determination to change detention regulations and detainee treatment. Although he uses executive orders to close Guantanamo, he still emphasizes that he explicitly denies using executive orders to assert his plans against the majority in Congress but instead underlines his willingness to work with Congress to restore detainee rights and strengthen the rule of law.

Even though Bush and Obama both express commitment to the *Geneva Conventions*, they both take part in a norm transformation process that leaves the United States with a new detention law (*Detainee Treatment Act 2005*; *Military Commissions Act 2009* [amendment to *MCA 2006*]). President Bush used the opportunities to project power and take the initiative in legal proceedings. Finally, the Supreme Court disagreed with his decisions on detainee rights. Even when working with Congress, Bush emphasized his leadership in the legislative process. On the contrary, President Obama was much more cautious to use executive power rather to start greater legislative projects and to emphasize the rule of law, leaving legislation to Congress. While the *Geneva Conventions* (1949) stay in effect for armed conflict between sovereign states, the new detention law adds regulations for terrorist captives in the war on terror including new regulations for status, treatment, and prosecution for terrorist detainees.

6.3 Setting Topics, Framing Issues, and Using Rhetorical Activities

The third building block for legitimation as a practice consists of topic-setting and issue-framing through rhetorical activities. As developed in the theoretical assumptions and shown in the evaluation by phases, topic setting and issue framing are key actions in legitimizing efforts in the norm transformation process. The presidents set topics in speeches or choose to entertain topics brought up by journalists. Moreover, the presidents frame issues in speeches by using rhetorical activities and using content-specific arguments. Topic setting and issue framing are key actions in building justificatory narratives for political actions and as such of legitimation as a practice. As described in theoretical considerations in Chap. 3, justification activities accompany legalization efforts by explaining, emphasizing, and attributing meaning to formal political steps. Justification consists of two components: rhetorical activities and substantive arguments. Like the previous considerations on legalization efforts, justification activities also in part depend on leadership style but are also bound by the restrictions of the office. Reconstructing topic settings of both presidents, subject codes show which topics appeared in frequency in detention-related speeches. Code relations between subject codes and rhetorical activities show how topics were produced. Building on these code evaluations, I further deepen the focus reviewing content-related arguments for justification. While this section mainly focuses on the framing of specific subjects by Bush and Obama, the subsequent section will focus on the use of rhetorical activities.

6.3.1 Bush—Setting Topics and Framing Issues

The topics Bush set himself or was presented with show in the evaluation of the subject codes over the entire period of Bush's time in office after 9/11. Figure 6.1 shows the appearance of the 12 subject codes in all selected speeches between 2001 and 2009 and the frequency in which these topics appear in detention-related speeches.[1] Noticeably, the trending topic above all else is the 'war on terror.' The subjects 'Guantanamo detainees,' 'Military Commissions Act/military tribunals,' and 'Usama bin Laden' appear in similar frequency. Less mentioned are the subjects 'CIA program,' 'treatment of prisoners/torture,' 'homeland security,'

[1] See Chap. 4 for a detailed description of coding and the Appendix provided in the Electronic Supplementary Material for coding guidelines.

'allies,' and 'intelligence.' Finally, least mentioned are the topics 'surveillance law,' '*Geneva Conventions*,' and 'constitutional presidential authority' (Fig. 6.1).

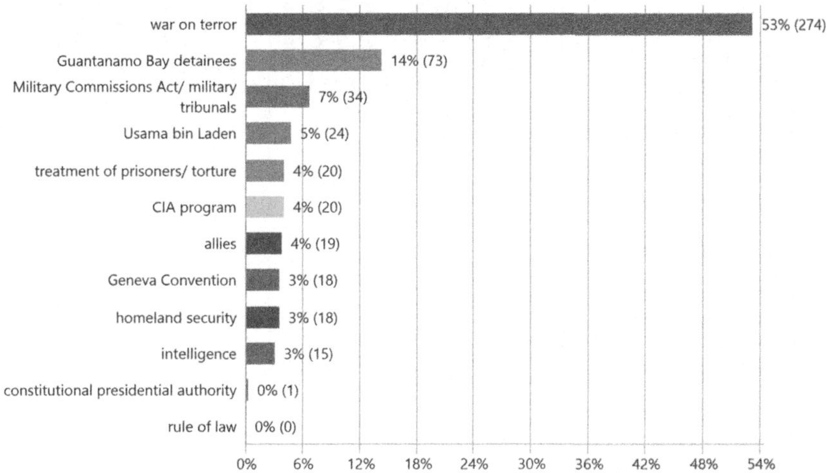

Fig. 6.1 Subject Codes Bush

Figure 6.1 shows the topics in detention-related speeches are not—as could be expected—dominated by legal topics like '*Geneva Conventions*,' 'rule of law,' 'Military Commissions Act/military tribunals,' or even 'presidential authority.' Rather dominant subject code is by far the topic 'war on terror' as the main conflict theater, and then far behind 'GTMO detainees,' 'Military Commissions Act/military tribunals,' and 'Usama bin Laden.' Detention and prosecution of GTMO detainees appear in line with security political topics, which is a first sign that Bush sets detention-related topics with a strong security political focus.

Further looking into the code relations between subject codes and rhetorical activities, reveals how Bush frames specific issues within the subject 'war on terror.' The rhetorical activities the president uses when addressing this topic are 'emphasizing security,' 'explaining security politics,' 'appealing to national values,' 'characterizing the enemy,' 'revoking national memory,' 'reporting on war progress,' 'explaining cooperation,' 'claiming pursuit to justice,' 'stressing newness of the war,' and 'expressing gratitude,' as the code-relations graphic shows (Fig. 6.2). These dominant activity codes are another sign for the security political framing of issues in the topic 'war on terror.'

Codesystem	Guantanamo Bay detainees	treatment of prisoners/ torture	Military Commissions Act/ military tribunals	Geneva Convention	rule of law	constitutional presidential authority	war on terror	Usama bin Laden	allies	CIA program	intelligence	homeland security	SUMME
admitting defeat													
admonishing													
announcing/commenting new detention law	3	1	19	4	2				1				30
appealing to national values	6	118	8	5	1	1		1	1	1			142
applying new detention law			3	4	2								9
applying the law	1	20	1					2					24
calling on Congress/working w Congress	5	17	25	7	3		4	7	1				69
characterizing the enemy	21	108	6	3	3	5	2	2		2			152
claiming presidential power	2	10	4	3	2	1	1	1					24
claiming pursuit to justice	20	48	22	2		6		5		2			105
commenting USSC/court decisions	19	1	13	2	3	1	3						42
committing to international law	3		11	2	13				2				31
criricizing democrats	1	15	1	3		1	1	1					23
criticizing Congress		1		12	1		3	1					18
criticizing past actions													
declaring a presidential order			1										1
denying/defending/offering alternative explanation	12	7	6		4	1			7				37
emphasizing accountability													
emphasizing legality	10	5	16	9	10	1			7				58
emphasizing rule of law	5	4	1	2		1	1						14
emphasizing security	37	219	37	34	4	8	6	23	2	3			373
emphasizing transparency	6	1											7
explaining prosecution of detainee maltreatment	5	1	2		1				6				15
explaining security politics	15	154	2	6		2	6	15	3	7			210
explaning cooperation	11	63	1			1	1		1	10			88
explaning/defending detainee treatment	67	19	21	35	10	2	5	1	9	1			170
expressing gratitude	4	22	4	1				1		4			36
(re-)interpreting the law	2	1	4		5								12
keeping secrets	2	10	1	8	2		2		4				29
listing acomplishments	2	21				1				2			26
proposing legislation	1	4	14	3	2		2	3					29
referring to quasi-law	3				1					1			5
reporting on war progress	8	81			2	3				1			95
revoking national memory	5	86	8	2		1	2	2	1	1			108
stressing newness of the war	1	25			1		3						30
SUMME	277	1062	231	147	72	36	42	65	45	35			2012

Fig. 6.2 Code Relations of Activities and Topics Bush

Bush dominantly uses 'emphasizing security' and 'explaining security politics' to connect national security with military operations in the 'war on terror.' Both activities are closely tied and to argue for the necessity of the use of force and application of violence in the war on terror. As Bush repeatedly states in this regard, the war on terror to him is "the calling of the 21st century" which remains his main claim for the U.S. lead war on terror. This vision is certainly fostered by personal experience of the 9/11 attacks and the surrounding insecurity as well as personal political convictions. With these rhetorical activities Bush underlines that fighting terrorism is not only the main security political challenge for the United States but also emphasizes the U.S. leadership role in the global fight against terrorism.

The president uses 'stressing newness of the war' to explain and justify actions in the war on terror which go beyond the established use of force or application of violence. This activity is used in connection with military tribunals, which are established outside the regular U.S. judicial system, with the non-application of the *Geneva Convention*s to GTMO detainees, justifying his exceptional decision-making and emphasizing his executive role in an extraordinary time, justifying the use of intelligence and CIA for terrorism prevention.

Bush also 'appeals to national values' and 'revokes national memory' when talking about the need to use force in countering terrorism. Both activities are used in connection with emotional anecdotes and personal stories about U.S. soldiers who gave their lives for the fight against terrorists. National memories are not only revoked when repeating the horrors of 9/11 and other terrorist attacks on U.S. soil, citizens, or institutions. Also, these activities are used to refer to past wars and overcome tyrannies, like World War II, and conflicts overcome in building the United States as a nation, like the Civil War. In connection with past security political obstacles, Bush uses national values, like liberty and freedom, to emphasize the importance of all efforts to win the war on terror. While stressing U.S. leadership, Bush emphasizes that not only American values and security are at stake, but also global security and civilization are in danger.

'Characterizing the enemy' and 'claiming pursuit to justice' are both used to argue for the necessity to use force in the war on terror and defend the application of violence. Referring to terrorists, Al Qaida members, or terrorism supporters, Bush characterizes the enemy as evil, unjust, immoral, knowing no rules, brutal, stateless, and faithless. The audience learns little about the actual persons involved, the possible motives, or conflict causing circumstances of the individuals accused of terrorist activities. Instead, the enemy is portrayed as an evil black box who remains a security threat to the nation and needs to be deterred, found out, and prevented from further attacks.

The hunt for Usama bin Laden is a case in point. Throughout Bush's time in office, Usama bin Laden remains an argumentative figure to defend the use of force, emphasize security, and argue for the continuance of the detention program for information gaining. This also shows in dominant rhetorical activities which are 'claiming pursuit to justice,' 'emphasizing security,' and 'characterizing the enemy.' 'Claiming pursuit to justice' is used in connection with military operations and not with legal proceedings. The capture or killing of bin Laden is seen as a security gain. Bush underlines the security political importance of finding bin Laden dead or alive and stresses that justice will be done. These statements not only show the security political understanding of justice but also reveal that justice according to Bush is not necessarily achieved though legal processing and court rulings but through military operations, including the options of capture and trial as well as killing. Characterizing Usama bin Laden as the enemy responsible for the 9/11 attacks, Bush justifies the use of force in the war on terror and the incarceration of the terrorist at GTMO. On the one hand Usama bin Laden serves as the personification of the terrorist threat, on the other hand, he remains an evil black box as the top searched terrorist. As the coded segments show, this topic is used to build an enemy figure throughout Bush's time in office which is subject for search and capture or kill missions and used to argue in favor of the use of force in continued military operations and application of violence in making captives mainly for information-gaining reasons to prevent future terrorist attacks.

When talking about allies, Bush mainly uses 'explaining cooperation' and thereby emphasizes the need for working with allies in the war on terror. Bush stresses the U.S. leading role in these cooperative efforts. Furthermore, explaining security politics, Bush stresses the need for cooperative efforts with allies in active combat. Also, cooperation with allies is necessary in cutting financial ties and searching for terrorists in countries other than the battlegrounds in Afghanistan (and later Iraq), eliminating safe havens, and surveilling communication. Talking about 'allies,' Bush not only regards cooperation but also divides into friends and foes. Either one is with the United States in fighting terrorism, or one is against the United States and thus an enemy. This rhetoric signifies a dichotomy of a post-Cold War world order of terrorism-fighting states against a terrorist network of non-state-aligned, post-sovereign acting diffuse enemies and collaborating states. Towards allies, Bush frequently expresses his gratitude and thanks state leaders for their cooperation and engagement. Yet, this activity is mainly used in situations during state visits where Bush follows the diplomatic protocol.

'Emphasizing security' and 'explaining security politics' are dominant rhetorical activities when Bush talks about 'homeland security.' The notion of security is moreover altered and extended after 9/11, as homeland security is used increasingly as synonym with national security. The topic 'homeland security' mainly deals with the reform of the security institutions which Bush emphasizes as one of his great projects after 9/11 in cooperation with Congress. 'Calling Congress to action,' Bush argues that the newly established Department of Homeland Security is the main reform necessary for an organized fight of terrorism and preparedness for new attacks. Installing the Department of Homeland security, Bush reacts to the failing of security institutions to cooperate which led to the terrorist attacks in the first place. With this innovation, Bush uses the activity 'claiming pursuit to justice' by granting law enforcement and intelligence agencies more authorization to pursue terrorism. Whereas national security used to entail boarder control and U.S. security measures outside U.S. mainland, homeland security is a wording that stands for both security through fighting terrorism abroad and measures on national soil, ensuring the security of American homes.

Concluding on Bush's rhetoric concerning the 'war on terror' and closely related subjects ('allies' and 'homeland security'), which mainly function as background-setting subjects, with regard to detention, he uses activities and arguments which mainly justify the use of force and application of violence. Moreover, the rhetorical activities are aimed at creating strong emotions of fear, uncertainty, insecurity, anger, hatred, mourning, grievance, comradery, nationalism, unity against an adversary, and determination.

Regarding the topic 'GTMO detainees,' most often acted out is 'explaining/defending detainee treatment' as humane and in line with the law. The subject code 'GTMO detainees' encompasses capture of terrorists and incarceration, detainee treatment, prosecution, and release as topics discussed in connection with the making of a new detention law. Instead of choosing the subject, Bush reacts defensively and 'offers alternative explanations.' Also, Bush often uses 'emphasizing security' when referring to Guantanamo detainees and detainee treatment which he mainly addresses as a security issue and less as matter of legal prosecution. 'Emphasizing security,' Bush explains that captivity of detainees serves national security in two ways. One argument presented by Bush is to take terrorists off the battlefield, and the other one is to gain information from detainees to prevent terrorist attacks. In this regard, military operations and the role of intelligence are emphasized.

'Guantanamo detainees' is a subject which mainly comes up in connection with the 'war on terror' and 'characterizing the enemy' as well as the 'CIA program' and the need for 'intelligence' in countering terrorism. Bush uses 'characterizing the enemy' to frame the enemy as an illegal combatant, who is culpable due to being on a battlefield, not a member of regular state forces, and not complying with the rule of warfare like wearing uniform to justify the denial of *Geneva Rights* and detention in GTMO. 'Claiming pursuit to justice' when talking about 'GTMO detainees,' Bush affirms that justice will be done. However, justice is mainly associated with the deprivation of liberty and indefinite detention, and for legal prosecution though military tribunals due to security reasons. Bush stresses the newness of the war and emphasizes that detainees are terrorists and not regular combatants. When asked why accepted violence-containing norms are not applied, he answers by emphasizing the legality of detainee treatment and stresses the newness of the war using quasi legal terminology and later new legal provisions for detention and detainee treatment. Additionally, GTMO appears in formal reporting duties to Congress, conveying prisoner counts or when addressing distinct prisoners and stories of their capture, like high-value detainees who were involved in the planning of 9/11.

Recalling the legal debate on detention in Guantanamo as discussed in Chap. 2 and the emergence of a new detention law as reconstructed in Chap. 5, legal rhetoric is expectable in President Bush's detention-related speeches. However, the evaluation of detention-related speeches shows low frequency in legal terminology in subjects and activity codes. Those topics which are directed at the legal dimension of the norm transformation play a rather subordinate role in the list of topics. Moreover, legal topics are dominated by security political arguments and activity codes, as the following evaluation of the subject codes on the 'treatment of prisoners/torture,' 'CIA program,' '*Geneva Conventions*,' and 'Military Commission Act/military tribunals' shows. Likewise, rhetorical activities which suggest legal arguments are used to make security political arguments.

Concerning the subject 'treatment of prisoners/torture,' Bush is reluctant to mention detainee abuse. When Bush is asked about torture and detainee maltreatment, the president's statements use 'explaining/defending detainee treatment.' Concerning torture allegations, Bush is clearly denying the accusation. He affirms legality of U.S. application of violence and denies torture by U.S. troops declaring cases of proven misconduct exceptions which will be prosecuted. The president reacts defensively, and keeps his answers short, unusually strict, and 'denying torture' or 'offering alternating explanations.' Moreover, Bush 'emphasizes legality' by committing to international law and stressing that the United States do not torture and comply with the *Torture Convention* and promises that maltreatment will be investigated, prosecuted, and punished. He further uses 'explaining security politics' to emphasize that the prisoners are treated well, even better than they would be in the places where they were captured (concerning food supply and medical care). Although Bush is very clear on his no-torture position, he is less clear on what constitutes torture. When questioned about specific interrogation techniques, Bush repeats the general denial of torture and refers to secrecy for security reasons, as he claims. However, referring to secrecy may also indicate a tactical argument to avoid answering in detail.

Concerning torture allegations, Bush makes a clear distinction between the cases in Iraq, which he describes as exceptions, and the general treatment of prisoners in GTMO. However, both subjects overlap, which also traces in similar rhetorical activity codes. In terms of information gaining, detainee treatment is an issue which is discussed in connection with the CIA program, torture, and enhanced interrogation techniques also relating to GTMO detainees. Although Bush denies torture and affirms commitment to international law, he avoids making clear statements on specific interrogation methods, like waterboarding, and thus it remains unclear what constitutes torture. Issues which are related to detainee treatment, like interrogation methods, torture, and the CIA program, apply to all U.S. detainees in the war on terror, including the ones held in GTMO.

The CIA program is a vital topic in the dispute over detainee treatment and a main topic in criticizing the Supreme Court deciding on GTMO detainee rights. As such, Bush uses 'explaining/defending/ offering alternative explanations' and 'emphasizing security' most when talking about the 'CIA program.' Bush argues for the program's necessity to uphold and provide national security and prevent future terrorist attacks by gaining intelligence which is argued to be the main factor for winning the war on terror. Although Bush 'emphasizes legality,' this does not mean that he argues for clarity on detainee rights in GTMO, but rather Bush 'emphasizes legality' to strengthen the legal position of the security personnel. Thus, legal issues here entail clarifying modalities for security personnel, to avoid prosecution for detainee maltreatment. In this regard, Bush uses 'keeping secrets' to avoid answering questions on detainee treatment based on security issues. 'Criticizing Congress,' Bush frames the continuance of the CIA program as the main test to the new detention law which is to be passed by legislation. In this regard, he campaigns strongly on the CIA program which had been put to hold due to legal issues. Although this is a legal matter, Bush mainly emphasizes security political issues and explaining the program's value to security politics. Moreover, this debate is not about containing violence against detainees, but the debate is about granting security personnel privileges in applying violence to detainees.

The term *Geneva Convention* rarely appears in detention-related speeches. Where mentioned, the subject is mainly used in connection with official international legal processes. Rarely, the '*Geneva Conventions'* are mentioned with reference to 'GTMO detainees' or in arguments for detainee rights and often in Question-and-Answer (Q/A) sessions with journalists. In these sections, Bush uses the rhetorical activities 'committing to international law' and 'denying/defending/offering alternative explanations.' He rejects allegations of breaking the law and affirms the importance of the '*Geneva Conventions.*' Bush emphasizes U.S. commitment to the *Conventions* and argues that GTMO detainees are not afforded POW status, as they are not combatants of states but pledged allegiance to an individual and are part of a terrorist network, outside the sovereign state system to which the law applies. 'Explaining and defending detainee treatment,' Bush argues that detainee treatment in Guantanamo is in line with the "spirit of the Geneva Convention" (Bush, The President's 2002-01-28: 125) and stresses that prisoners would still be treated humanely. Bush supports his position by 'characterizing the enemy' as killers and operating outside state structures, following an ideology, and declaring them illegal non-combatants, *unlawful enemy combatant*, and "types of combatants we have never faced before" (Bush, The President's 2006-07-07: 1339). Despite Bush 'emphasizing legality' of the U.S. treatment of prisoners, dispute arises concerning the interpretation of *Common Article 3*. Particularly in the argument over the interpretation of *Common Article 3*, Bush 'emphasizes security' for U.S. security personnel and calls on Congress to support legislation that clearly prevents prosecution of security personnel.

Concerning military tribunals and the *Military Commissions Act*, the activity used most is 'emphasizing security.' As Bush argues, it is a national security interest to have the option "within the confines of our Constitution" (Bush, Remarks Following 2001-11-19: 1426) not only for secret keeping in military operations but also for the safety of the judicial personnel. As the evaluation by phases showed, the subject 'Military Commissions Act/military tribunals' peaked when the law was in the process of passing in Congress. Thus, Bush uses 'calling Congress to action' when urging the legislation to decide on the use of military commissions for detainee prosecution. Bush argues, 'claiming pursuit to justice,' that military tribunals are but one option to achieve justice. Bush also clarifies, while 'explaining and defending detainee treatment,' that military commissions are a means to try terrorists in a war with the Department of Defense in charge of the judicial proceedings. The subject is closely connected to legal issues, especially in 2006, when the Supreme Court rulings are awaited, and the *Military*

Commissions Act 2006 is discussed and passed by Congress. In this context, Bush uses 'announcing and commenting new detention law' to emphasize his role in providing for military tribunals, critically 'commenting the USSC decisions,' 'asking Congress to pass legislation' on military commissions, and to announce the *Detainee Treatment Act 2005* and the *Military Commissions Act 2006* as security relevant law. Bush also 'emphasizes the legality' of the detainee prosecution and stresses his efforts to work towards safety guaranteeing legal proceedings in detainee prosecution.

Concluding these evaluations, Bush chooses topics and frames issues with a clear security political focus. Bush frames detention and detainee interrogation as solutions for security challenges in the war on terror and for preservation of national security and safety of the security personnel. Although Bush speaks to several topics using a wide variety of rhetorical activities, the core security political arguments appear in repetition and often not only similar argumentative sense but also similar in phrasing and wording. This not only shows in the subject codes but especially in Bush's use of rhetorical activities, which are mainly suited to frame issues as relevant for national security, threat perceptions, and safe-keeping of U.S. security and judicial personnel. Even subjects which are genuinely legal matters, like detainee prosecution ('Military Commissions Act/ military tribunals'), the application of domestic and international law ('*Geneva Conventions*'), and treatment of prisoners (GTMO detainees' status and torture allegations) are mainly dominated by security political arguments (Fig. 6.3).

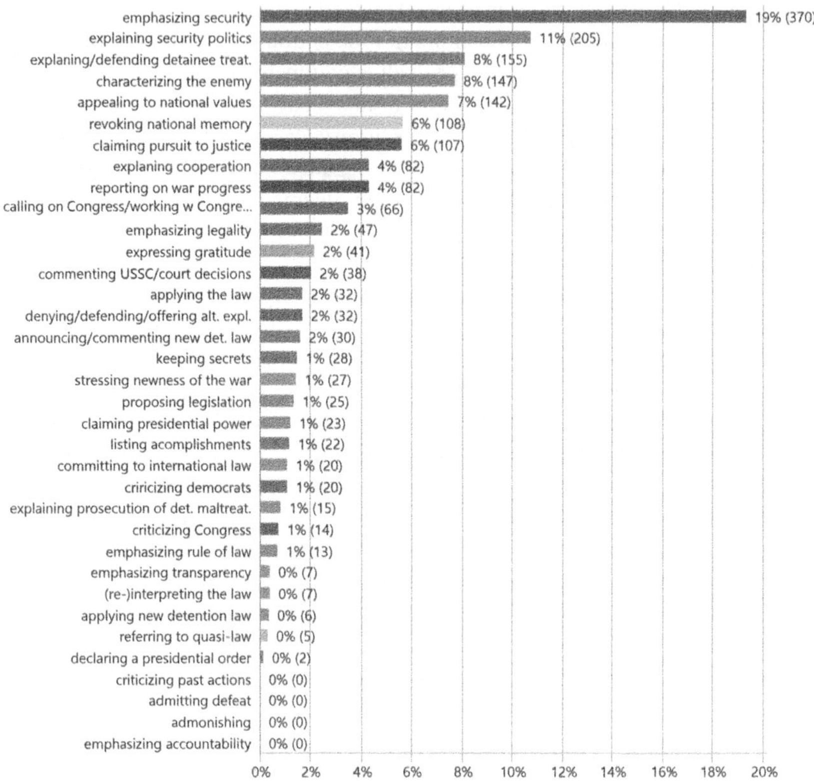

Fig. 6.3 Rhetorical Activity Codes Bush

The main question Bush has to answer with regard to detention is why a new detention law is necessary, since national law, international criminal law, and international war law offer such robust frameworks for dealing with terrorists. The narrative Bush crafts by setting topics and framing issues entails that a new, special regulation is necessary to deal with an unknown and unprecedented evil enemy in a new kind of warfare. These legal changes include reserving core decisions on detention, treatment, and prosecution to the president's discretion, referring legal prosecution to the Department of Defense to conduct military tribunals, and declaring the enemy an *unlawful enemy combatant*, thus, depriving them of *Geneva Rights*. Although Bush's detention policy was challenged in court, he hardly changed course during his presidency. According to Bush, these special provisions are necessary, as this is the only way to guarantee national security, pursue justice, prevent future terrorist attacks, and fight and deter terrorist enemies in the world. Secrecy as part of security procedures is necessary to keep security personnel safe, even though this safety may come at the expense of transparency and accountability. Moreover, Bush affirms that his policies are legal and that he follows the law, while preserving national security which is his duty as president and commander in chief.

The subject 'war on terror' is the main topic framed by Bush for the change in detention law which provides the background to embed the arguments for a new detainee treatment and ultimately a new detention law. Generally, Bush is reluctant to engage in legal discussions and refers to lawyers, legal advisors, judges, or other judiciary institutions for legal assessments of detainee treatment and the interpretation of detention law. The need for legal change or new regulations he reasons with security needs rather than with legal arguments. Concerning legal questions, legality of detention, detainee treatment, and prosecution are relevant topics. These two topics are domestic legal issues which mainly concern the *habeas rights* of detainees before U.S. courts and *due process*; and internationally the question is whether and how the *Geneva Conventions* apply to GTMO detainees. Whereas these topics are related to legal interpretation of constitutional, U.S. criminal and military law, and international law, Bush's rhetoric hardly uses legal activities. Instead, when concerning legal questions, Bush usually avoids clear answers by either emphasizing his presidential power to decide upon the matter at a later point in time and based on his empowerment as president and commander in chief or by referring legal questions to legal personnel, i.e. lawyers and legislative or judicial institutions.

Even though Bush obeys the Supreme Court rulings and follows the court mandate by starting to work on legislation for detention and detainee treatment with Congress, he clearly criticizes the other branches of government. Emphasizing his own efforts in legally regulating detention matters, Bush criticizes the Supreme Court for making law instead of purely interpreting the law, thus of overstepping the courts mandate, and Congress (dominated by a majority of the Democrats) for not acting on in the best interest of national security.

Concluding, in Bush's rhetoric, the law is mentioned but clearly subordinate to means to achieve and preserve national security. Whereas Bush emphasizes the superiority of the U.S. legal system, constitution, and national values compared to the enemy, he does not frame countering terrorism in terms of the rule of law. Although Bush's rhetoric emphasizes the rule of law, adhering to the rule of law is often placed at odds with the proposed security strategy, which is based on the use of force and application of violence in an exceptional situation of a new kind of war. Furthermore, Bush advocates the idea of an exclusiveness of protective and constitutional rights for U.S. and allied citizens.

6.3.2 Obama—Setting Topics and Framing Issues

The distribution of subject codes, as displayed in Fig. 6.4, shows the topics mentioned by or entertained by Obama in detention-related speeches during both terms in office. The graphic shows that Obama entertained eleven subjects in detention-related speeches between 2009 and 2017.[2] Noticeably, two subjects are dominant in detention-related speeches: 'war on terror' and 'GTMO detainees.' Next in mentioning appears the subject 'allies,' followed by 'treatment of prisoners/torture,' 'constitutional presidential authority,' and 'rule of law.' Less often mentioned are 'Usama bin Laden' and 'homeland security.' Least often appear the subjects 'Military Commissions Act/military tribunals,' '*Geneva Conventions*,' and 'intelligence.' Not mentioned is the subject 'CIA program' (Fig. 6.4).

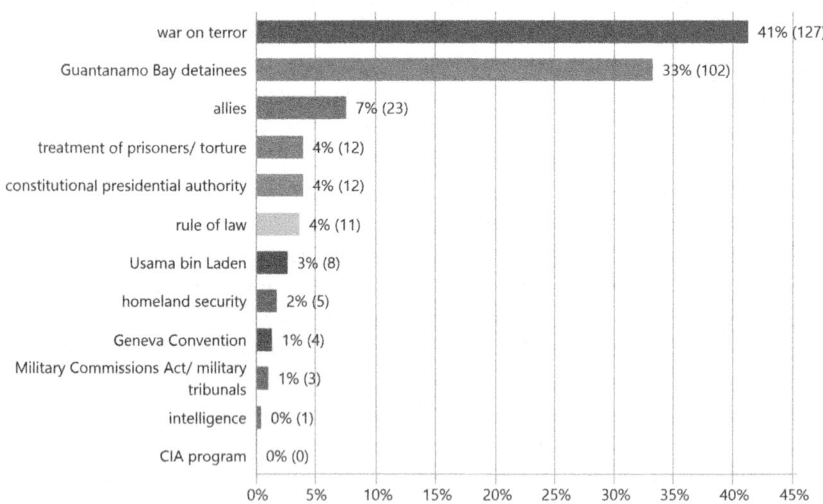

Fig. 6.4 Subject Codes Obama

[2] See Chap. 4 for a detailed description of coding and the Appendix provide in the Electronic Supplementary Material for coding guidelines.

The figure reveals that the distribution of topics is different from Bush's choice of topics. At first glance, the list of topics suggests a similarity to Bush's security political focus, with the two dominant topics being 'war on terror' and 'Guantanamo detainees.' Contrary to his predecessor, concerning the 'war on terror,' Obama's main argument is the reduction of U.S. engagement in active combat. Regarding 'GTMO detainees,' Obama stresses the closures of the detention facility and the return to the rule of law. Thus, Obama sets dominant topics with the focus on establishing security by reducing the use of force and applying the rule of law. Although security remains a top priority, the strategic focus of Obama shifts towards an approach of shared responsibility in a global framework of cooperative security under U.S. leadership.

Further looking into the code relations between subject codes and rhetorical activities, reveals how Obama frames specific issues within the single subjects (Fig. 6.5). As the graphic shows Obama not only sets topics differently than Bush but also frames issues differently with rhetorical activities in detention-related speeches. Code relations show which rhetorical activities were used in specific subjects and thus offer insights as to how specific topics are framed in terms of activities and in terms of substantive arguments adding to a practice of legitimation in action and content. Bush pursued a strategy favoring the use of force and application of violence in the war on terror and used norm transformation to support his strategy. Instead, Obama follows an approach guided by the rule of law to support his strategy of peace through justice. Although Obama's efforts are designed to reverse the norm transformation of the Bush administration, Obama ends up amending detention norms and institutionalizing norm transformation.

Codesystem	Guantanamo Bay detainees	treatment of prisoners/ torture	Military Commissions Act/ military tribunals	Geneva Convention	rule of law	constitutional presidential authority	war on terror	Usama bin Laden	allies	CIA program	intelligence	homeland security	SUMME
admitting defeat	1							2					3
admonishing	2												2
announcing/commenting new detention law	13	7	2		2	3							27
appealing to national values	47	42	7	9	1	2	1	1	5		1		116
applying new detention law	10	21			1								32
applying the law	2	15											17
calling on Congress/working w Congress	33										1		34
characterizing the enemy	3	15		1			1	2		1			23
claiming presidential power	18	10	6	2		6							42
claiming pursuit to justice	29	1	2	1	4	1	1						39
commenting USSC/court decisions	3		1			1							5
committing to international law	2	1								4			7
criricizing democrats													
criticizing Congress	42	5				4							51
criticizing past actions	7		11	2	1								21
declaring a presidential order	4	1	2										7
denying/defending/offering alternative explanation	2	1	2		1								6
emphasizing accountability		2	1	1		4							8
emphasizing legality	6	1									1		8
emphasizing rule of law	27	12	4	3	1				1	1			49
emphasizing security	90	136	16	4	1	7	6	6	8				274
emphasizing transparency	3		2			6							11
explaining prosecution of detainee maltreatment			4	1	1								6
explaining security politics	20	127	3	2	1		3	11	11	1			179
explaning cooperation	21	53	1					4	23				102
explaning/defending detainee treatment	138	25	15		4		1			1			184
expressing gratitude	8	1		1					6				16
(re-)interpreting the law					1								1
keeping secrets	5	12	7			7							31
listing acomplishments	2	7		1			1						11
proposing legislation						2							2
referring to quasi-law													
reporting on war progress	7	47					1	1					56
revoking national memory	10	18		3			1	1					33
stressing newness of the war		3											3
SUMME	555	563	86	31	19	43	16	28	54	8	3		1406

Fig. 6.5 Code Relations of Activities and Topics Obama

Concerning the 'war on terror,' Obama takes a different position than his predecessor. 'Emphasizing security' and 'explaining security politics,' Obama calls for a "new era of American leadership" (Obama, Remarks Following 2009-01-22; Obama, Remarks at 2009-01-22). During Obama's time in office, the 'war on terror' remains the main topic in detention-related speeches. Whereas Bush started the wars in Afghanistan and Iraq, Obama wants to end American engagement in active combat and reduce military spending in war. Similarly to Bush, Obama uses 'emphasizing security' and 'explaining security politics' most frequently. However, Obama's strategic positioning, which he also emphasizes in speeches, is to withdraw troops, bring them home, stop active combat, reduce war expenditure, and to continue U.S. leadership in the war on terror by engaging in civil military activities and lead cooperative security efforts with international partners. Regarding the war on terror, Obama implements a strategic shift, coining collective security in Afghanistan and emphasizing building regional and local civilian capacities, calling for strong partnerships with allies considering a comprehensive strategy including regional responsibilities in an understanding of shared security. Like Bush, Obama also stresses his commander in chief responsibility to national security. However, Obama 'emphasizes the rule of law' and trust in constitutional institutions as well as commitment to international law as main principles to achieve security before the use of military power.

The changing security environment during Obama's time in office is reflected in the way he talks about the war on terror. He emphasizes that the United States is at war with Al Qaida and admits to terrorist threat scenarios. He also admits that measures are necessary to preserve national security. In this regard, he stresses the importance of national values, like freedom, equality, dignity and fairness, as a strength in the fight against terrorism. Whereas Bush used a strong image of an evil enemy to mobilize support for the war on terror, Obama's use of enemy references is rather case specific and related to specific events and not for constructing an enemy figure in connection with detention policy and GTMO. 'Characterizing the enemy' Obama names Al Qaida as main adversary and affirms that the United States remain at war with terrorism. As conflict scenarios and the security environment change during Obama's time in office, he also clarifies that the network is evolving and splintering into smaller cells which complicates the detection of attacks. 'Explaining security politics,' Obama distinguishes terrorist networks who operate in the name of God and in the name of Islam, from the Muslim religion, clarifying that terrorists share no principles of any religion. Furthermore, Obama clearly acknowledges Muslims as the victims of terrorism. 'Emphasizing security,' Obama promises a systematic approach in countering terrorism including targeting leadership and infrastructure of terrorist networks as well as dealing with homegrown terrorism as threat scenarios shift. While this approach continues to involve military force, efforts will also extend to law enforcement, diplomacy, and cooperative security measures.

Detention of terrorists in Guantanamo Bay Detention Camp is a decisive component in Bush's strategy in the war on terror. Although for some detainees Obama includes the possibility of indefinite detention, detaining terrorists without charges or prospects is not part of Obama's counterterrorism strategy. Instead, Obama's efforts are directed at reviewing detainee's status and work towards release, transfer, or prosecution. Overall, the detention-related strategy is to return to the rule of law. In line with this conviction, Obama already campaigns for the presidency with the declared goal to shut down GTMO. Thus, for Obama, GTMO is an inherited security liability and a stain on U.S. reputation, which he tries to resolve. In Obama's speeches, the topic 'GTMO detainees' is mainly associated with closing GTMO, and all other detention related issues are subordinated under this leading goal. The remaining detainees in Guantanamo pose a security political problem, which needs a well-planned solution.

Concerning 'GTMO detainees,' Obama uses most frequently 'explaining/defending detainee treatment,' 'emphasizing security,' 'appealing to national values,' and 'criticizing Congress.' Like Bush, Obama uses 'explaining/defending detainee treatment' when referring to detention and detainee rights. However, on his first day in office, Obama signs three executive orders, ordering the closure of GTMO and ameliorating detainee treatment, reestablishing the rule of law in detention policies. Due to this lack of rule of law, Obama criticizes the Bush administration for making GTMO a recruitment tool of Al Qaida terrorists. Criticizing the idea of a prison outside the legal system and reminding of the respective Supreme Court rulings, Obama sees the Bush administration's detention policy as undermining the rule of law, causing a setback for U.S. moral authority, and continued detention as a factor of insecurity. Acknowledging concerns for national security in connection with detainee releases, Obama 'emphasizes security' and promises procedures to assure safe releases. Regarding detainee prosecution, Obama 'criticizes past actions' and especially the inefficiency of Bush administration in prosecuting detainees, as only three military commissions were accomplished in seven years.

Next to release of cleared detainees and prosecution, repatriation to countries of origin and third-party countries remains a diplomatic issue for Obama, as Congress blocks the transfer of GTMO detainees to U.S. mainland. In favor of using existing legal channels of prosecution in the U.S. court system, Obama proposes the idea of not only prosecuting the detainees on U.S. mainland but also using an Illinois detention facility for the detention of convicted terrorist. As the conflict with Congress finances continues, Obama 'criticizes Congress' with reference to U.S. budgetary problems, arguing that running GTMO is unnecessary and too expensive. Obama further argues that the U.S. could use those funds in the current economic and financial crisis the United States faced in domestic politics. Thus, repatriating detainees remains an issue for cooperation with allies and in line with the *Torture Convention.*

Failing to close GTMO, Obama 'appeals to national values' and emphasizes that GTMO signifies a continued breach with core U.S. national values. Whereas Bush emphasized the war on terror and detention policy as the calling of the 21st century and the security political responsibility for the United States, Obama stresses that should the U.S. fail to close GTMO, "history will cast a harsh judgement" on the United States (Obama, Remarks at 2013-05-23: 488). Emphasizing U.S. responsibility to the rule of law, Obama repeats up to the end of his presidency that GTMO should be closed. Nevertheless, Obama not only fails to realize closing GTMO but also does not fully reverse the norm transformation in detention law, leaving indefinite detention a reality for the remaining prisoners and a legal option for following administrations.

Regarding relations to 'allies,' Obama uses 'explaining cooperation' and 'explaining security politics' before 'emphasizing security.' Whereas Bush's threat perception was strongly focused on global terrorist networks and collaborators, Obama acknowledges a complex threat environment including the global climate crisis, nuclear proliferation and conflicts with Iran and North Korea, next to terrorism, and war zones as well as armed conflict zones in Afghanistan, Pakistan, Iraq, Somalia, Libya, and Syria. In contrast to Bush, Obama pursues a strategy of peace with justice based on diplomacy and cooperative security, rejecting unilateral solutions. Like Bush, Obama also offers U.S. responsibility in leadership and admits that peace often cannot be achieved without the use of force. Yet, he stresses the importance of continued U.S. responsibility in global security politics, like the prevention of mass atrocities and for the protection of human rights. However, these global challenges he considers shared burdens which are to be solved by shared responsibility. The use of force according to Obama is thus a coordinated effort with partners for peace, and peace is to be achieved through strengthening international organizations and security alliances like in NATO or the UN. Overall Obama stresses the need for diplomacy underlined in his diplomatic meetings and expressed gratitude to allied state leaders and as part of the diplomatic protocol. 'Appealing to national values,' Obama emphasizes that security efforts should be motivated by hope instead of fear. 'Emphasizing the rule of law,' the president underlines the importance of international treaties to achieve what he calls peace in justice.

Whereas 'homeland security' was a major topic for Bush, encompassing not only the institutional joining of forces but also becoming a synonym for national security, Obama does not set this specific topic. Rather, Obama refers to 'homeland security' in the context of the department's responsibility of preventing terrorist attacks. As such, 'homeland security' comes up in connection with the attacks of Christmas Day 2009 and the investigations afterwards. In this regard, Obama explains the security political failures to analyze the collected data.

'Usama bin Laden' functioned as an enemy figure in defending the security political strategy by Bush, however, Obama hardly refers to the subject. Like Bush, Obama 'emphasizes security' and when 'explaining security politics,' he continues to acknowledge that the United States remain engaged in a war with Al Qaida under the leadership of Usama bin Laden. Also, Obama stresses efforts to continue searching for bin Laden as capturing or killing the terrorist leader remain top priorities. Obama clearly lists bin Laden's death as an accomplishment but also as a unique security mission. Although killing bin Laden is a gain in security, Obama also stresses that terrorist threats remain a security problem. Obama uses 'appealing to national values' to underline that the U.S. people are resilient against terrorist enemies who continue to pose threats which have become a reality to be dealt with as a part of normal everyday life and not in terms of an exceptional, permanent state of emergency.

Whereas the 'war on terror' and 'GTMO detainees' are more associated with a security political focus, the topics 'constitutional presidential authority,' 'rule of law,' 'Military Commissions Act/military tribunals' have a genuine legal character. Regarding the constitutional presidential authority, Obama addresses two issues: the state secret privilege and the conflict with Congress regarding closing GTMO. In connection with the state secret privilege, Obama mainly uses 'emphasizing security,' 'keeping secrets,' 'claiming presidential power,' and 'emphasizing transparency.' Concerning the state secrets privilege, Obama had criticized the Bush administration of overusing and disguising law-breaking policy as security relevant. Thus, Obama argues in favor of more transparency of the president in security politics, while preserving national security and improving accountability and congressional oversight.

The activities 'criticizing Congress' and 'announcing/commenting new detention law' Obama mainly uses in connection with the conflicts with Congress concerning the funds to close Guantanamo and the president's right to realize detainee transfers to U.S. mainland. Bush criticized Congress and the Supreme Court not only concerning specific issues but also for exceeding competences. Obama stresses the importance of the division of responsibilities between government branches and criticizes Congress only in certain issue-related aspects.

Overall, Obama emphasizes the importance of government institutions and strengthens the rule of law, opposing exceptions.

Obama strongly 'emphasizes the rule of law and legality, referring to the constitution and its historical significance, reminding the audience of national values and a shared identity. Whereas Bush also mentions the rule of law and uses references to national values to argue for the use of force in defense of the country's security, Obama sets the 'rule of law' as a topic which he frequently repeats in security political arguments in detention-related speeches. For Bush, the constitution and its principles were subject to security political efforts and needed defense and safekeeping with extraordinary measures. To the contrary, Obama strongly argues for the rule of law, which is deeply rooted in the nation's history and is the decisive feature of the American people and democracy. Like Bush, Obama 'revokes national memories.' However, Obama features the rule of law in overcoming tyrannies in World War II and as a guarantee for fair treatment to surrendering forces in past armed conflicts. 'Emphasizing accountability and transparency' of the government, the president underlines the importance of strengthening U.S. institutions, for example Congress for oversight and to judge on power abuses. Overall, Obama 'emphasizes security' by the means of the rule of law, not only by adhering to national values but also regarding international norms. In this regard, Obama emphasizes the uniqueness of the U.S. as world power willing to commit to self-restraint in the use of force and application of violence in the pursuit of building international norms. 'Explaining security politics' and 'criticizing past actions,' he frames the rule of law as a strength and not as a weakness.

Concerning the '*Military Commissions Act* and military tribunals,' Obama uses 'explaining and defending detainee treatment' as well as 'claiming pursuit to justice' and refers to the use of military tribunals for the prosecution of wartime criminals throughout the history of the United States. Taking office, Obama clarifies that prosecution and administering justice are judicial tasks, and thus he refers the authority for detainee prosecution from the Department of Defense to the Attorney General (Executive Order 13492; Executive Order 13493). In this regard, Obama admits to the advantages of military courts in terms of security and the admission of evidence compared to federal courts. 'Criticizing past actions,' Obama explains that he had strong reservations against the military commissions ordered by the Bush administration, as they lacked provisions for *due process.* Referring to the Bush administration's new detention laws, Obama claims that reforms were made by his government to provide rule of law standards and especially exclude testimony and evidence received through the use of cruel, inhuman, or degrading interrogations. With these adjustments, military commissions are to be used for prosecution and for achieving justice.

Obama's commitment to the rule of law also extends to international law. Unlike Bush, who has to argue for his commitment to the *Geneva Conventions*, Obama is not in conflict with international law. In his speech receiving the *Nobel Peace Prize*, Obama emphasizes: "Even as we make difficult decisions about going to war, we must also think clearly about how we fight it" (Obama, Remarks on 2009-12-10: 1801). Moreover, since Obama frames the subject GTMO detainees mainly as issue regarding the closure of the detention center, he does not frame detainee status, prosecution, or treatment in captivity as an issue of international legal conflict. Rather he frames issues genuinely related to the *Geneva Conventions* as in line with the rule of law and international provision.

When talking about the treatment of prisoners, a topic that is mainly related to the problem of torture and interrogation methods bordering on torture, Obama most often uses 'emphasizing security' and explaining detainee treatment' as well as 'criticizing past actions.' 'Emphasizing security' and the prioritizing America' safe-keeping, Obama bans torture and 'criticizes past actions.' Bush's position on torture was a clear commitment to the *Torture Convention* while leaving open what exactly constitutes torture. Obama clearly states that torture remains illegal and that waterboarding constitutes torture. Enhanced interrogation methods Obama opposes as a violation of U.S. ideals and values and as constituting torture, stressing that his administration stopped interrogation methods and he calls past legal reasonings of such methods a mistake (Obama, The President's 2009-04-29: 587). Moreover, Obama still 'emphasizes security,' stating that neither torture nor enhanced interrogation led to more security. He explains that violence against detainees is a security risk for U.S. troops, makes captures and surrenders in the battlefield less likely, and functions as a recruiting argument for terrorist networks. As torture would undermine U.S. counterterrorism efforts, Obama explains that intelligence could still be gained without enhanced interrogation methods. Moreover, Obama stresses the importance to uphold U.S. national values and restore the U.S. moral standing in the world, especially in challenging situations. 'Appealing to national values,' 'keeping secrets,' 'claiming presidential authority,' and 'explaining prosecution' of are used similarly often. Using these activities, Obama explains prosecution of detainee maltreatment and promises that investigations are conducted, and the security personnel will be taken accountable for detainee maltreatment.

Concluding these evaluations, Obama choses topics and frames issues with a clear focus on the rule of law. Compared to Bush, Obama inherits detention-related topics, however, he chooses to reframe detention-related topics to match his strategy of peace with justice. As shown on his first day in office, Obama's main topics are the closing of Guantanamo, the amelioration of detainee treatment, and the return to the rule of law in detainee prosecution. In this regard, Obama focuses largely on improvements in the security system, stressing improved regulations for transparency and accountability within the constitutional framework, a cooperative comprehensive security approach with counterterrorism as one aspect of threats, and the reduction of the use of force and application of violence in favor of diplomatic efforts and legal prosecution.

Whereas Bush focuses on defending his deviation from *Geneva Rights* and argues for a new detention law, Obama stresses his intention to reverse detention policies, close GTMO, stop enhanced interrogation, and improve regulations of military commissions to improve detainee rights in prosecution. These subjects remain dominant in Obama's detention-related rhetoric with a stable line of arguments. He wants to close Guantanamo, which he sees as a liability and security threat as well as damaging the U.S reputation. Attempts to relocate prisoners remain complicated, due to resistance in Congress to sign off on transfers to U.S. mainland, the impossibility to return detainees to their homelands for possible violation of the *Torture Convention,* and the reluctance of other countries to accept former detainees.

Bush frames detention-related topics in terms of security politics and uses the same dominant arguments in every topic; instead, Obama acknowledges the complexity of security political and detention related issues and engages in issue-related explanations. Thus, Obama focuses on the dimensions of topics, explaining decision-making processes, and reasoning resulting policies. This also shows in less speeches and rhetorical activities overall (see Fig. 6.6). However, Obama reveals his strategic positions in few key speeches which are often event related and are characterized by explanations of complex situations and based on factual evidence. Reviewing single activity codes reveals strategic differences in presidential justification rhetoric. Although both presidents use 'emphasizing security,' 'explaining security politics,' and 'explaining/defending detainee treatment,' the evaluation has shown that these activities were used for different lines of argument.

These different rhetorical strategies also show in the use of the rhetorical activities 'characterizing the enemy' and 'pursuit to justice.' Bush portrayed an evil enemy and argued for the use of force and application of violence in interrogations to achieve justice as a retaliation for the victims and preservation of national security. To the contrary, Obama argues in a more nuanced way, clearly naming the adversary Al Qaida and distinguishing them from Muslims. While 'emphasizing the rule of law' in the pursuit to justice through legal prosecution, Obama 'emphasizes security' which is to be achieved in a comprehensive approach. So, for Obama, serving justice is a judicial task that is achieved by applying national and international law and not by using force and applying violence by the military.

Obama's security approach moreover shows in the references to national security by emphasizing national values, the rule of law, and the moral standing of the United States in the world. 'Appealing to national values' is used by Obama as emphasizing shared values, a common national identity, and understanding of the importance of the rule of law as guiding principles of policy making and to explain efforts for transparency and accountability as principles of good governance. Whereas Bush argued for changes in detention laws to allow for the use of force, Obama wants to return to the rule of law on the national level and to the commitment to international law and argues for restrictions on violence as a security enhancing strategy. Thus, he frames detention mainly as the problem of closing GTMO by releasing, transferring, or prosecuting detainees. Where Bush framed detention as a necessity for persevering national security, Obama frames GTMO as a liability and unnecessary and as an unlawful camp that needs to be closed. As a replacement, Obama proposes the return to the rule of law either by

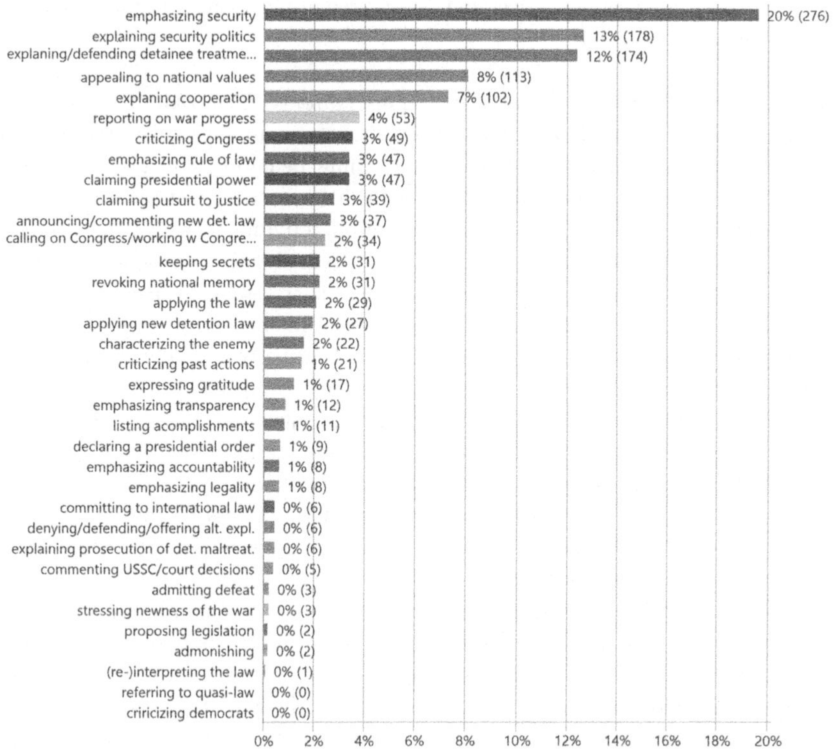

Fig. 6.6 Rhetorical Activity Codes Obama

using the U.S. legal system or through amended military commissions for prosecution of terrorists. In any case, Obama argues for the prosecution of detainees, to restore the U.S. reputation in the world, and to guarantee national security through law and justice. According to Obama, justice is a legal process administered by the judiciary and not by applying military force. In the end, Obama fails not only to close Guantanamo Bay Detention Camp due to restrictions imposed by Congress but also in reversing the norm transformation in detention law. Instead, he institutionalizes an amended yet transformed detention law including military commissions, the status of alleged terrorists in detention, and the possibility of indefinite detention. Moreover, not only the written law remains transformed, but also the underlying values, ideas and beliefs regarding legitimate violence have been changed permanently.

Concluding on Topic Setting and Issue Framing through Rhetorical Activities
As the detailed presentation of the norm transformation process shows, both presidents follow a different strategy concerning detention policies in the war on terror. Although the presidents dealt with different stages of the norm transformation process, both engaged in legitimation activities to realize legalization goals and to justify the use of violence. Clearly, Bush and Obama are perceived as fundamentally different presidents; yet, they share some formal commonalities concerning the presidency and the commander in chief position, the legal and strategic challenges of the war on terror both domestically and internationally, the issue-framing and dealing with violence and security in the war on terror, and the formal legal possibilities to shape detention-related law and influence normative understanding. In short, they have the position in common, the legal framework, and the rhetorical justification activities available to them.

Yet, they differ in role interpretation, topic setting, and issue framing through rhetorical activities. Hence, they used different strategies and practiced legitimation differently. As the evaluation of the topics has shown, in detention-related speeches not legal reasoning is dominant but rather emotion-appealing rhetoric. Concerning the war on terror and GTMO detainees, both presidents emphasize security and explain security politics. Yet, both presidents follow different approaches. Bush frames detainee rights as a security political issue and argues for violence-enabling regulations for detention and interrogation to gain information and enhance U.S. national security. While acknowledging the importance of the rule of law, Bush argues for the limitation of detainee rights and stresses the necessity of the use of force and application of violence. Overall, Bush follows a strategy of the rule of force for security gains. To the contrary, Obama frames detention mainly in terms of the closure of GTMO to return to the rule of law, restore the moral standing in U.S. security politics, and restore the U.S. reputation in the world. Following a strategic approach of peace with justice, Obama argues to establish regulations for more transparency and accountability, as the rule of law is a core U.S. value which will increase security and safety.

6.4 Legitimation as a Practice in Norm Transformation

Legalizing this violent act of indefinite detention encompassed a complex process including all branches of government—the executive, the legislative, and the judicative—contributing to a transformation in detention law on the national level, with spill-over effects on the interpretation and use of international provisions of detainee treatment.[3] In the report presented in Chap. 5, I gave an overview of the findings in the case study of legalization and justification activities by Presidents Bush and Obama in the process of transforming the detention law from violence-containing to violence-enabling regulations. Following the conceptual understanding put forward in this study, I looked at legitimation activities which consist of legalization activities and justification activities. Tracing the norm-transformation process, I analyzed activities of the presidents in the material world and in rhetoric over time. Further evaluating presidential actions, I analyzed legalization activities and institutionalized actions, and rhetorical actions in topic setting and issue framing with rhetorical activities. In this section, I draw a conclusion regarding the results from the empirical case study report and present a conceptual understanding of legitimation as a practice in a norm transformation process.

Towards a Practice of Legitimation

Building on the theoretical assumptions presented in Chap. 3, I conceptualize legitimation as a complex security political practice encompassing several activities which are, when performed competently, recognizable as intentional and meaningful, thus as political actions. These actions may be institutionalized and/or based on personal ideas, values, or beliefs. Although performed by a powerful state actor, who is acting in an assigned role, legitimation in security politics can be practiced in a variety of ways. Variations may include staging factors as well as performative activities. Whereas staging factors include actions which are suited to frame situations and provide background-setting information, I understand legitimation activities as a container for all legitimacy-seeking actions performed by a specific person or a group of actors concerning a norm transformation.

---

[3] As discussed in detail in Chap. 2, this process is described as the emergence of a new detention norm; and as discussed in Chap. 3, I consider this process a norm-transformation towards a new detention law.

Table 6.1 Conceptual Components—Practices of Legitimation

Role Interpretation and Leadership Style	
leadership	interpretation of executive powers and use of means
cooperation	cooperative towards others or in conflict with others
mindset	values, beliefs, and ideas
Informal and Formal Legalization	
secrecy	using force and applying violence despite normative restrictions and without detection
open-breach and violation	continued use of force and application of violence while knowingly and openly in breach with normative restrictions despite criticism of respective audience
legal re-interpretation and re-framing	using offensive and defensive topic setting and issue framing to consolidate use of force and application of violence with a norm-conform interpretation and using rhetorical justification and setting precedent
legal innovation	proposing a new legal approach to cover the use of force and application of violence under a newly formalized legal and normative understanding and use rhetorical justification to convince the audience that this innovation is right and just
Topic Setting and Issue Framing with Rhetorical Activities	
standing commander in chief position and presidential authority	emphasizing security
	explaining security politics and committing to cooperation
	declaring presidential order
	claiming presidential power
	Strengthening one's position by keeping secrets for national security reasons
appealing to national values and shared history	appealing to national values
	revoking national memories
	report on commonly achieved progress and list accomplishments

(continued)

Table 6.1 (continued)

Role Interpretation and Leadership Style	
	mourning losses and emphasizing grace for sacrifice for the nation
establishing special circumstances and reason your solution	stressing newness of the conflict situation
	denying criticism, defending decisions, offering alternative explanations
blaming a common adversary	characterizing the enemy
	claiming pursuit to justice
	explain and defend use of force and application of violence
criticizing opponents	other parties
	past decisions
	the judiciary and specific rulings
	a divided legislative
claiming compliance to norms, law, and institutions	calling on legislative and propose legislative innovation
	applying the law
	committing to international law
	using law-like terminology and innovative interpretation of the law
	emphasizing rule of law, accountability, legality, transparency

Concluding from the analysis, practicing legitimation in norm transformation involves (but may not be limited to) the following building blocks of activities. Legitimation as a practice in norm transformation consists of three groups of actions: role definition and leadership style, informal and formal legalization activities, and topic-setting and issue-framing with rhetorical activities to legalize and justify norm transformation (see Table 6.1).

Role Interpretation and Leadership Style

The first group of actions for political state actors includes defining one's role in political leadership and interpreting one's scope of power in the current position. Role interpretation and leadership style are based on an actor's mindset in terms of ideas, values, and beliefs. Role understandings function as the general moral, ideational, and strategic framework which determines the security political and legitimation strategy of a powerful state actor. An actor's role also defines the relationship with other actors, on the international level or on the national level.

As for Bush and Obama, both claimed leadership and responsibility for security politics mainly in the role of commander in chief. Yet, they also interpreted their scope of action very differently. While Bush mainly relied on the AUMF to claim leadership and determine detainee rights in the war on terror, Obama emphasized the rule of law and his willingness to involve the people represented by Congress to determine detainee rights. Although certain aspects of position are legally prescribed, like executive rights, duties, and responsibilities, the person in office has a certain leeway to interpret the role of power. Legitimation thus depends on how powerful state agents interpret their role in terms of leadership, cooperation with other actors, values, beliefs, and ideas as well as norm adherence.

Legalization Activities

The second group of actions encompasses powerful state agents to use their position and available means to engage in norm transformation through informal and formal legalization activities suitable in the current transformation stage. Legalization activities divide into informal and informal institutionalized legalization actions which are accompanied by rhetorical legalization. As presented in Chap. 5, norm transformation evolves in several sequential steps over time involving many legalization activities. The sequence of events in a norm-transformation process and official legalization process may include, but not be strict in order or completion, the following stages and involve the following activities:

- *Ignorance and secrecy*: In this initial stage of a norm transformation process powerful state actors use force and apply violence despite normative restrictions and without detection by others. Activities in this stage may include non-referencing of norm-violation or non-mentioning of the illegality of the actions to others, and secret consulting on application of legal provisions in given circumstances and discussing the possible application of precedent cases.
- *Open breach and norm violation*: This stage involves the continued use of force and application of violence, however knowingly, openly, and observably in breach with normative restrictions despite criticism of a respective audience. Activities in this stage may include the expressive and deliberate denial of protective rights and non-application of existing law in the commonly agreed upon interpretation despite an arguable applicability to the case in the circumstances.

- *Legal (re-)interpretation, reframing, and innovation*: This stage encompasses powerful state agents presenting alternating interpretations of existing law and norms as well as plausible arguments. Arguments may include quasi-legal terminology, resembling the law in wording and phrasing but not inherently part of existing written law used to reason for the preferred course of political actions. Referring to legal precedent or actively setting legal precedent are activities used in support of the re-interpretation efforts.
- *Normalizing quasi-legal terminology*: In this stage, legal innovations are normalized through repeated use of quasi-legal terminology in communication through official channels and may be complemented by proposing new institutions and/or proceedings.
- *Formalizing legal innovation by initiating change in legal provisions*: This step formally completes norm transformation and includes state actors formally proposing new rules to the legislative institutions and actively working with the legislative branch to pass new law. Proposed legislation includes provisions to cover the use of force and application of violence under a newly formalized violence-enabling legal and normative understanding.
- *Institutionalizing and normalizing the new law*: This final stage includes politically engaging with the new law by referencing the new law, amending the new law, and causing rulings on the law without formally abolishing or completely reversing the new law in meaning.

Legal interpretation efforts are furthermore supported by offensive and defensive topic-setting and issue-framing to consolidate the use of force and application of violence with a norm-conform interpretation. Rhetorical activities are designed to convince the audience that the proposed legal innovation is right and just. However, legalization efforts are but one part of a wider legitimation strategy involving legitimacy-seeking actions in speech. In the following, I conceptualize speech related legitimation efforts which involve topic setting and issue framing through rhetorical activities.

Justification Activities—Topic Setting and Issue Framing with Rhetorical Activities
Whereas legalization is a rather sequential process in norm transformation, justification runs in all phases of the norm transformation process. As defined in Chap. 4, I understand legitimation as a political practice showing in observable performance patterns of intentional action and rhetoric designed to persuade a designated audience that political actions are right, necessary, and just. Concluding on the observed actions by Bush and Obama, the concept of the practice of

legitimation in norm transformation combines these actions in and on the material world with rhetorical patterns in speech.

After role interpretation and informal and formal legalization, the third group of actions involves engaging in topic setting and issue framing using rhetorical activities for background and stage preparation, legalization, and justification. Subject introduction and addressing are up to the presidents in most parts. Overall, setting the subject and acting in issue framing are vital parts of legitimacy-seeking rhetorical strategies. Choosing which topics to talk about as a main frame of arguments is a huge part of setting the tone for legitimation and a first step in narrative building.

As the analysis shows, justification is mainly acted out in rhetorical activities which frame issues in favor of the envisaged violence-enabling norm transformation. Rhetorical activities may include the following sets of actions:

- *Standing the commander in chief position and presidential authority* by emphasizing security, explaining security politics, committing to cooperation, declaring a presidential order, claiming presidential power, and strengthening a position by keeping secrets for national security reasons.
- *Appealing to national values and shared history* by naming values and revoking national memories, reporting on commonly achieved progress and listing accomplishments, mourning losses, and emphasizing grace for sacrifice for the nation.
- *Establishing special circumstances and reasoning solutions* by stressing newness of the conflict situation, denying criticism, defending decision, and offering alternative explanations.
- *Blaming a common adversary* by characterizing an enemy, claiming pursuit to justice, and explaining and defending the use of force and application of violence.
- *Criticizing opponents* by criticizing other parties, criticizing past decisions, criticizing the judiciary and specific rulings, criticizing the legislative and specific law initiatives.
- *Claiming compliance with norms, laws, and institutions* by calling on the legislative to act and proposing legislative innovation, applying the law, committing to international law, using quasi-legal terminology and innovative interpretation of the law, and emphasizing rule of law, accountability, legality, and transparency.
- *Keeping secrets and declaring issues or decisions as secret* by rarely and scarcely answering to specific questions on certain security issues; denying specific information and offering general information on security relevant

questions; explaining necessity of secrets with preserving national security, keeping security forces safe, and not giving up advantages to the enemy; emphasizing the duties as commander in chief and state secret privilege.

With topic setting and issue framing powerful state agents have great influence on the public perception of a political action. One of the strongest issue-framing examples is Bush framing the 9/11 attacks as acts of war. Bush continued to frame terrorist networks as imminent security threat and barbaric, extremely brutal, ruthless enemies, against whom the United States need to defend and protect their people by all available means. To the contrary, Obama framed his political decisions as always in line with the rule of law. Unlike Bush, to whom Guantanamo was the answer to a war in which gaining information through detainees is a key to national security. Obama framed Guantanamo as a security threat and liability because it mobilizes terrorists. Furthermore, Obama argued that failing to close GTMO leaves a stain on the U.S. reputation as a democratic state that is committed to the rule of law and protective international legal standards. Building strong narratives, which are designed to justify the means of violence, and repeating these lines of argument make a great part of the legitimation practice.

Concluding, the analysis has shown that a practice of legitimation in norm transformation consists of two components: (in-)formal legalization and rhetorical justification which concern topic setting and issue-framing through content-related rhetorical activities. These activities make up the legitimation strategy of a powerful state agent who chooses from offensive and defensive activities based on a personal role definition and strategic approach. Offensively, state actors can practice legitimation to place topics on the public agenda and frame issues to the strategic favor of envisaged security politics to foster norm transformation. On the defensive, these activities can be practiced defending against accusations, answering provocative questions, and arguing in favor of a course of action that may be politically challenging. Overall, a legitimation practice is designed to gain support from a designated audience for a changed norm interpretation and proposed norm innovation leading up to a norm transformation.

Practices of Legitimation—Towards Building Theory

7

In this chapter, I synthesize the results from the empirical case study report towards a conceptual understanding of practices of legitimation. In the following section, I thus present the building blocks for theory advancements. In the subsequent sections, I discuss the relevance and contribution of these research results regarding theoretical and practical implications as well as methodological points of concern and present issues for further research.

7.1 Practices of Legitimation—Building Blocks for Theory Advancement

In Chap. 6, I presented the findings of the case study analysis of legalization and justification activities by Presidents Bush and Obama in the process of transforming the detention law from violence-containing regulations to violence-enabling regulations. Beyond the case specific outcomes, the results have implications for theory advancement as building blocks for a general conception of legitimation practices. Following the presented definition of legitimation and practices, the empirical data adds to a general conception of legitimation practices by providing further insights as to the activities used for legitimacy-seeking efforts. Thus, the results offer a how-to for analyzing government officials' legitimation activities in relation to engagement with legal references up to the active changing of law and norms through transformative efforts. Thus, the conception of a strategic legitimation practice in norm transformation adds an actor-centered, action-focused conception to norm dynamics over time and in qualitative content.

A practice approach to legitimation thus has several advantages. The concept combines legalization actions in the material world and justification actions in rhetoric, which both form necessary parts of legitimacy-seeking actions. Thus,

D. Hühnert-Hugendubel, *Between Rules of War and Rule of Law*,
https://doi.org/10.1007/978-3-658-49121-5_7

legitimation as a process of gaining legitimacy becomes more transparent and understandable as often both levels are considered separately. Neither the actions themselves nor the language alone constitutes the full effect of legitimation. Only in combination of observable changes in legislation and rhetorical justification, the entire effect of legitimation in terms of changing underlying ideas, beliefs, and values of the designated audience unfolds.

A How-to on Legitimation as a Strategic Practice

Legitimation practices are used as motor for norm transformation, in every stage of a norm's transformation, and to transform the qualifying content of a norm. The results of this study provide a deeper understanding of how legitimation of *rule* is realized by referring to legitimate *rules* and by gradually adapting the rules. Thus, what the study offers is not only a manual on how legitimation is practically performed but also an insight as to how legitimation is strategically used by powerful actors concerning the following aspects. Legitimation as a strategic practice thus shows:

- *How political actors build a comprehensive security narrative based on background-setting as well as issue and event framing.* This activity mainly contains topic framing of conflicts or situations as an argumentative basis to reason the necessity for the use of force, application of violence, or implementation of new regulations. Stressing the newness of a conflict situation is a main argument in reasoning new procedures. Illustrating situational framings with individual stories that are emotionally relatable, that successfully overcoming major obstacles, that give examples for great heroism and national value support, or that relate to shared memories, create a connection for the target audience.
- *How political actors rationalize political decisions by explaining procedures referring to common reason and transparency.* This is the most basic activity of explaining and showing transparency by sharing information on investigations. An empirical example is the reporting on the commission investigating 9/11. Another example from the Obama administration is the repeatedly presented explanation for the return to the rule of law.
- *How position-specific arguments referencing and using the power vested in the political position are used to gain strategic advantages.* In the U.S. case, the president as commander in chief has a duty to prioritize national security very highly and thus also emphasize that and how they are fulfilling the responsibility to protect the nation. Arguments in this regard use stirring fear by

emphasizing threats and cautioning the people. Especially in times of inner-state political power quarrels, like after events of crisis when leadership may be questioned and in times of election campaigns, criticism of democratic institutions and/or processes is common. However, the presidents stay within the constitutional boundaries of the office and within the framework of lawfully granted actions (presidents do not break the law knowingly or admit to wrongdoing).

- *How keeping secrets is connected to emphasizing the security need and responsibilities for safekeeping of the military.* This mainly entails keeping specific information secret for national security or military safekeeping and offering general information instead. This is often used passively in response to (unwelcome) questions as well as actively a position uplifting strategy.
- *How referring to commonly shared background knowledge with high emotional value is used to gain support and appeal to empathy.* In the case of the United States this reference usually concerns a commonly shared history of becoming one nation and a praise of constitutional values. The shared history and historical narratives serve as a great reference, containing stories of obstacles overcome, wars fought, independence and the development of freedom values, painting a picture of a shared history of struggle, battles and memories of great, unifying results. Whereas some historical arguments span back centuries, other historical references are more event-related and reference to recent commonly shared grievance. For instance, the shared trauma of 9/11 and other commonly shared traumatizing (terrorist or war-related) events. References include shared values like the American dream, and freedom. Also, social community values like families, communities, military, and veterans are often referred to.
- *How the use of personal anecdotes or the telling of individual, emotional stories creates an appeal to empathy.* Often the presidents refer to their experience with survivors or next of kin when reporting on war progress. Also, the presidents tell stories of war participants or relatable situations that were overcome to create a relatable image in support of an argument.
- *How creating an image of a common enemy segregating a higher valued 'we the people' from a less worthy 'them the evil enemy.'* Characterizing the enemy mainly includes activities and arguments designed to mobilize against an evil and dangerous enemy who is hard to fight but defeatable through joint effort. Thereby, 'we, the people' is usually associated with superiority in values, morals, humanity, kindness, rule-following, and other generally as 'good' regarded attributes. In this separation, values are kept apart by referring to the

civilized law-and-order free world as opposed to a respectless rogue enemy, who knows no mercy, no rules, and no god.

Three Categories of Legitimacy-seeking Practices in Norm Transformation

As the study shows, legitimation is not a sequentially performed practice, but rather legitimation activities are performed in every stage of the norm transformation process to benefit the progress. Legitimation activities can be sorted into categories of legitimacy-seeking actions in every stage: secrecy, contesting, and validating. The first category of 'secrecy' contains all clandestine actions as well as admittedly secret actions. Secrecy shows in the non-mentioning and clandestine acting and the mentioning that public disclosure would harm national security or endanger security personnel. Furthermore, this category includes hiding military actions and classifying actions and evidence thereof.

The second category of 'contesting' includes activities of denial, marginalization, or banalization and is often used in reaction to accusations or critical questioning. Denial shows in negating that an act signifies as a grave violation of the law (see arguments on enhanced interrogation methods) or claiming that something is legal despite criticism. Marginalizing or banalizing often entails putting accusations in perspective. This may entail arguing for justice (referring to criminal status or enemy character) or attempting to normalize a situation which was claimed to be exceptional (like housing conditions in Guantanamo for instance).

The third category of 'validating' includes framing actions like declaring exceptions, characterizing the enemy, legal reasoning, legalization activities, and norm-interpretation. Contesting, framing, and declaring exceptions include references to newness (of technology, situation, actors), declaring that rules do not apply due to extraordinary circumstance, and official actions that proclaim a state of emergency. Characterizing the enemy may include barbarizing the enemy and painting an image of a brutal, uncivilized, and illegally acting foe. Based on such characterizations denial of basic rights may be argued. Moreover, dehumanizing the enemy may occur in characterization and by arguing for and committing inhumane treatment. Legalization and norm-interpreting activities may include reasoning for the legality of the actions with reference to domestic, foreign and international law or referencing favorable precedent as well as actively setting precedent for legal changes. In terms of formal legalization, pressing legislation to change the law in favor of the political strategy and realizing legal changes by executive measures may be used. Norm (re-)interpreting may include arguing how the norm applies to a given situation and how a given action falls within the margins of the rule in defense of the violent action and an attempt to establish a suitable regulation.

Offering a comprehensive approach to legitimation as a strategic practice, the results of this study have added value regarding the discussed debates on norm dynamics, legal issues, and legitimation as a legitimacy-gaining practice for political actions as well as power positions in the international system. The findings offer an action-focused and action-centered concept of interest-driven political actions towards norm transformation. This conception thus complements existing models of norm dynamics by offering insights as to how deliberate change is induced over time and how the quality of norms can be influenced by powerful actors. By providing an in-depth analysis of the U.S. presidents' actions, the study presents insights into the use of legitimation as a strategic instrument in U.S. security politics. Furthermore, the analysis shows how the office of the presidency determines legitimation and how individual office holders can shape security political strategies on the use of force and legalization, regarding presidential topic choices and issue framings designed for a change in narratives and justifications.

The practice approach contributes to a conceptual understanding of how legitimation is used domestically and internationally to legitimize rule through transforming rules and thus securing own power positions on the international level and govern the positions and possibilities of others. The arguments made by both administrations show that legitimation is a tool for inner stability, persuasion for support, and gaining empathy. At the national level, legitimation practices in the war on terror contributed to a gradual legalization of a violence-enabling perspective on the use of force and application of violence against terrorists, the limitation of rights, and the extension of re-establishing justice by law and by force. In this sense, the United States not only legitimize their own actions but also attempt to gain support and acceptance as well as stabilize their international power position. At the international level the legitimation practices working towards a norm transformation have regulatory and constitutional effects on the international order of legitimate violence. Regulatory effects concern the use of force and application of violence against declared terrorists and the interpretation of protective norms. Constitutional effects concern interpretations of status determinations, choice of law regarding conflict determination, and terrorist criminal prosecution. Legitimation practices as a strategic political performance to change the law or norms' perceptions not only show how norms are transformed over time and in character but also indicate a change in underlying mindsets including ideas, beliefs, and values, within the United States as well as among international audiences.

7.2 Discussing Relevance and Contributions

This section reflects the results of the study placing the findings in the context of broader debates of related concepts and theoretical implications of scholarship on legitimacy, international law, and IR norm research and practice-theory approaches. As I argued in Chap. 2, I consider the war on terror a security political discourse, during which violence-containing norms and underlying ideas, values, and beliefs are re-defined. This assumption is based on a wider political and legal scholarly debate on legitimacy and legitimate violence in the war on terror. Security crises, like the one produced after 9/11, are motors for norm transformation, as they allow for the political framing and basis for legitimation narratives. Based on these assumptions, one main contribution of the results of this study is that the concept of legitimation as a strategic practice provides a deeper understanding of state actors influence on the discourse on legitimate violence during the war on terror. The practice perspective provides a conceptual clarification of how state leaders use rhetorical justification actions to set topics and frame issues to facilitate changes in the law and normative perceptions of what is legal and just. Whereas the critical legal debate suggests that political justifications mainly rely on legal reframing, the analysis of the legitimation rhetoric and legalization activities of Bush and Obama reveals that legal references are rather rare. To the contrary, specific legal reasoning is left to lawyers, as the Bush administration clearly states. Although Obama is a lawyer by profession, in the position of the president he refrains from engaging in detailed legal arguing, referring to legal authorities, apart from general appeals to return to the rule of law. Although formal legalization is part of the legitimacy-gaining strategy, legitimacy as a political struggle to win hearts and minds who will eventually grant legitimacy is rhetorically speaking not won by legal arguments but instead dominated by emotion-appealing justification activities. However, the analysis also shows that both sides are necessary for norm transformation. On the one side, legalization through informal and formal acts as well as precedent-setting violent acts fostered norm transformation towards violence-enabling detention norms, and on the other hand, justification activities interpreting and framing detention norms in terms of enabling the application of violence occurred. While the Bush administration clearly worked on a transformation towards violence-enabling detention norms for terrorists, the Obama administration showed a tendency to reverse this development. However, ideas of exclusiveness of the law and enemy characterizations justifying violence to ensure security seem to have worked their way into social and political convictions. Although Obama pursued a path back to the rule of law and the containment of violence, his efforts were hindered by a political environment which had turned in favor of a less protective legal framework for terrorists. Although Obama's partially successful efforts show that political decisions leading to the transformation towards violence-enabling norms are reversable, the stumbling blocks Obama failed to overcome also signify the tendency in social beliefs, ideas, and values leaning towards favoring interpretations of norms on legitimate violence which enable violence.

Overall, the case study is an example of the phenomenon of many norm conflicts in the war on terror where normative meaning was deliberately reframed. The study confirms that legal framing is a vital part of legitimation practice in transforming detention norms in the war on terror. Moreover, blurring the lines between good and bad and right and wrong opens room for interpretation on several violence-related levels and shows how terminology and issues are strategically framed. Especially the Bush administration used the same strategy of swapping meanings and working with similarities in terminology. Prominent examples of Bush's war on terror reframing of violence-containing terminology are the terms *pre-emptive*, *unlawful enemy combatant*, and *enhanced interrogation methods*. However, Obama also disguised deviations from violence-containing norms by speaking of *targeted lethal actions* in connection with targeted killings by drones which conflict with the assassination ban. However, focusing on the United States as a norm-transforming entrepreneur, two aspects remain outside the study's scope. First, the results cannot account for the perception of the norm transformation by other states, and second, the results cannot account for the permanence or quality of the changes in the overall effect on the normative order of legitimate violence. Actions of legitimation seem to have contributed to a change in the social perception of what legitimate violence is. Complementary to this study's results, an analysis on the perception and reproduction of the use of force and application of violence in the war on terror should focus on statements regarding the justification of violent acts and connotations of right and wrong.

The findings of the study contribute to bridging the gap between norm research and the critical legal debate concerning norm conflicts on legitimate violence in the war on terror. The results of this study add to a conceptual understanding of how political actors engage with norms and law to realize security political goals. The study shows in detail how political actors attempt to strategically position violent actions within the legal framework. Yet, the study also demonstrates how political actors influence the law and normative meanings to expand the scope for political action. In the case of detention law, provisions on conventional warfare remain in effect and continue to be an important pillar of war law, while provisions for status and treatment of terrorists were added. Treatment of detainees in captivity might have suffered from a possible weakening of the torture norm and possibly from a growing acceptance for so-called enhanced interrogation techniques. Also, the application and meaning of *Common Article 3* may change in armed conflicts as arguments of the Bush administration questioned provisions on general protection. However, the Obama administration's attempts to reinforce commitment to international humanitarian law which contains rather than enables the use of force and application of violence shows that transformation steps are reversable to a certain degree depending on political and social willingness.

Critically reflecting the research process regarding the nexus of the legal and the political, both—the connection and the clear separation of norm and legal research—are helpful depending on the purpose of research. A connection between the two spheres of research is helpful in clarifying the deviation of political actions from common legal interpretation and contrasting how political actions work towards a differing interpretation and scope of actions, thus underlining the political aspect of the politics of international law. On the contrary, clear separation is helpful to avoid a mix-up in spheres of competence and keep checks and balances in place. While politics make the law, political action still needs checking, which is usually guaranteed by a three-pillar system of checks and balances. However, each branch has distinct competences as to interpreting or making law. Depending on the specific strategic goal of political actions, political actors adapt legitimation activities. Although political actions must stay within the legal framework, political actors use their power to interpret the legal frame in favor of the envisaged action, thereby changing the meaning of the law. This process often happens by changing the reading of the rules instead of the writing of the rules. While interpreting the rules and using legitimacy-seeking rhetoric may involve consulting and preparation, adapting the law by rhetorical interpretation is less time-consuming and capacity-consuming than law-changing through official legislative procedures, especially on the international level where consensus is harder to reach due to multiple stakeholders and diverging interests.

The results of this study thus encourage a stronger normative perspective in legal reviews of political actions as well as a sensitivity to the complexity and dimensions of political legal interpretation in order to distinguish between the political use of the language of the law for legitimacy-gaining actions and the commonly accepted meaning of the law. However, the law, which in case-specific debates is tied to a dichotomy of legal and illegal, should on the one hand continue to be applied to judge political action, since politicians are also subject to the law and should be held accountable. On the other hand, legal scholars might benefit from insights as to the political use of the law for legitimacy-seeking purposes and be more sensitive to the political exploitation of legal debates. This requires an openness to political use of the law for strategic purposes and the meaning of quasi-legal talk as well as emotional mobilization for normative and legal change and approval.

Consequently, the strength of the proposed conceptual approach is the combination of two spheres: the legal and the political, the political debate on existing law and agreed-upon normative meaning on the one side and the legal modification through political interest-maximizing strategy to change normative values, ideas, and beliefs on the other. As the concept reveals how politics work the law and change the law for strategic purposes, the conflict remains that politicians claim to be in line with the law while critics accuse otherwise. Whereas practices of legitimation help understand how politics work through legal references, the findings cannot settle conflicts on the contested legality of violent actions or disputed legal interpretations by political stakeholders. As the Bush administration has proved, the judicial path is also only partly helpful in this regard, when critical rulings on government actions are overturned by ex-post legalization through legislation. The critical legal debate and the legitimation practices of U.S. presidents in the war on terror display the legal and political struggle for legitimacy over how to use force and apply violence in a right and just manner. Since all struggling parties are referring to the same legal regulations, the critical legal debate is necessary to interpret political actions on the grounds of original normative intent—that is protective in terms of granting basic human rights despite the individual's actions, universal protection, and containment of state violence—of norms on legitimate violence. At the same time, the critical legal debate has to account for politics as strategic actions to change the argumentative and eventually even written meaning of laws and international norms.

The results further add to an overall understanding of norms on violence being in flux in the international system and under the influence of powerful actors. Thus, legitimation as a strategic action to foster norm transformation influences the normative order of legitimate violence by changing regulatory meanings and on the hierarchic order by changing constitutional norms assigning actor qualities and positions. In the considered case the norm transforming legitimation activities of the U.S. not only changed regulations on detention and detainee treatment but also changed the status definitions for participants in armed conflict and changed the legal perception of declared terrorists as individual and collective participants in combat.

7.3 Limitations of Methods and Findings

Critically reflecting the findings, I discuss the limits of the analysis signaled in the research design and the relevance for theory advancement. For one, the rhetorical analysis does not include material beyond the presidential record. Whereas the findings display well how the presidents argued in self-selected topics and issues raised by journalists, the results cannot speak to contradicting positions and facts, as these are not included in the analytical focus. For example, the study presents Bush's denial of torture, which stands uncontested, as no account of the chain of command on enhanced interrogation and no independent assessment of the applied methods is included in the analyzed material. Likewise, the speeches analyzed here only give an account of Obama's intentions to improve transparency and accountability but do not include an account of how well this promise is kept in *Military Commissions* or in targeted killings which are increasingly used instead of dangerous operations on the ground. Moreover, the analysis is limited to presenting legitimation activities which were used by the presidents. Thus, the results give no account of how these strategies were developed, which kind of compromise was reached beforehand, or why these positions, arguments, and activities were formed and used. Although the analysis accounts for individual choices of Bush and Obama as beholders of the office, the influence of personal experiences on specific role interpretations remains outside the analytical scope. Nevertheless, expectable is that the personal experiences Bush and the members of the administration made on 9/11 and in the days after the attacks had an effect on threat perceptions and political decisions on the use of force and application of violence. On the contrary, Obama could probably benefit from a certain degree of professional distance to the terrorist attacks and did not have to make decisions out of the situation of an acute attack.

As critically mentioned in the research design, I consider the chosen case a 'talking pig.' With the singularity of the specific case comes a certain lack of similarity to other cases. Singularity concerns the role and power position of the United States among the state community, the uniqueness of Guantanamo Bay as a U.S. detention center on leased territory, and the small number of cases to which indefinite detention applies who remain captive in Guantanamo. A less unique case selection concerning actor capabilities and norm conflict would allow for a broader comparability to other cases. Among the international state community, the United States have a specific position as a powerful democratic state. With this power position and the historical role of the United States as norm entrepreneur for violence-containing norms since World War II comes a certain responsibility and exemplary function regarding the interpretation, use, and legitimation of normative prescriptions. As not many states, if any, are capable of copying this role and act similarly in the transformation of norms on legitimate violence, the transferability of the analytical results to other states is limited. Yet, a certain imitation effect is possible. Although it seems unlikely that U.S. legitimacy-seeking efforts were aimed to encourage imitation, the effect may nevertheless occur—in cases of other states imitating violence-enabling norm interpretations—and is thus worth studying. Furthermore, due to the powerful position, U.S. activities have a signaling effect for the international state community. For the development of international law the U.S. use of force, application of violence, and interpretation of norms is a signal towards a possible overall tendency within the international system to interpret restrictions on state violence less strict and towards a norm interpretation favoring violence-enabling norms, especially concerning the treatment of terrorists. Thus, analyzing an extreme case of applied violence by a single, powerful and thus influential, state, a talking pig, may not have much value regarding comparability. However, the results offer insights as to other factors, like overall tendencies towards possible norm interpretations and imitations of a less limited use of force and less restricted application of violence.

Similarly, the choice of analyzing indefinite detention in Guantanamo Bay shows some unique features which limit the comparability to a larger case base. Admittedly, Guantanamo Bay is a unique prison for its special geographic and legal prerequisites. Moreover, after the efforts to close the detention camp, very few prisoners remain at the site and indefinite detention is thus limited to very few cases. Although comparability may be low and indefinite detention may be a specific act of violence, the resulting practices of legitimation have a conceptual benefit as these patterns may apply and/or be found in other legitimacy-needy debates.

A broader empirical basis including more cases to compare would have allowed for a stronger base to build theory from case study results. The analysis builds on the method of building theory from cases (Eisenhardt 1989; Eisenhardt 2021) which I adapted to meet my study's needs. Projects using the Eisenhardt method usually rely on a larger base of comparable cases and involve a team of investigators providing a large basis of data and analytical results from which to build theory. In comparison, working on a research project alone is associated with certain restrictions and limitations in terms of work capacity and analytical scope. Teams of several investigators have the advantage of more human resources to investigate more cases and evaluate more data including cross-checking of evidence, coding, and feedback loops to improve quality and validity. Also, research teams have the advantage of relying on more eyes and a larger base for background knowledge from which the interpretation can benefit. Although a single-handed single-case approach cannot claim the same analytical scope as a multi-investigator large case base design, this case study still offers conceptual building blocks to advancing theoretical approaches on norm transformation and practices of legitimation. These building blocks are valid starting points to develop theses for further research. These may then be validated in larger research projects to evaluate data for comparable cases to enhance theory building.

In the case study design, I made several research practical decisions, which were necessary reductions of complexity. Yet, the results of this study could provide starting points for further research and in-depth comparison. One of these decisions concerns the choice of actors. Despite a multitude of actors showing in the documentation of the timelines, I limited the study's focus on the actions of the presidents. Although this step is necessary to ensure workability and is thus a practical research decision, it also leaves many actors and their contribution to legitimacy-seeking activities of the government out of consideration. Further research could focus on other vital actors or actor groups. The presented study also has a clear time limit. Further research could incorporate other cases in the same timeframe either conducted by the U.S. or by other states to collect more insights on the application of violence and legitimation activities in this period. Further analysis could focus on entirely different time frames to compare practices of violence and practices of legitimation. Opting for a case with a broad database, I excluded related cases of violent acts in the war on terror, like torture, extraordinary renditions, and targeted killings. However, the results provided in this study may be used for testing even with smaller databases on the cases listed above. As such, the contribution of this study should be considered as a conceptual contribution to norm research and additionally as a starting point for further practice-oriented research on legitimation.

Concerning the organization of the research process, a couple of practical research decisions left out some opportunities for further research considering fieldwork and deskwork. Concerning fieldwork, practice theory approaches offer a multitude of methods to be explored in further research. For this project, I specifically excluded certain methods, yet such methods could offer added value to the research fields of legitimation practices and norm transformation. Further research focusing on actor motives and strategic planning behind the scenes would benefit from personal insights and institutional observations gained through expert interviews. Whereas this research project heavily relied on transcribed speech material, practice theory is open to multimedia approaches including other sources, like social media feeds, and filmed documentation which would allow for the inclusion of further aspects of performance which focus on bodily or other background information (i.e. stage setting, crowd, formalities, clothing) to gain a comprehensive picture of a comprehensive practice.

As discussed, concerning the results of the study several limiting factors should be considered. However, within the limits outlined above, the results constitute a concept applicable in further research and provide blocks for theory-building worth testing in further research. As possibilities for application of the concept practices of legitimation are too complex to list here, a couple of building blocks worth following up on include norm conflict, U.S. domestic normative interpretations, and international norms. In the following, I discuss the practical implications and opportunities for further research.

7.4 Implications and Issues for Further Research

In addition to the theoretical implications of the findings and the discussed methodological limitations, the research results have practical implications which indicate issues for further research. Proposing a concept for legitimation practices in norm transformation, the results add to norm research on dynamic changes in norm compliance and norm quality. Since the presented concept adds an actor-focused and action-focused approach to legitimacy-seeking as a strategic political set of actions, the concept cannot account for the perception, processing, and granting of the designated audiences. As I limit the research project to reviewing government, and even closer limited only presidential legitimacy-seeking activities, I cannot draw any conclusions as to how successful the activities were. Indicators for mixed resonances are the controversial debates among scientific communities, legal practitioners, and the public. Civil society's protest against Guantanamo and critical debates raised on specific legal issues as discussed in Chap. 2 as well as the controversial election debates during the run-up of Obama in 2008 display a rather negative resonance of legitimation efforts of the Bush administration. In the analyzed material international discomfort showed in repeated questions for release of certain prisoners. Obama repeatedly argues that U.S. reputation has suffered from the Bush administration's detention policy. However, the analysis did not focus on international acceptance and/or criticism of Bush's or Obama's policies. Acknowledging that legitimation is a reflexive process, further research should focus on a systematic evaluation of the legitimacy-granting side of the legitimacy-gaining process. Investigations should include the resonance of the government activities in the United States evaluating different interest groups as well as among the international state community. Furthermore, the long-term effects of norm transformation should be subject to further research in order to clarify whether the discussed phenomena remain conflict-specific or whether some aspects of the (attempted) norm transformations are also relevant in other conflict scenarios.

The results of this case study concerning detention and the legal status of detainees contribute to debates on legitimate violence and counterterrorism strategies in armed conflicts. Since this study mainly focused on legitimation strategies of applied violence, operative strategizing and application of violence in the field were left aside. Nevertheless, legal and political legitimation is closely tied to counterterrorism strategies and this nexus should be investigated in further research regarding the violence-containing quality of norms on legitimate violence. The legal status of participants in combat has effects on their treatment and on the use of violence on the battlefield. While the international state community still struggles to agree on common terminology and definitions on terrorism, the norm interpretation and application of violence during the war on terror has precedent-setting effects for the status of terrorists as participants in attacks and active combat not only for U.S. law but also on the international level. Although the codification on the international level has not changed in writing, the U.S. have challenged the agreed upon interpretation of the detention law with alterations such as the *unlawful enemy combatant* and the *unprivileged enemy belligerent*. However, the traces 20 years of U.S. anti-terror politics have left in the international system should be further investigated regarding the use of violence against declared terrorists by the United States and other states and thus the commitment to violence-containing norms. Repeated legal precedents referring to these status regulations by the United States and other states would contribute to fixing these status determinations and consequent legitimation of violence against enemies declared as terrorists. Such fixed violence-enabling interpretations would erode the protective norms of the *Geneva Conventions* in use over time and may result in permanent violence-enabling status determination on the international level.

Thus, further research should evaluate whether and how the status and its implications on detainee rights and images continue to be used in pursuit of global terrorism by the United States and in other conflicts involving sovereign states and declared terrorist enemies. This concerns inner state anti-terrorism policies as well as international activities (targeted killings or military activities in counterterrorism). Furthermore, investigations should focus on the transformative effects on other states' treatment of enemies in international and non-international armed conflicts. This should also include whether or not other states have adopted the term in their justification of violence regarding alleged terrorists or terrorist groups (i.e. China, Russia, or Israel). In this regard, the progress of the transformation of violence-containing norms towards violence-enabling norms should be further investigated extending to other norms challenged during the war on terror, concerning torture, assassinations, and pre-emptive defense.

Additionally, the nexus between enemy characterization and the legitimation of exceeding the limits of legitimate violence should be further investigated. As the analysis shows, characterizing the enemy is a rhetorical justification activity for the application of violence. Furthermore, the results reveal that in the war on terror, especially during the Bush administration, new links are determined between status labels and categories for culpability. Terrorists are not only found guilty for planned or executed attacks which constitute acts of crime but also indefinitely detained for their capabilities in training and their ideologically based intent to do harm. This idea of culpability is present in both administrations' arguments for indefinite detention. As this enemy characterization goes along with the legal view of a criminal law based on conviction rather than on criminal offenses, characterizing an enemy as a terrorist is also a strategic act of labeling for the legitimation of violence which exceeds the boundaries of legitimate violence. Further research should investigate the use and legitimation of pre-emptive captivity and indefinite detention and pre-emptive assassinations and targeted killings. Investigations should also inspect the use of the label 'terrorism' as legitimation for the use of force and application of violence which further blurres the lines between combat-engaged individuals and armed groups and neutral civilians.

One implication of this study's findings is that further research in U.S. policy analysis should be conducted on secrecy. Whereas secrecy mainly posed a practical research problem for this study, in politics a growing tendency to secrecy in connection with state violence without transparent explanation may have serious effects. Secrecy prevents and renders prosecution of wrongdoing impossible and thus allows for state arbitrariness. Furthermore, a lack of transparency and accountability hinders democratic principles concerning checks and balances and civil society's participation. Obama launched a campaign on the state secret privilege and demanded more transparency and accountability. The state secret privilege builds on the idea the sometimes secrecy is necessary for security reasons and that the government is entrusted not to break that trust by acting illegally. However, the cases in the war on terror show that often secrecy hints to norm-deviating behavior, and too often secrecy is a disguise for illegality and an exploitation of the immunity-granting government position. Moreover, the political quarrels in the war on terror over the use of force and the application of violence also shows that secret government actions were not only what the people wanted. Although trust in the state secret privilege is necessary, control in terms of democratic oversight must be established. Secrecy needs to be the exception and conditions for keeping actions secret need to be spelled out clearly. Since the Obama administration claimed to have worked towards more transparency and accountability, further research should be aimed at the legitimation activities of secret-keeping and clandestine activities. This includes the treatment of whistleblowers and dealing with leaked security information. In this regard, further practice-oriented research could focus on secret-keeping activities, such as the practice of redactions and classifying information especially regarding legal prosecution *in absentia.*

Moreover, leaked or declassified material poses a chance to reconstruct decision-making processes and learn about behind-the-scenes legitimation. Legitimacy-seeking activities as presented by the presidents or secretaries are the product of a complex process involving a multitude of actors in consulting and administration. Analyzing papers which document this opinion-forming process behind closed doors helps understand the mindsets and interpretations of legal consultants and the strategic positioning and political opinions of stakeholders. As leaked documents provide a still to be explored data source and more material will become available as classifications may be lifted, this source should be used for further research.

Conclusion 8

This research project shows—legitimation matters! The question I wanted to answer is—how does legitimation work, though? The puzzle this study started out on is that the use of force and application of violence in the war on terror needed consolidation with violence-regulating norms. This research project then asked how the Presidents Bush, Jr., and Obama have practiced legitimation to consolidate the conflict between security interests and violence-containing norms. Building on the discussion of an extensive body of research on norm conflicts in the war on terror in political and legal science in Chap. 2, I discussed legitimation as a strategic political practice in consolidating norm conflicts and innovatively transforming violence-containing norms towards violence-enabling norms. In the following Chap. 3, I focused on norm transformation as my theoretical assumption for the empirical case study. This conceptual approach to norm dynamics accounts for both changes in normative acceptance during a norm's life cycle and qualitative adaptations in norms' meaning and use.

Following the methodological approach laid out in Chap. 4, the single-case study was conducted using a combination of evidence-gathering and qualitative content analysis. The case of indefinite detention was chosen because in the case of the transformation of the detention norm a full norm transformation cycle is visible, and the quality of the norm is changed from violence-containment to violence-enablement. Indefinite detention in Guantanamo thus qualifies as a well-documented case of norm transformation. Working on the question of how the presidents managed and realized this reconciliation, the case study analysis used the approach of building theory from cases combined with interpretative methods

Supplementary Information The online version contains supplementary material available at https://doi.org/10.1007/978-3-658-49121-5_8.

D. Hühnert-Hugendubel, *Between Rules of War and Rule of Law*,
https://doi.org/10.1007/978-3-658-49121-5_8

to trace legitimation activities in terms of legalization and justification during the two presidencies between 2001 and 2017, as presented in Chap. 5. As the empirical case study shows, the Bush and the Obama administration have fostered norm transformation in detention norms in several stages—from preparatory to initial over legalization and institutionalization. Norm transforming activities included informal and formal legalization as well as justification actions. Both presidents engaged in legitimation activities of legalization and justification to change this norm's meaning and use and thus reframe the meaning of norms on legitimate violence in the security political discourse of the war on terror. The Bush administration was criticized for detainee treatment and for exceeding the original intent of the legal interpretation of detention laws and altered detention law in writing and in general meaning. Although Obama promised a return to the rule of law and established ameliorations in detention law early on in his time in office, he remained criticized for institutionalizing and fostering a 'secret' detention law and finally institutionalized new detention laws. Thus, both presidents engaged in legalization and justification activities to reconcile the application of violence with national and international law.

The empirical case study examined how President Bush and President Obama legitimized the norm transformation in detention law concerning GTMO detainees. The resulting patterns in activities in and on the material world and in rhetoric added up to a comprehensive conceptualization of practices of legitimation as traced in Chap. 5 and evaluated in Chap. 6. The evaluation of the norm transformation process over time in Chap. 5 and the evaluation of political activities in Chap. 6 result in a comprehensive conceptualization of legitimation as a strategic political practice. This concept functions as a building block to developing further theoretical approaches to legitimacy, legitimate violence, and legitimation in norm transformation processes, as I critically discussed regarding potential for further research and methodological challenges in Chap. 7. In the following, I present the answers to the research question and an overview of the relevance of the findings and contributions to the field. Finally, I offer an outlook for further research on legitimation practices and possible fields of application of the concepts found in this case study.

8.1 Research Results: A Strategic Practice of Legitimation in Norm Transformation

Acknowledging norm conflicts in the war on terror, the starting point of this project was the puzzle of how U.S. presidents bridged the gap between the violence-containing norms and the application of violence. More precisely, I wanted to understand how legitimation works in practice. Therefore, the research question of this study asked which legitimation practices the Presidents George W. Bush, Jr., and Barack Obama exercised to foster the transformation of violence-regulating norms in the war on terror. As stated in the Introduction, my driving motivation in this research project was to examine legitimation in practices used to advance transformation processes from violence-containing towards violence-enabling norms. To this end, the analytical focus in this study lay on the activities designed to promote the norm transformation processes. Moreover, the assumed U.S. aim was to shape the interpretation and underlying mindsets, ideas, and values to encourage general agreement with the use of violence against the declared enemy. Following a practice-oriented research process, I came to the following research results.

Conceptually, legitimation practices constitute a complex set of actions which are competently performed based on background-knowledge by legitimacy-seeking actors who attempt to adapt and add to detention norms. Legitimacy-seeking activities appear as a set of meaningful, purposeful, deliberate, and intentional actions performed in repeated patterns and routines. Legitimation consists of legalization mainly showing in activities in and on the material world, and justification actions which mainly trace in speeches as rhetorical activities, which are designed for and aimed at a legitimacy granting audience. First, legitimation depends on a powerful actor's interpretation of the power position and leadership style concerning cooperation as well as core values, beliefs, and ideas. These factors influence key positions on foreign and security policies as well as the importance of the rule of law and constitutional boundaries, all of which wheigh into the strategic positioning and guiding principles of the person's decision-making. Second, legitimation depends on the powerful actor's actions enforcing informal and formal legalization including secrecy, open-breach and violation, legal re-interpretation and re-framing, as well as legal innovation. Legalization activities include but may not be limited to the following most prominent ones: event-induced denial of rights and refusal to apply regulations to a given situation, introducing quasi-legal provisions, and executively working towards the legalization of new rules on a given situation and/or subject, engaging in a formal legalization process and working within the institutionalized legalization process towards the realization of the proposed new rules, and passing the new rules and defending them as security relevant gain in the legal system. Legalization actions mainly occur in activities following official tracks of government-prescribed procedures but also entail a preparatory stage. Third, legitimation depends on topic setting and issue framing with rhetorical activities. These justification actions are mainly acted out in speeches as rhetorical activities which prepare, argumentatively support, and praise the legalization and security political activities. This encompasses formal language, accompanying official legalization activities, as well as justification activities which involve finding supportive rhetorical actions, background knowledge activating, emotional arguments, and subject-supporting, rational arguments. These rhetorical activities that add up to legitimation practices include but may not be limited to the following most prominent ones: emphasizing security, explaining security politics, characterizing the enemy, reporting on war progress, listing accomplishments, revoking national memory, and appealing to national values.[1]

Concerning the meaning and use of legitimation as a strategic political practice, the study revealed the following characteristics for legitimation in practice.

Legitimation is stable in the core following a decisive security doctrine and strategy but also partially adaptable to short notice changes in critical situations and security environment. As the analysis of both presidential activities shows, both presidents stick to core behavior and arguments, which remain stable over time, despite upcoming political issues, voiced criticism, or changes in the security environment. As the evaluation of the norm transformation process showed, certain core characteristics in terms of strategic positioning remained stable over time concerning national security and commitment to national values for instance. However, rhetoric was adapted due to the shifts in the security environment or challenges to the strategic positioning, like Bush reacted to Supreme Court rulings and Obama reacted to Congress decisions.

Legitimation is determined by the government prescribed role, inscribed in the role as a duty and as such a formal and often institutionalized act. While the presidents have the possibility to shape justification to some degree, some aspects of legitimation are determined by the office. For instance, the role as commander in chief determines an emphasis on national security and the constitutional division

[1] For a detailed listing of the activities found see Chap. 6 and the Appendix provided in the Electronic Supplementary Material. For a discussion on generalizability and further research see Chap. 7.

of branches demands a certain respect for Supreme Court rulings. Both presidents fulfill the duty of their office and provide explanations unsolicited and not only in response to questions but also with the aim of protecting the presidency from harm. Often formalized legalization processes are connected to justification in speeches, and the other way around some speeches are mandatory, for example, in connection with signing legislation. Legitimation in legalization and accompanying speech is often an orchestrated, institutionalized activity which is routinized and officially prescribed.

Legitimation is a contestable part of political discourse, subject to political positioning and strategizing and thus often highly emotional. As the analysis showed, both presidents faced discussions regarding legitimation activities. While Bush faced USSC rulings restricting his application of violence and interpretation of detention laws, Obama's legitimation strategy regarding detention policy and interpretation of laws provoked conflict with Congress. Especially in election years, the evaluation of activities and rhetoric showed changes in legalization and justification activities. Whereas points of interest are emphasized, critical issues and problematic topics are avoided in speeches. Although factual explanations play a role in logical argumentations, many speeches contain language designed to appeal to support-generating emotions like compassion or empathy and strong, mobilizing emotions like fear or anger.

Legitimation as a discursive process involves negotiation in a complex political system which is extremely multi-layered and versatile. Given the complexity of the entire process of legitimation efforts of a government, narrowing the focus to a few key individuals in a powerful position was, among other aspects, a practical research decision. However, focusing on the presidents' legitimacy-seeking activities does not account for the whole process but rather for a specific focal point of power, even though probably an influential one. Also, the diversity—in terms of a multitude of political actors and interests involved –, the multi-layered character—in terms of bureaucratic structures and power levels –, and the complexity involving the interplay with other actor groups—like media, non-governmental organizations, and civil society (social media)—who influence legitimation processes are not displayed in this study. Although a schematic concept of the exchange of legitimacy-seeking activities and legitimacy-grating actors is relational, legitimation is not a linear process but one that may involve twists and turns and is the product of a negotiation and thus constitutes a compromise rather than a single actor's position.

Legitimation is strongly connected to legality and (codified and non-codified) norms but legitimacy-seeking rhetoric is mainly emotion-appealing. Although the debate on acts of violence in the war on terror is largely a legal debate, the presidents' legitimacy-seeking rhetoric does not refer to legal provisions as much as the critical legal debate would suggest. In legitimation rhetoric legality of government actions is emphasized, and accusations of wrongdoing are refuted. When talking about specific acts of violence, legality is emphasized, and government lawfulness is accentuated. Instead, legitimacy-seeking efforts are strongly directed at achieving rational and emotional persuasion. This entails aiming at changing the beliefs, ideas, and feelings which support a violence-enabling normative system and thus allow for a transformation in violence-regulating norms. Hence, the attempts at legitimization are not aimed at gaining approval for a specific change in the law, rather legitimacy-seeking efforts are aimed at changing the underlying convictions within the legitimacy-granting audience. Thus, a change in law becomes approvable due to a changing attitude towards the kind of violence which is considered as right and just. By changing the core values, a change towards violence-enabling norms becomes possible.

8.2 Contribution and Relevance of the Findings

The main contribution of this research project is the comprehensive conception of legitimation as a strategic political practice in norm transformation processes. The results present building blocks for a theory on legitimation and an actor-centered and action-focused concept of norm transformation in quality and as development over time and thus provide building blocks for the development of theory. Concerning approaches to legitimacy, legitimate violence, and legitimation, the findings provide a conception of legitimation as a political set of strategic actions towards the transformation of norms. Regarding the empirical case analysis, this study contributes to a deeper understanding of how state officials act out legitimation to justify and legalize security political actions. Empirically, the case study provides a detailed account of how Bush and Obama argued for the legitimate detention and detainee treatment while affirming yet changing and eventually transforming detention norms. In a narrower sense, the results of the study offer insights as to how state leaders argue for the legitimate use of violence in legally and socially controversial cases of the use of force and application of violence during the war on terror. On this intersection of political and legal issues this conception of legitimation speaks to debates in IR norm research, U.S. foreign and security policy, exceptionalism, and international law.

These research results add to debates in IR norm research dealing with compliance, norm life cycle stages, or the normative character of norms by providing an actor-centered approach to dynamic and qualitative norm change, as discussed in Chaps. 2 and 3. For one, the results complement existing theories and concepts of norm transformation with action-focused conceptions on the legitimacy of norms and strategic change through legalization and justification activities. Thus, the results add a practice approach to norm transformation in IR by offering an action-focused perspective on the role and function of legitimacy-seeking activities of norm entrepreneurs in the process of transforming normative mindsets and eventually altering legal provisions. Conceptually clarifying practices of legitimation enhances theoretical understanding of how powerful states can practically take an influence in norm shaping processes. The results further elaborate the role of the U.S. as a norm entrepreneur towards the development of violence-enabling norms. Thus, the findings of this study contribute to research on the norm life cycle and to the question as to how norms develop over time, whether norms change in use, possibly die, or transform, and the role state actors can play in these processes. For another, the conceptual results can be used as a starting point for further research on cases which are suitable for further developing the theorizing of legitimation practices. Where norm and international legal research intersect, the distinction provided in the concept of legitimation practices—as legalization and justification activities—may contribute to realizing a stronger connection and granting more distinction between the legal and political aspects of government actions. Whereas legalization aspects display the legal discourse and represent arguments regarding written law, justification aspects add to the normative sphere of the security political discourse, allowing to factor in underlying considerations of what is right and wrong.

Regarding U.S. foreign and security politics, the case study adds to research on U.S. policies in the war on terror as a prolonged state of emergency and discourse on legitimate violence. The results contribute to a deeper understanding of how U.S. foreign and security politics are justified and legalized and how the presidents fulfill their roles consolidating security interests and legal restrictions. In a narrow sense, the findings of the case study offer detailed insights into the transformation of detention norms and thus contribute to a better understanding of legitimation concerning detention and detainee treatment in GTMO. Thereby, the results add to the body of existing research on new detention law and the legal debate on Guantanamo, as discussed in Chap. 2. Moreover, this study provides a building block for related cases of U.S. legal debates on the use of force and the application of violence in conventional war and international armed conflict, like targeted killings or extraordinary renditions.

Considering 9/11 as an event triggering an ongoing situation of national emergency, this study also adds to the body of literature on crisis management in states of emergency and situations of prolonged exceptionalism. The case study shows how democratic institutions work through emergency-related legal solutions and how exceptions affect constitutionally granted fundamental rights and freedoms. The findings of the analysis contribute to a deeper understanding of how crisis management functions within a democratic state. Moreover, the findings help understand how administrations communicate to convince the respective audience within a state but also among international audiences concerning the legitimate use of force and application of violence. The case study thus contributes to a deeper understanding of political communication and persuasion, nationally and internationally. In this regard, this analysis provides a building block for research on long-term effects of national security crises and prolonged states of emergency. Providing a deeper understanding of how state actors practically perform legitimation activities, in deeds and argumentatively, the results inform how processes in norm change are induced and fostered within a democratic system and against adversaries. Using a practice-oriented approach, the findings of this research project add a body of pragmatic research projects and practice theory studies.

8.3 Outlook on Further Research

Understanding the main result of legitimation as a strategic political practice and as such as a comprehensive concept and a building block to further theories on legitimacy and legitimation, further research should include testing and further competitive or similar case work. For example, the concept of legitimation practices could be applied to or tested on other norms, other state or non-state actors, and in other legal spheres. The same holds for aspects of legitimation focusing on norm transformation which could be researched in other norm issue areas. The results could also be used to investigate other security political discourses in the United States, like the Cold War or World War II, the Covid-19 pandemic, or domestic discourses like the death penalty or discrimination issues, for instance.

Closer related to the case studied in this study, one of the issues for further research concerns the long-term consequences of normative changes during the war on terror regarding violence-containing norms and the reception on the international level. As this study mainly looked at the norm entrepreneurship stage up to the institutionalization of a new detention norm mainly in U.S. domestic law, the long-term effects on international law could not be analyzed to the same extent. Moreover, although this study covered a period of 16 years, the timespan is rather short considering that determining stability of norms is usually measured in longer timeframes or including the compliance behavior of a wider range of actors. Further research should thus include long-term effects concerning the development of detention law within the United States, compliance with violence-containing norms on the international level, and further attempts to establish violence-enabling readings of violence-regulating norms.

One possibility for direct transfer and comparability in testing results offer related acts of violence in the war on terror, like torture and enhanced interrogation or assassinations and targeted killings. In the case of torture, further research should include testing for similar legitimation strategies used by the Bush administration in other cases of norm conflict, focusing on legal advisors and leading personnel in the Department of Defense and in conflict zones like Afghanistan, Pakistan, Somalia, and Yemen. In the case of targeted killings, further research should compare the Bush and Obama administrations concerning arguments on lethal force and strategies of secrecy. Considering the growing advancements in military technology, the debate on legal limitations in targeted killings, which is close to the legitimation issues of the detention debate has already shed some light on issue areas that need further regulations on violence. With developments in drones, autonomic weapons, and other technical systems that are remotely controlled by military personnel or designed to operate autonomously, based on artificial intelligence, regulations for the use of such technology and a normative restriction on lethal force are necessary. The possibility for states to argue that existing normative frameworks which would probably rather restrict the use of such technological advancements do not apply is high. While the use of such technologies partly also defines rules by setting precedents, further research should investigate normative developments and political legitimation strategies challenging core principles of the international normative order.

Regarding standards on legitimate violence, further research should focus on state and non-state practices of violence within or exceeding the legal and normative boundaries of the normative order of legitimate violence. Further research should include effects of state violence which contradicts the general idea of containment of state violence in the international system and thus extend to other cases of violence-enabling norm transformations, other zones of conflict, and include other actors. Cases for testing the results presented here or for open investigation of the application of violence in breach of violence-containing norms should include torture, targeted killings, extraordinary renditions in other conflict zones, like Afghanistan, Pakistan, Somalia, and Yemen. Research in this regard should not be limited to the United States, but extend to other powerful states, like Russia or China, and other democratic states, like France, the United Kingdom, or Israel. Especially European states were divided on security political position during the U.S.-led war on terror. Analyzing how European democracies dealt with terrorist threats using a similar research design or testing the results of this study presents an opportunity for further research. Subject to legitimation efforts in addition to detainee treatment would be inner state surveillance and the characterization of terrorists in legal terms and security political strategies for terrorist prevention.

Further research should focus on the effects of legitimation and norm transformation on U.S. domestic law, on core legal principles like the rule of law, and on the use of force and application of violence in foreign and security policies of subsequent administrations under Presidents Trump and Biden. Especially concerning constitutional rights in the U.S., during the war on terror, debates on surveillances and data protection were sparked. With growing technological advancements in big data evaluation and surveillance these debates continue to be relevant in terms of balancing civil rights and states' obligations concerning national security. Further research into the normative change concerning protective norms could build on the presented conception of legitimation practices. Further research should not only include democratic states but also cover states with less developed constitutionally granted protective rights and weaker legal provisions on data protection and privacy, like China or Russia.

This research project is situated in the specific conflict environment of the war on terror, yet, since 2017 the security environment has evolved with new developments in threat perceptions, conflict scenarios, and actor constellations. The war on terror seems to have lost significance and no longer appears as a dominant security political discourse. With this change in security priorities, the focus on norms, which are challenged by upcoming crises, also shifts. Reaching beyond the narrow security political focus, the results of this research project speak to inner state debates on states of emergency which challenge basic civil rights and freedoms. Thus, the results of this research project could be tested in further research on norms regarding constitutional rights, the rule of law, and general debates on fundamental rights and freedoms in states of emergency. Also, further research connected to practices of legitimation should cover U.S. debates on hard-won rights, like anti-discrimination norms and women's rights.

Although the war on terror is no longer the dominant security political discourse, terrorism continues to play a role in international armed conflicts, inner state conflicts, and transnational armed conflicts. In such cases, further research could address the justification of violence especially against civilians, the characterization of the declared enemy, and on the positioning of governments towards violence-containing norms.

However, as important as legitimation is, the controversial debates in political and legal scholarship, in politics, and in the public during the war on terror also underline the value and power of granting legitimacy to political leaders. The war on terror has changed the general understanding of what legitimate violence is. Although detention in Guantanamo seems to be an almost closed case, with only a small number of remaining detainees, the normative questions raised in the war on terror concerning the regulation of state violence remain up to date. Nevertheless, the war on terror fosters a normative belief based on the idea that protective rights are exclusive, nationally bound, and conditional instead of basic, universal, human rights. As status lines were increasingly blurred in the war on terror, the violence-related debates seem to have added multiple conditions on receiving protection in an armed conflict, which indicate that a claim to protection is granted by birth (U.S. citizens would not be incarcerated at Guantanamo), can be lost due to wrongdoings (like terrorism activities dehumanizing a person, whereas based on the GC humanity cannot be lost, see Common Art. 3), or has to be earned instead of grated due to protection-worthy status.

Even though the case study focuses on two presidents as leading state actors, the analysis also shows that norm transformation is not the product of individuals but rather a political process which involves a multitude of actors and a wide legitimacy-granting audience. Although the tracing of events over time may in a simplified reading suggest a linear process, norm transformation is not necessarily a linear nor always a successful process. Whether or not transformative efforts are successful depends on a comprehensive adaptation of norms and the core of shared beliefs of a society, which is a very complex non-linear process. However, as the extensive study of justificatory rhetoric has shown, legitimation is worked hard for, which also shows how important gaining support for political and legal ambitions is for political leadership. As this research project has mainly focused on legitimacy-seeking activities concluding that legitimation matters to political leadership, the receptive side of these legitimacy-seeking efforts, the side granting legitimacy may matter even more. Powerful actors may seek legitimacy, but whether or not they are granted legitimacy is up to the people.

9/11 not only remains a security-relevant event that marks the beginning of the war on terror but also is a reminder that the 'how' in political justification and legalization sets the course for the use of force and application of violence. Through the politics and legitimation practices applied in the war on terror, the discourse on legitimate violence has changed throughout the past two decades. The results of this study, I consider a starting point and a building block to follow up on these norm transformations as a general trend among the international state community to foster violence-enabling policies. Strategic political practices of legitimation as applied during the war on terror by Bush and Obama have contributed to the transformation of violence-regulating norms. Although alterations in codified law are limited, transformation moreover encompasses not only the meaning and use of violence-regulating norms but also extends to transformations of underlying ideas, values, beliefs, and social perceptions of what is considered right and just and thus legitimate violence.

Literature

Acharya, A. (2004). How Ideas Spread: Whose Norms Matter? Norm Localization and Institutional Change in Asian Regionalism. *International Organization, 58*(2), 239–275.

Adler-Nissen, R., & Pouliot, V. (2014). Power in practice: Negotiating the international intervention in Libya. *European Journal of International Relations, 20*(4), 889–911. https://doi.org/10.1177/1354066113512702

Adler, E. (2008). The Spread of Security Communities: Communities of Practice, Self-Restraint, and NATO's Post-Cold War Transformation. *European Journal of International Relations, 14*(2), 195–230.

Adler, E., & Pouliot, V. (2011). International Practices. *International Theory, 3*(1), 1–36.

Agamben, G. (2004). *Ausnahmezustand* (Dt. Erstausgabe, 1. ed.). Frankfurt am Main: Suhrkamp.

Ahmad, M. (2014). The Use of Drones in Pakistan: an Inquiry into the Ethical and Legal Issues. *The Political Quarterly, 85*(1), 65–74.

Al Jazeera. (2022). Timeline: 20 years of Guantanamo Bay. *AlJazeera.com.* Retrieved from https://www.aljazeera.com/news/2022/1/10/timeline-20-years-of-guantanamo-bay-prison

Alexander, J. C. (2013). The Law-Free Zone and Back Again. *University of Illinois Law Review, 2013*(2), 551–624.

Alston, P., Morgan-Foster, J., & Abresch, W. (2008). The Competence of the UN Human Rights Council and its Special Procedures in relation to Armed Conflicts: Extrajudicial Executions in the 'War on Terror'. *The European Journal of International Law, 19*(1), 183–209.

Amnesty International. (2013). Elf Jahre Guantánamo: Chronik. Retrieved from https://www.amnesty.de/2013/1/10/elf-jahre-guantanamo-chronik

Aradau, C. (2007). Law Transformed: Guantánamo and the 'other' exception. *Third World Quarterly, 28*(3), 489–501. https://doi.org/10.1080/01436590701192298

Aradau, C., & van Munster, R. (2009). Exceptionalism and the 'War on Terror'. Criminology Meets International Relations. *The British Journal of Criminology, 49*(5), 686–701.

Arend, A. C. (2003). International Law and the Preemptive Use of Military Force. *The Washington Quarterly, 26*(2), 89–103.

Axelrod, R. (1986). An Evolutionary Approach to Norms. *The American Political Science Review, 100*(4), 682–683.

D. Hühnert-Hugendubel, *Between Rules of War and Rule of Law*,
https://doi.org/10.1007/978-3-658-49121-5

Banka, A., & Quinn, A. (2018). Killing Norms Softly: US Targeted Killing, Quasi-secrecy and the Assassination Ban. *Security Studies, 27*(4), 665–703. https://doi.org/10.1080/09636412.2018.1483633

Banks, W. C., & Raven-Hansen, P. (2003). Targeted Killing and Assassination: The U.S. Legal Framework. *University of Richmond Law Review, 37*(3), 667–749.

Barnett, M., & Duvall, R. (2005). Power in International Politics. *International Organization, 59*(1), 39–75. https://doi.org/10.1017/s0020818305050010

Ben-Josef Hirsch, M. (2014). Ideational change and the emergence of the international norm of truth and reconciliation commissions. *European Journal of International Relations, 20*(3), 810–833.

Bially Mattern, J., & Zarakol, A. (2016). Hierarchies in World Politics. *International Organization, 70*(3), 623–654. https://doi.org/10.1017/S0020818316000126

Björkdahl, A. (2002). Norms in International Relations: Some Conceptual and Methodological Reflections. *Cambridge Review of International Affairs, 15*(1), 9–23.

Bourdieu, P. (1976). *Entwurf einer Theorie der Praxis auf der ethnologischen Grundlage der kabylischen Gesellschaft*. Frankfurt am Main: Suhrkamp.

Bourdieu, P. (1977). *Outline of a Theory of Practice*. Cambridge: Cambridge University Press.

Bourdieu, P. (1990). *The Logic of Practice*. Stanford, CA: Stanford University Press.

Bueger, C. (2014). Pathways to practice: praxiography and international politics. *European Political Science Review, 6*(3), 383–406. https://doi.org/10.1017/S1755773913000167

Bueger, C. (2016). Practice. In X. Guillaume & P. Bilgin (Eds.), *Routledge Handbook of International Political Sociology* (pp. 328–337). Abingdon, Oxon; New York, N. Y.: Routledge.

Bueger, C., & Gadinger, F. (2014). *International Practice Theory. New Perspectives*. London: Palgrave Macmillan.

Bueger, C., & Gadinger, F. (2015). The Play of International Practice. *International Studies Quarterly, 59*(3), 449–460.

Bueger, C., & Gadinger, F. (2018). *International Practice Theory* (Second ed.). Cham: Palgrave Macmillan.

Büger, C., & Gadinger, F. (2008). Praktisch gedacht! Praxistheoretischer Konstruktivismus in den Internationalen Beziehungen. *Zeitschrift für Internationale Beziehungen, 15*(2), 273–302.

Bull, H. (2012). *The Anarchical Society. A Study of Order in World Politics* (4th ed.). New York, N. Y.: Palgrave Macmillan.

Butler, J. (2006). *Precarious Life. The Powers of Mourning and Violence*. London: Verso.

Butler, J. (2015). Human shields. *London Review of International Law, 3*(2), 223–243. https://doi.org/10.1093/lril/lrv011

Clark, I. (2003). Legitimacy in a global order. *Review of International Studies, 29*, 75–95. https://doi.org/10.1017/S0260210503005904

Clark, I. (2005). *Legitimacy in International Society*. Oxford: Oxford University Press.

Crawford, E. (2010). *The Treatment of Combatants and Insurgents under the Law of Armed Conflict*. Oxford; New York, N. Y.: Oxford University Press.

Cronogue, G. (2012). A New AUMF: Defining Combatants in the War on Terror. *Duke Journal of Comparative & International Law, 22*, 377–406.

De Londras, F. (2008). Guantánamo Bay: Towards Legality? *Modern Law Review, 71*(1), 36–58. https://doi.org/10.1111/j.1468-2230.2008.00680.x

Deibert, R. J., & Crete-Nishihata, M. (2012). Global Governance and the Spread of Cyberspace Controls. *Global Governance, 18*, 339–361.

Deitelhoff, N., & Zimmermann, L. (2020). Things We Lost in the Fire: How Different Types of Contestation Affect the Robustness of International Norms. *International Studies Review, 22*(1), 51–76.

Denbeaux, M., & Boyd-Nafstad, C. (2007). The Attorney-Client Relationship in Guantanamo Bay. *Fordham International Law Journal, 30*, 491–608.

Department of Defense. (2005). National Defense Strategy: GlobalSecurtiy.org.

Dombrowski, P., & Payne, R. A. (2006). The Emerging Consensus for Preventive War. *Survival*, 115–136.

Donnelly, J. (1998). Human rights: a new standard of civilization? *International Affairs, 74*(1), 1–24.

Dooley, L. M. (2002). Case Study Research and Theory Building. *Advances in developing human resources, 4*(3), 335–354.

Dörmann, K. (2003). The legal situation of 'unlawful/unprivileged combatants'. *IRRC, 85*(849), 45–74.

Downes, C. (2004). 'Targeted Killings' in an Age of Terror: The Legality of the Yemen Strike. *Journal of Conflict and Security Law, 9*(2), 277–294.

Drumbl, M. A. (2003). Self-Defense and the Use of Force: Breaking the Rules, Making the Rules, or Both? *International Studies Perspectives, 4*(4), 409–431.

Drumbl, M. A. (2005). Guantánamo, Rasul, and the Twilight of Law. *Drake Law Review, 53*, 897–922.

Dunlap, C. J. J. (2001). Law and Military Interventions: Preserving Humanitarian Values in 21st Conflicts. Retrieved from https://scholarship.law.duke.edu/cgi/viewcontent.cgi?article=6193&context=faculty_scholarship

Dunne, T. (2007). 'The Rules of the Game are Changing': Fundamental Human Rights in Crisis After 9/11. *International Politics, 44*, 269–286. https://doi.org/10.1057/palgrave.ip.8800188

Eberl, O. (2008). Zwischen Zivilisierung und Demokratisierung: Die Exklusion der 'Anderen' im liberalen Völkerrecht. *Soziale Systeme, 14*(2), 349–369.

Eisenhardt, K. M. (1989). Building Theories From Case Study Research. *The Academy of Management Review, 14*(4), 532–550.

Eisenhardt, K. M. (1991). Better Stories and Better Constructs: The Case for Rigor and Comparative Logic. *The Academy of Management Review, 16*(3), 620–627.

Eisenhardt, K. M. (2021). What Is the Eisenhardt Method, really? *Strategic Organization, 19*(1), 147–160.

Eisenhardt, K. M., & Graebner, M. E. (2007). Theory Building from Cases: Opportunities and Challenges. *Academy of Management Journal, 50*(1), 25–32.

Eisenhardt, K. M., Graebner, M. E., & Sonenshein, S. (2016). Grand Challenges and Inductive Methods: Rigor Without Rigor Mortis. *Academy of Management Journal, 59*(4), 1113–1123.

Esch, J. (2010). Legitimizing the "War on Terror": Political Myth in Official-Level Rhetoric. *Political Psychology, 31*(3), 357–391.

Evers, M. M. (2017). On Transgression. *International Studies Quarterly, 61*(4), 786–794. https://doi.org/10.1093/isq/sqx065

Finnemore, M. (1996). Norms, culture, and world politics: insights from sociology's institutionalism. *International Organization, 50*(2), 325–347.

Finnemore, M., & Sikkink, K. (1998). International Norm Dynamics and Political Change. *International Organization, 52*(4), 887–917.

Fisk, K., & Ramos, J. M. (2014). Actions Speak Louder Than Words: Preventive Self-Defense as a Cascading Norm. *International Studies Perspectives, 15*(2), 163–185.

Fletcher, G. P. (2004). Black Hole in Guantánamo Bay. *Journal of International Criminal Justice, 2*(1), 121–132.

Florini, A. (1996). The Evolution of International Norms. *International Sudies Qarterly, 40*(3), 363–389.

Förster, A., & Lemke, M. (2016). Die Legitimation von Ausnahmezuständen. Eine Analyse zeitübergreifender Legitimationsmuster am Beispiel der USA. In M. L. e. al. (Ed.), *Legitimitätspraxis* (pp. 13–22). Wiesbaden: VS Springer.

Frakt, D. J. R. (2012). Prisoners of Congress: The Constitutional and Political Clash over Detainees and the Closure of Guantantmo. *University of Pittsburgh Law Review, 74*, 179–262. https://doi.org/10.5195/lawreview.2012.195

Freedman, L. (2003). Prevention, Not Preemption. *The Washington Quarterly, 26*(2), 105–114.

Friedrichs, J., & Kratochwil, F. (2009). On Acting and Knowing: How Pragmatism Can Advance International Relations Research and Methodology. *International Organization, 63*(4), 701–731. https://doi.org/10.1017/S0020818309990142

Gerring, J. (2004). What Is a Case Study and What Is It Good for? *American Political Science Review, 98*(2), 341–354.

Glaser, B. G., & Strauss, A. L. (1967). *The Discovery of Grounded Theory: Strategies for Qualitative Research.* Chicago: Aldire.

Goddard, S. E. (2006). Uncommon Ground: Indivisible Territory and the Politics of Legitimacy. *International Organization, 60*(1), 35–68.

Goddard, S. E., & Krebs, R. R. (2015). Rhetoric, Legitimation, and Grand Strategy. *Security Studies, 24*(5), 5–36.

Goertz, G. (2006). *Social Science Concepts. A User's Guide.* Princeton, NJ: Princeton University Press.

Goertz, G., & Diehl, P. F. (1992). Toward a Theory of International Norms. Some Conceptual and Measurement Issues. *The Journal of Conflict Resolution, 36*(4), 634–664.

Gong, G. W. (1984). *The Standard of 'Civilization' in International Society.* New York, N. Y.: Oxford University Press.

Gozzi, G. (2007). History of International Law and Western Civilization. *International Community Law Review, 9*(2007), 353–373.

Gray, C. (2004). *International Law and the Use of Force* (2 ed.). Oxford: Oxford University Press.

Greenberg, K. J. (Ed.) (2006). *The Torture Debate in America.* New York, N. Y.: Cambridge University Press.

Greenberg, K. J., & Dratel, J. L. (Eds.). (2005). *The Torture Papers. The Road to Abu Ghraib.* New York, N. Y.: Cambridge University Press.

Greenberg, K. J., Dratel, J. L., & Grossman, J. S. (2008). *The Enemy Combatant Papers: American Justice, the Courts, and the War on Terror*. New York, N. Y.: Cambridge University Press.

Gregory, D. (2006). The Black Flag: Guantánamo Bay and the Space of Exception. *Geografiska Annaler: Series B, Human Geography, 88*(4), 405–427.

Gregory, T. (2017). Targeted killings: Drones, noncombatant immunity, and the politics of killing. *Contemporary Security Policy, 38*(2), 212–236.

Großklaus, M. (2017). Friction, not erosion: Assassination norms at the fault line between sovereignty and liberal values. *Contemporary Security Policy, 38*(2), 260–280.

Guiora, A. N. (2011). Determining a Legitimate Target: The Dilemma of the Decision Maker. *Texas International Law Journal, 47*, 315–334.

Haas, M. C., & Fischer, S.-C. (2017). The evolution of targeted killing practices: Autonomous weapons, future conflict, and the international order. *Contemporary Security Policy, 38*(2), 281–306. https://doi.org/10.1080/13523260.2017.1336407

Hajjar, L. (2014). The Long Shadow of the CIA at Guantánamo. *Middle East Report, 273*, 20–26.

Hattem, J. (2016). Gitmo timeline: How we got here. *The Hill*. Retrieved from http://thehill.com/policy/national-security/270417-gitmo-timeline-how-we-got-here

Heller, R., & Kahl, M. (2013). Tracing and understanding 'bad' norm dynamics in counterterrorism: the current debates in IR research. *Critical Studies on Terrorism, 6*(3), 414–428.

Heller, R., Kahl, M., & Pisoiu, D. (2012). The 'dark' side of normative argumentation—The case of counterterrorism policy. *Global Constitutionalism, 1*(2), 278–312.

Hühnert, D. (2016). *New Kind of War—New Kind of Detention? How the Bush Administration Introduced the Unlawful Enemy Combatant*. Münster: LIT Verlag.

Hurd, I. (1999). Legitimacy and Authority in International Politics. *International Organization, 53*(2), 379–408. https://doi.org/10.1162/002081899550913

Hurd, I. (2007a). *After Anarchy: Legitimacy and Power in the United Nations Security Council*. Princeton, NJ: Princeton University Press.

Hurd, I. (2007b). Breaking and Making Norms: American Revisionism and Crises of Legitimacy. *International Politics, 44*, 194–213. https://doi.org/10.1057/palgrave.ip.8800184

Hurd, I. (2016). The permissive power of the ban on war. *European Journal of International Security, 2*(1), 1–18.

Hurd, I. (2017). Targeted killing in international relations theory: Recursive politics of technology, law, and practice. *Contemporary Security Policy, 38*(2), 307–319.

ICRC. (2024). General Bibliography on IHL. Retrieved from https://casebook.icrc.org/law/general-bibliography-ihl

Ingebritsen, C. (2002). Norm Entrepreneurs. Scandinavia's Role in World Politics. *Cooperation and Conflict, 37*(1), 11–23.

Johns, F. (2005). Guantánamo Bay and the Annihilation of the Exception. *The European Journal of International Law, 16*(4), 613–635.

Johns, F. (2013). *Non-Legality in International Law. Unruly Law*. Cambridge: Cambridge University Press.

Johns, F., Joyce, R. J., & Pahuja, S. (2011). *Events: The Force of International Law* (Vol. 80). Oxon, New York, N. Y.: Routledge.

Jose, B. (2016). Bin Laden's targeted killing and emerging norms. *Critical Studies on Terrorism, 10*(1), 44–66. https://doi.org/10.1080/17539153.2016.1221662

Jose, B. (2017). Not completely the new normal: How Human Rights Watch tried to suppress the targeted killing norm. *Contemporary Security Policy, 38*(2), 237–259. https://doi.org/10.1080/13523260.2017.1334856

Kaplan, A. (2005). Where is Guantánamo? *American Quarterly, 57*(3), 831–858.

Kasher, A., & Yadlin, A. (2005). Assassination and Preventive Killing. *SAIS Review of International Affairs, 25*(1), 41–57.

Keating, V. C. (2014). Contesting the International Illegitimacy of Torture: The Bush Administration's Failure to Legitimate its Preferences within International Society. *The British Journal of Politics & International Relations, 16*(1), 1–27. https://doi.org/10.1111/1467-856x.12024

Kelly, L. M., & Cordeiro, M. (2020). Three principles of pragmatism for research on organizational processes. *Methodological Innovations, 13*(2), 1–10. https://doi.org/10.1177/2059799120937242

Keohane, R. O. (1986). Reciprocity in international relations. *International Organization, 40*(1), 1–27.

Koskenniemi, M. (2001). *The Gentle Civilizer of Nations. The Rise and Fall of International Law 1870–1960.* Cambridge: Cambridge University Press.

Krahmann, E. (2013). The United States, PMSCs and the state monopoly on violence: Leading the way towards norm change. *Security Dialogue, 44*(1), 53–71.

Krasner, S. D. (Ed.) (1983). *International Regimes.* Ithaca and London: Cornell University Press.

Kratochwil, F. V. (1989). *Rules, Norms, and Decisions. On the conditions of practical and legal reasoning in international relations and domestic affairs.* Cambridge: Cambridge University Press.

Krebs, R. R., & Jackson, P. T. (2007). Twisting Tongues and Twisting Arms: The Power of Political Rhetoric. *European Journal of International Relations, 13*(1), 35–66.

Kretzmer, D. (2005). Targeted Klling of Suspected Terrorists: Extra-Judicial Executions or Legitimate Means of Defence? *European Journal of International Law, 16*(2), 171–212.

Krook, M. L., & True, J. (2010). Rethinking the life cycles of international norms: The United Nations and the global promotion of gender equality. *European Journal of International Relations, 18*(1), 103–127. https://doi.org/10.1177/1354066110380963

Kurnaz, M. (2007). *Fünf Jahre meines Lebens* (1st ed.). Berlin: Rowohlt.

Kutz, C. (2014). How Norms Die: Torture and Assassination in American Security Policy. *Ethics & International Affairs, 28*(4), 425–449.

Langley, A., & Abdallah, C. (2016). Templates and Turns in Qualitative Studies of Strategy and Management. *Catedra Corona 25, 21*(1–20), 201–235. Retrieved from https://repositorio.uniandes.edu.co/server/api/core/bitstreams/e4d335f8-f707-47f5-9d37-61ca71044e87/content

Lantis, J. S., & Wunderlich, C. (2018). Resiliency dynamics of norm clusters: Norm contestation and international cooperation. *Review of International Studies, 44*(3), 570–593.

Levi, M., Sacks, A., & Tyler, T. (2009). Conceptualizing Legitimacy, Measuring Legitimating Beliefs. *American Behavioral Scientist, 53*(3), 354–375.

Liese, A. (2009). Exceptional Necessity. How Liberal Democracies Contest the Prohibition of Torture and Ill-Treatment when Countering Terrorism. *Journal of International Law and International Relations, 5*(1), 17–47.

Luban, D. (2008). Lawfare and Legal Ethics in Guantánamo. *Stanford Law Review, 60*(6), 1981–2026.

Lynham, S. A. (2002). The General Method of Theory-Building Research in Applied Disciplines. *Advances in developing human resources, 4*(3), 221–241.

MacKay, J. (2019). Legitimation Strategies in International Hierarchies. *International Studies Quarterly, 63*(3), 717–725.

Maran, R. (2006). Detention and Torture in Guantanamo. *Social Justice, 33*(4), 151–181.

March, J. G., & Olsen, J. P. (1998). The Institutional Dynamics of International Political Orders. *International Organization, 52*(4), 943–969.

Maxwell, M. D. M., & Watts, S. M. (2007). 'Unlawful Enemy Combatant': Status, Theory of Culpability, or Neither? *Journal of International Criminal Justice, 2007*(5), 19–25. https://doi.org/10.1093/jicj/mql100

McKeown, R. (2009). Norm Regress: US Revisionism and the Slow Death of the Torture Norm. *International Relations, 23*(1), 5–25. https://doi.org/10.1177/0047117808100607

McNeal, G. S. (2009). Organizational Culture, Professional Ethics and Guantanamo. *Case Western Reserve Journal of International Law, 42*(1), 125–149.

Meisels, T. (2007). Combatants—Lawful and Unlawful. *Law and Philosophy, 26*, 31–65. https://doi.org/10.1007/s10982-005-5917-2

Münch, S. (2016). *Interpretative Policy-Analyse. Eine Einführung*. Wiesbaden: Springer VS.

Murphy, R., & Radsan, A. J. (2009). Due Process and Targeted Killing of Terrorists. *Cardozo Law Review, 31*, 405–450.

Nadelmann, E. A. (1990). Global prohibition regimes: the evolution of norms in international society. *International Organization, 44*(4), 479–526.

National Security Archive. (2008). Torturing Democracy Timelines. Retrieved from https://nsarchive2.gwu.edu/torturingdemocracy/timelines/index2.html

Neocleous, M. (2006). The Problem with Normality: Taking Exception to 'Permanent Emergency'. *Alternatives: Global, Local, Political, 31*(2), 191–213.

Neumann, I. B. (2005). To Be a Diplomat. *International Studies Perspectives, 6*(1), 72–93. https://doi.org/10.1111/j.1528-3577.2005.00194.x

New York Times. (2024). The Guantamao Docket. Retrieved from https://www.nytimes.com/interactive/projects/guantanamo

O'Connell, M. E. (2010). The Choice of Law Against Terrorism. *Journal ofNational Security Law and Policy, 4*, 343–368.

Oldopp, B. (2013). *Das politische System der USA. Eine Einführung* (2., aktualisierte und erweiterte Aufl. 2013 ed.). Wiesbaden: Springer Fachmedien Wiesbaden.

Oxford Learner's Dictionaries Online. (2023). Transform verb. Retrieved from https://www.oxfordlearnersdictionaries.com/definition/american_english/transform

Panke, D., & Petersohn, U. (2012). Why international norms disappear sometimes. *European Journal of International Relations, 18*(4), 719–742. https://doi.org/10.1177/1354066111407690

Panke, D., & Petersohn, U. (2016). Norm challenges and norm death: The inexplicable? *Cooperation and Conflict, 51*(1), 3–19.

Paust, J. J. (2003). War and Enemy Status After 9/11: Attacks on the Laws of War. *The Yale Journal of International Law, 28*, 325–335.

Payne, R. A. (2001). Persuasion, Frames and Norm Construction. *European Journal of International Relations, 7*(1), 37–61.

Pouliot, V. (2010). *International Security in Practice. The Politics of NATO-Russia Diplomacy* (Vol. 113). Cambridge: Cambridge University Press.

Pouliot, V. (2013). Methodology. Putting Practice Theory into Practice. In R. Adler-Nissen (Ed.), *Bourdieu in International Relations. Rethinking Key Concepts in IR* (pp. 45–58). Abingdon, Oxon and New York, N. Y.: Routledge.

Pratt, S. F. (2015). Crossing off names: the logic of military assassination. *Small Wars & Insurgencies, 26*(1), 3–24.

Pratt, S. F. (2018). Norm transformation and the institutionalization of targeted killing in the US. *European Journal of International Relations, 25*(3), 723–747. https://doi.org/10.1177/1354066118812178

Price, B. C. (2012). Targeting Top Terrorists. How Leadership Decapitation Contributes to Counterterrorism. *International Security, 36*(4), 9–46.

Proulx, V.-J. (2005). If the Hat Fits, Wear It, If the Turban Fits, Run for your Life: Reflections on the Indefinite Detention and Targeted Killing of Suspected Terrorists. *Hastings Law Journal, 56*(5), 801–900.

Radsan, A. J., & Murphy, R. (2011). Measure Twice, Shoot Once: Higher Care for CIA-Targeted Killing. *University of Illinois Law Review, 2011*(4), 1201–1241.

Raymond, G. A. (1997). Neutrality Norms and the Balance of Power. *Cooperation and Conflict, 32*(2), 123–146.

Reckwitz, A. (2002). Toward a Theory of Social Practices. A Development in Culturalist Theorizing. *European Journal of Social Theory, 5*(2), 243–263.

Reus-Smit, C. (2003). Politics and International Legal Obligation. *European Journal of International Relations, 9*(4), 591–625.

Reus-Smit, C. (2007). International Crises of Legitimacy. *International Politics, 44*, 157–174. https://doi.org/10.1057/palgrave.ip.8800182

Reus-Smit, C. (Ed.) (2004). *The Politics of International Law*. Cambridge: Cambridge University Press.

Rose, D. (2004). *Guantánamo Bay: Amerikas Kriege gegen die Menschenrechte*. Frankfurt am Main: S. Fischer.

Rosert, E. (2019). Salience and the emergence of international norms: Napalm and cluster munitions in the inhumane weapons convention. *Review of International Studies, 45*(1), 77–99.

Rosert, E., & Schirmbeck, S. (2007). Zur Erosion internationaler Normen. Folterverbot und nukleares Tabu in der Diskussion. *Zeitschrift für Internationale Beziehungen, 14*(2), 253–287.

Rumsfeld, D. H. (2001). A New Kind of War. *New York Times Online*. Retrieved from http://www.nytimes.com/2001/09/27/opinion/27RUMS.html

Rumsfeld, D. H. (2002). Secretary of Defense Donald Rumsfeld and Air Force General Myers, Chairman, Joint Chiefs of Staff, briefed February 12 at the Pentagon [Press release]

Sadat, L. N. (2006). Ghost Prisoners and Black Sites: Extraordinary Rendition Under International Law. *Case Western Reserve Journal of International Law, 37*(2), 309–342.

Sadat, L. N. (2007). Extraordinary Rendition, Torture, and Other Nightmares from the War on Terror. *The George Washington Law Review, 75*(5/6), 1200–1248.
Sadat, L. N., & Geng, J. (2010). On Legal Subterfuge and the So-Called 'Lawfare' Debate. *Case Western Reserve Journal of International Law, 43*, 153–161.
Sall, M. A. (2013). Classified Opinions: Habeas at Guantánamo and the Creation of Secret Law. *Georgetown Law Journal, 101*(4), 1147–1170.
Sandholtz, W. (2008). Dynamics of International Norm Change: Rules against Wartime Plunder. *European Journal of International Relations, 14*(1), 101–131. https://doi.org/10.1177/1354066107087766
Sassòli, M. (2004). The Status of Persons Held in Guantánamo under International Humanitarian Law. *Journal of International Criminal Justice, 2*(1), 96–106.
Sassòli, M. (2006). Query: Is There a Status of 'Unlawful Combatant'. *International Law Studies, 80*, 57–67.
Scheinkman, A., McLean, A., Ashkenas, J., Tse, A., & Harris, J. (2018). The Guantánamo Docket. Retrieved from https://www.nytimes.com/interactive/projects/guantanamo/timeline
Schwartz-Shea, P., & Yanow, D. (2012). *Interpretive Research Design. Concepts and Processes*. New York, N. Y.: Routledge.
Seawright, J., & Gerring, J. (2008). Case Selection Techniques in Case Study Research. A Menu of Qualitative and Quantitative Options. *Political Research Quarterly, 61*(2), 294–308.
Senn, M., & Troy, J. (2017). The transformation of targeted killing and international order. *Contemporary Security Policy, 38*(2), 175–211. https://doi.org/10.1080/13523260.2017.1336604
Shannon, V. P. (2000). Norms Are What States Make of Them: The Political Psychology of Norm Violation. *Interntional Studies Quarterly, 44*, 293–316.
Shannon, V. P., & Keller, J. W. (2007). Leadership Style and International Norm Violation: The Case of the Iraq War. *Foreign Policy Analysis*(3), 79–104.
Smith, C. S. (2005, 21 November 2005). Inside Guantanamo. *New Statesman*, 14–17.
Smith, C. S. (2007). Gitmo: America's black hole. *Los Angeles Times*. Retrieved from https://www.latimes.com/archives/la-xpm-2007-oct-05-oe-smith5-story.html
Spillius, A., & Willis, A. (2012, 11. January 2012). Guantánamo Bay 10-year anniversary: timeline. *The Telegraph*. Retrieved from https://www.telegraph.co.uk/news/worldnews/northamerica/usa/9006682/Guantanamo-Bay-10-year-anniversary-timeline.html
Stephens, D. (2011). The Age of Lawfare. *International Law Studies, 87*, 327–357.
Steyn, J. (2004). Guantanamo Bay: The Legal Black Hole. *International & Comparative Law Quarterly, 53*(01), 1–15. https://doi.org/10.1093/iclq/53.1.1
Suchman, M. C. (1995). Managing Legitimacy: Strategic and Institutional Approaches. *The Academy of Management Review, 20*(3), 571–610.
Thomas, C. A. (2014). The Uses and Abuses of Legitimacy in International Law. *Oxford Journal of Legal Studies, 34*(4), 729–758.
Venzke, I. (2009). Legal Contestation about 'Enemy Combatants'. On the Exercise of Power in Legal Interpretation. *Journal of International Law and International Relations, 5*(1), 155–184.
Venzke, I. (2012). *How Interpretation Makes International Law. On Semantics and Normative Twists*. Oxford: Oxford University Press.

Wachtel, H. A. (2005). Targeting Osama bin Laden: Examining the Legality of Assassination as a Tool of U.S. Foreign Policy. *Duke Law Journal, 55*(3), 677–710.
Wajner, D. F. (2019). 'Battling' for Legitimacy: Analyzing Performative Contests in the Gaza Flotilla Paradigmatic Case. *International Studies Quarterly, 63*(4), 1035–1050.
Walen, A., & Venzke, I. (2007). Detention in the 'War on Terror': Constitutional Interpretation Informed by the Law of War. *ILSA Journal of International & Comparative Law, 14*(1), 46–97.
Weber, M. (1925). *Wirtschaft und Gesellschaft: die Wirtschaft und die gesellschaftlichen Ordnungen und Mächte: Nachlaß. Gemeinschaften. Tbd. 1*: Mohr Siebeck.
Wiener, A. (2004). Contested Compliance: Interventions on the Normative Structure of World Politics. *European Journal of International Relations, 10*(2), 189–234.
Wiener, A. (2007). Contested Meaning of Norms: A Research Framework. *Comparative European Politics, 5*, 1–17.
Wiener, A. (2017). A Theory of Contestation. A Concise Summary of Its Argument and Concepts. *Polity, 49*(1), 109–125. https://doi.org/10.1086/690100
Wiener, A., & Puetter, U. (2009). The Quality of Norms is What Actors Make of It. Critical Constructivist Research on Norms. *Journal of International Law and International Relations, 5*(1), 1–16.
WikiLeaks. (2011). The Guantanamo Files. Retrieved from https://wikileaks.org/gitmo/
Wilde, R. (2005). Legal 'Black Hole'? Extraterritorial State Action and International Treaty Law on Civil and Political Rights. *Michigan Journal of International Law, 26*(3), 739–806.
Wilson, R. J. (2003). United States Detainees at Guantánamo Bay: The Inter-American Commission on Human Rights Responds to a 'Legal Black Hole'. *Human Rights Brief, 10*(3), 2–5.
Wittes, B., Chesney, R., & Benhalim, R. (2010). The Emerging Law of Detention. The Guantánamo Habeas Cases as Lawmaking. *Governance Studies at Brookings.*
Wonka, A. (2007). Um was geht es? Konzeptspezifikation in der politikwissenschaftlichen Forschung. In T. Gschwend & F. Schimmelfennig (Eds.), *Forschungsdesign in der Politikwissenschaft. Probleme-Strategien-Anwendungen* (pp. 63–89). Frankfurt: Campus Verlag.
Wunderlich, C. (2013). Chapter One. Theoretical Approaches in Norm Dynamics. In H. Müller & C. Wunderlich (Eds.), *Norm Dynamics in Multilateral Arms Control. Interests, Conflicts, and Justice* (pp. 20–48). Athens, Georgia: University of Georgia Press.
Yin, R. K. (1981). The Case Study Crisis: Some Answers. *Administrative Science Quarterly, 26*(1), 58–65.
Yin, R. K. (2009). *Case Study Research: Design and Methods* (4th ed.). Thousand Oaks, CA: Sage.
Yoo, J. (2011). Assassination or Targeted Killings after 9/11. *N. Y.L. Sch. L. Rev., 56*, 57–79.
Young, M. (2014). Death from Above: The Executive Branch's Targeted Killing of United States Citizens in the War on Terror. *University of Illinois Law Review*(3), 967–1011.
Zachary, S. (2005). Between the Geneva Conventions: Where Does the Unlawful Combatant Belong? *Israeli Law Review, 38*(1–2), 378–417.
Zimmermann, L. (2016). Same Same or Different? Norm Diffusion Between Resistance, Compliance, and Localization in Post-conflict States. *International Studies Perspectives, 17*(1), 98–115.

The manufacturer's authorised representative in the EU is Springer Nature Customer Service Centre GmbH, Europaplatz 3, 69115 Heidelberg, Germany. If you have any concerns regarding our products, please contact ProductSafety@springernature.com

Printed and bound by CPI Group (UK) Ltd, Croydon, CR0 4YY
30/09/2026
02225494-0005